Climbing

Books by Raymond Bridge

THE COMPLETE SNOW CAMPER'S GUIDE

AMERICA'S BACKPACKING BOOK

FREEWHEELING: The Bicycle Camping Book

*A CAMPER'S GUIDE TO ALASKA, THE YUKON,
AND NORTHERN BRITISH COLUMBIA*

CLIMBING: A Guide to Mountaineering

Climbing

A GUIDE TO MOUNTAINEERING

Raymond Bridge

CHARLES SCRIBNER'S SONS · NEW YORK

Library of Congress Cataloging in Publication Data

Bridge, Raymond.
    Climbing: a guide to mountaineering.

    Bibliography p. 390
    Includes index.
    1. Mountaineering. I. Title.
GV200.B74   796.5′22   75–38571
ISBN 0–684–14430–1

To MADDIE,
AN UNFAILINGLY CHEERFUL COMPANION
IN THE MOUNTAINS AND IN LIFE

CONTENTS

Climbing

I

Introductory

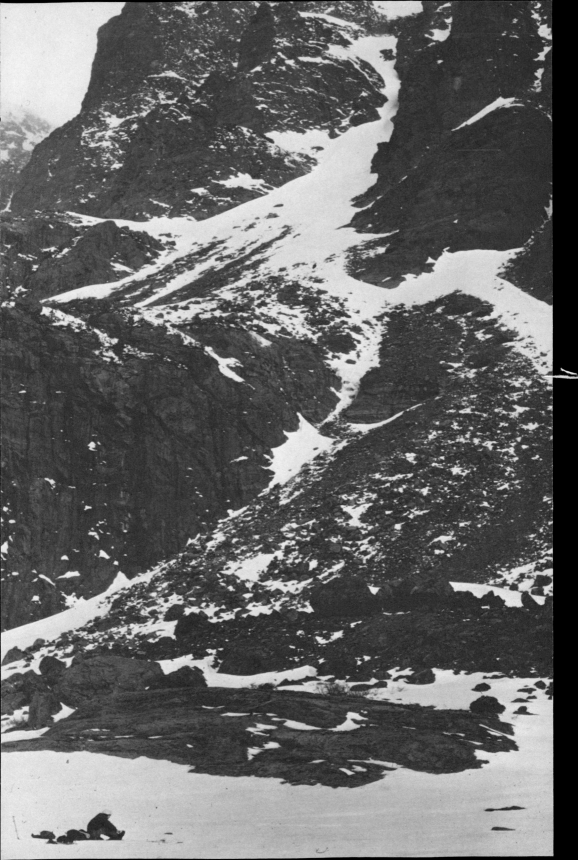

INTRODUCTION

"Climb the mountains and get their good tidings. Nature's peace will flow into you as sunshine flows into trees. The winds will blow their own freshness into you, and the storms their energy, while cares will drop off like autumn leaves."

—John Muir

This book is about some of the techniques used to climb mountains and their smaller relatives, cliffs, frozen waterfalls, and crags. The mountains have been good to me. In the many hours I have spent among the peaks I have found escape, solitude, adventure, and beauty. I have enjoyed a companionship with others that is too rare in modern life, because in our times we rarely have the opportunity to share the intense experiences that occur in climbing. Nor do we often deliberately and personally trust our lives to others in the way that mountaineers frequently do.

I have also been lucky enough sometimes to sense the beating of great rhythms among the mountains, the operation of natural forces so powerful, so tremendous, and so terribly beautiful that human beings and their works pale to insignificance in the presence of something far larger and more important. The experience is one of real humility. Yet paradoxically it is also renewing, leaving one more at peace with oneself and other men and women than one was before. There is something about the mountains that brings perspective and allows the soul and consciousness to grow.

Mountains have always loomed large in the human imagination, whether as sources of terror, awe, or beauty or as a strange challenge combining all these and more. The great ranges are the crests of waves formed by storms in the crust of the Earth, and in their higher reaches life struggles tenuously for a hold in elemental rock and ice. In the high peaks one finds a terribly harsh environment and some of the purest beauty that we know.

This book has several aims. It is an attempt to present basic American climbing technique in a logical and systematic way. It is not comprehensive, in that there is no effort made to discuss every way of solving each climbing problem that may arise, to analyze every way of using a handhold, nor to detail all the techniques that may be used in various specialized types of advanced climbing. Such an encyclopedic compilation would be virtually impossible. But I have tried to make this book a solid, basic manual covering modern technical climbing and the equipment used, both for the guidance of beginning and intermediate climbers and for reference by more experienced mountaineers.

Since this is a book about technique, a "how-to" book, it is bound to be somewhat pedestrian. The meaning of the mountains may often slip away, buried under the information on methods and equipment, but those interested in modern climbing must be willing to master the necessary technical skills to achieve reasonable safety. Climbing is an exacting passion and a haphazard approach is likely to be disastrous. An older and simpler style of climbing is to stay off the vertical walls and icy gullies; this allows one to appreciate the mountains with fewer impediments. It seems to be the nature of some people, however, to perpetually try to come into more intimate contact with the great vertical lines of the peaks, and for this various sorts of hardware and the skills of using it are necessary.

It has been said many times that one cannot learn to climb from a book. In this respect this book is no different from others on climbing and on other activities requiring physical skills and rapid, precise judgments. One cannot learn to sail a boat, paddle a kayak, or play a violin from a book, but books can be helpful, and I hope this one will help people to learn to climb or to climb better, more safely, or more naturally. If so, it will have served its purpose.

A NOTE TO THE BEGINNER

Climbing is a potentially dangerous sport, and it is one that requires a lot of time and effort to learn. This is one of the many reasons why it is so satisfying. Every good mountaineer keeps learning new things about climbing for as long as he continues to go to the mountains. There is no easy way to become an expert climber or mountaineer, and there are no real short-cuts.

The best way to learn to climb, and the fastest, is to apprentice yourself to good climbers. Try to find some people who have been climbing for a long time to take you out and teach you the skills you need to know. Books like this one can supplement what you learn on the rocks and the snow and they can keep you from wasting your experienced friends' time by allowing you to learn a lot of basic skills, such as knots, on your own.

You may be able to find a club which runs a climbing school free or at a nominal cost. This can be an excellent way of learning basic skills, and some such schools are quite thorough. Courses range from short basic rock climbing courses to year-round mountaineering schools. Examples of the latter are the courses run by the Seattle Mountaineers and the Boulder Group of the Colorado Mountain Club. There are also many commercial climbing schools these days. Learn as much as you can from experienced climbers and try to develop your own judgment. Most important, remember that good mountaineering judgment comes only with a lot of climbing experience.

One of the reasons that it is best to learn climbing with experienced people is that in the beginning it is important to leave a very wide margin of safety. Many of us learned to climb with others no more experienced than ourselves, or even less so. To climb safely in these circumstances one must be very conservative, because it is very easy to make serious mistakes. This means that one either takes frightening risks or progresses very slowly. The more one can learn from experienced climbers, the more quickly one can progress to doing more difficult, more interesting climbs. This book is written to help you learn more quickly and to help you develop your judgment. It can never be a substitute for experience or judgment. A climbing book is not like a cookbook or a chemistry lab manual. It cannot be used to provide formulae to get you up a rock or a mountain, only to help you learn the principles of climbing.

Mountaineering and climbing are enjoyable activities, challenging and exciting, but usually quite safe if good judgment is used. One of the attractions of climbing is that the climbing team is wholly self-reliant—committed to their own skill and knowledge, literally staking their lives on it. Safety is discussed a good deal in this book, because good safety techniques allow us to enjoy many adventures and wilderness experiences without taking serious risks. Good safety techniques and progressively more accurate knowledge of our own abilities, combined with lots of practice close to the ground, allow us to push closer and closer to the limits of our ability.

It is important to note too, though, that not all climbing and mountaineering is safe. Some climbs cannot and should not be made safe. There is a great deal of difference between difficulty and danger in climbing. There are extremely difficult climbs which are very safe, and there are very dangerous climbs which are relatively easy. The climbs that present some sort of ultimate challenge are those which are both difficult and dangerous. (This is not a challenge that most American climbers are willing to undertake, however.) This book makes no value judgment on whether the risks entailed on some of the more serious climbs are worth taking, but it does assume that beginners should stay off dangerous climbs until they have enough experience to understand the risks involved. One of the purposes of this book is to help you sharpen your judgment of hazards that may be involved.

Many advanced climbing techniques are discussed in this book on the assumption that the more information and knowledge the novice can acquire about mountaineering techniques, the better off he will be. Many such methods and the equipment used will be of no use in the first, or even second, climbing season. Beginners will not need jumar ascenders or big wall techniques, but I do not think that these are out of place even in a book written primarily for the neophyte. I hope that this book is complete enough so that as the reader progresses towards more serious climbs he will at least be able to find enough information here to enable him to ask the right questions and make some evaluation of various techniques, tactics, and styles of climbing. There often seems to be too large a gap between books designed mainly for beginners, covering only the most elementary climbing techniques, and arguments in print between long-time climbers on the merits of a particular ax or a particular ethical position.

A WORD OF THANKS

The climbing techniques described in this book derive from a long tradition of wilderness mountaineering in the U.S. and Canada. This tradition is quite different from the European one, although much American climbing has evolved from the older Alpine base. Many of the best climbers in both Canada and the U.S. at various times have been European immigrants or visitors who brought their skills from the continent. Others have been very much in the tradition of American exploration.

There is not really space here to trace all the special roots of American climbing, but among other distinguishing features there has been a strong emphasis on safety techniques here, partly because of the usually safe nature of many of our mountains, and partly because of the critical and ingenious eye that many Americans have turned towards both equipment and methods. As a result, the last couple of generations of Americans have contributed some superb equipment and techniques to the international climbing world.

Another special root of American climbing is the wilderness tradition. Climbing in the U.S. and Canada has always had strong links with wilderness travel. Access to many climbing areas requires backpacking long distances and camping at the base of the climb. Even though there are many rock climbing areas which are close to the roads, much American climbing is wilderness climbing, and many climbers here feel that the best climbs are those done in a true wilderness setting, far from the nearest roads.

American climbing has also generally been guideless climbing, done by friends who climbed together in their spare time and on vacations. There haven't been too many professionals in American climbing, with some notable exceptions. The safety consciousness mentioned earlier is partly an outgrowth of the fact that people who can climb only occasionally are more likely to feel a need for equipment to back them up in case of a misjudgment than would guides who climb all through the season.

These and other factors have produced many outstanding and original climbers in many parts of North America. They put up the routes that modern climbers repeat and they developed the techniques which we now use. The more of the classic climbs in the U.S. and Canada that one does, the more one appreciates the tremendous daring and skill it took to first climb them, often with greatly inferior equipment. Whether one is climbing routes put up by Salathé in California, Ellingwood or the Stettners in Colorado, or Kain in British Columbia, one is humbled. Whatever merit there is in this book is the result of the contributions of all those who have made up the American climbing tradition, and I would like to thank them, from old masters to young tigers. Good climbing.

1

THE FINE EDGE

Climbing is one of the most absorbing sports ever devised by the restless human mind. Because it often requires an unusual amount of commitment, because it is practiced in some of the most beautiful, remote, and savage places in the world, because it is rather esoteric and serves no useful purpose, and because it frequently requires great effort, stamina, and agility, physical and intellectual, it is often as much of a religion, a philosophy, a way of life, or an aesthetic as it is a sport. The fact that it holds no attraction at all for many of his fellows does not bother the climber in the least. Whether he is an individualist or merely an élitist, he is likely to revel in the fact that climbing is not a mass sport.

The question "Why?" has always plagued climbers. It may come from newspaper writers or from worried spouses. Most often it comes from the back of one's own mind in some particularly scary or uncomfortable place, but then it is usually phrased: "What the hell am I doing up here?" There have been a lot of answers given, most of them not very satisfactory. I will not try to answer the query here, except to say that most people who climb enjoy it a lot. Like most really worthwhile things in life, climbing involves its share of hardship, difficulty, and sometimes danger. People who climb very much find that the rewards are more than commensurate with the negative aspects. They have the opportunity to live for a while in some of the most beautiful and awe-inspiring spots on earth, to experience a kind of fusion of mind and body, to coordinate their

9

A climber on a moderate snow slope, using crampons and climbing in balance.

own actions with those of their companions in a situation of real mutual dependency and trust.

THE MANY FACETS OF MOUNTAINEERING AND CLIMBING

Mountaineering as a sport began in the nineteenth century in Europe, when upper-class Englishmen discovered the Alps. These English climbers and their Continental guides developed the art of mountaineering. Some of the traditions of European climbing were imported directly to America. Edward Whymper, who made the first ascent of the Matterhorn, traveled in the Canadian Rockies, and European guides were imported to that area in order to make it into a Continental-style climbing resort. Many of the greatest American climbers originally came from Europe and brought much of their technique with them. By and large, however, climbing and mountaineering in North America has grown up with a tradition of its own, borrowing many methods from Europe, but maintaining a strong association with wilderness travel and exploration. The general pattern has been to climb peaks by backpacking in and camping at the base rather than developing a system of huts and climbing spas. Although many climbing areas in the United States and Canada have had professional guides, climbing here has usually been guideless. Most of the development has been by amateurs climbing with other amateurs. The American climber is a self-reliant animal. He plans his own trips, picks his companions, hauls his equipment and supplies to base camp, cooks his meals, and climbs his own mountains.

The field of mountaineering has many associated skills, some of them quite specialized. Many have developed into sports in their own right, separated in a number of respects from the parent art of mountaineering, although continual interaction remains. One of the most obvious offshoots is skiing. Most downhill skiers these days have never skied in the backcountry or climbed a large slope under their own power. The art of wilderness skiing remains a part of the mountaineering tradition, but downhill skiing and even cross-country skiing are separate specialized sports. Many types of climbing have developed into separate specialities, too, although they remain more in the general tradition of mountaineering than skiing. Rock climbing, which is one aspect of greater mountaineering, is often practiced on cliffs and pinnacles by highly skilled climbers who have never been up a mountain. It has even developed its own yet more specialized offshoots, such as bouldering on extremely difficult routes near the ground. Some of the best bouldering specialists never climb more than 30 feet above the base of a rock.

The particular bias of this book is toward the mountains. The skills discussed are largely of a technical kind, but the assumption is that the most interesting use of those skills is among high peaks. Some attention is paid to various specialties, but climbing is presented as a whole, with the understanding that many aspects can be satisfying when practiced alone. Mountaineering is a sport with many, many facets. The experiences available to the climber are wide and varied. On one trip, he may climb a sandstone pinnacle in the great desert region of the Southwest. He may spend days climbing on boulders or frozen waterfalls near home, ski in to ascend a peak in the Sierra Nevada in winter, and later go on a two-month expedition to Alaska. The techniques are so varied from one of these climbs to another that the differences defy description, yet there are also common strains.

THE FINE EDGE

The similarities among the many kinds of climbing tend to bring one back to the question of what climbing is all about. One factor which lends character to the sport is the overcoming of difficulties and dangers through the personal effort and will of the climbers. The surmounting of obstacles by nerve, by perseverance, by strength and agility, by mental and physical dexterity, seems to be an essential ingredient of climbing. The climber may do many routes which are easy for him, but the act of stretching his own limits, of overcoming them, of reaching out and experiencing some of the raw edge of life is one of the most characteristic features of climbing. It is the subjective side of this experience which is most important. Difficulty is purely relative. A climb which will be trivial to one climber may tax the skill and the nerves of another, whether because of different skills, variations in conditions or equipment available, or simply different mental states.

Several other factors lie at the core of the climbing experience. The stark beauty of the environment and the climber's ability to accommodate himself to his surroundings are vital. The aesthetics of the act of climbing itself and of the line of a route are important, and all the normal athletic pleasures involving physical exertion and control play a part. Most important of all, perhaps, is testing oneself in the crucible of great and impersonal natural environments. The element of danger is always present, although it plays a smaller role than is generally thought.

Some of these contributing features may not be present on many climbs. They are like individual types of yarn being used to weave a tapestry; all play their part in creating the whole picture, even if they do not appear in many portions. Their relative importance will vary also, but their variety provides the proverbial spice in climbing, as in life.

Climbing seems always to provide a concentrated taste of life. The climber lives somewhere on the fine edge of existence, where feelings and experiences are distilled to a rich broth far too strong for many palates. Climbing is at the same time a primary experience, partaking of the most basic issues and feelings of life and death, and a quite useless pastime, setting the participant apart from the real world of affairs. Yet a sense of perspective about the real needs of the mind and the body, of the animal and the thinking man, can be obtained on a climb as in very few other situations. The climber's life depends on his own actions and judgment and on those of his companions. His comfort and well-being rest with the whims of nature and with his own foresight in anticipating and dealing with them. His wants and joys are reduced to a level of simplicity rare in modern society. He may achieve a feeling both of personal wholeness and of oneness with the world around.

DANGER AND THE QUESTION OF SAFETY

Climbing is not by its nature a dangerous sport. The safety record of competent American mountaineers and rock climbers is quite good. To leave the matter with that statement, however, would be dishonest, for as in some other sports, danger plays an important role in the essence of climbing; it cannot be separated as a purely fortuitous ingredient. Danger is present in swimming, but it rarely plays any sort of central part. While the climber rarely courts death, there is a dark side to the sport.

To begin with, he frequently places himself in situations which are potentially very hazardous; he uses his technique, equipment, judgment, and skill to maintain an adequate margin of safety under these circumstances. One of the pleasures of the sport is precisely that one depends on one's own resources (and those of the rest of the party) for safeguards. Serious mistakes in judgment will not be rectified by the intervention of a legislative agency or a bureaucratic organization. On a high and difficult rock climb, if the climber and his companions do not belay properly and climb well, someone is likely to be killed. The climbers are the masters of their own fate. Even the mountaineer walking up an easy mountain must use his own judgment about the weather—when lightning strikes a mountaintop he had best be somewhere else.

The upshot of all this is that if climbing is a relatively safe sport, it is safe because the climbers are so. Baseball can be made safer by setting up rules about equipment and play. No one can legislate climbing safety. The climber retains the wonderfully human privilege of being a damned fool and killing himself.

On a more restricted level, a mountaineer who knows what he is about faces many choices in his career in the matter of safety. As in life, the elements of the unforeseen and the unpredictable play their part in mountaineering. Most of the craft, however, aims at removing these elements of chance, so that risks are calculated with reasonable accuracy and the climber can maintain whatever margin of safety he feels appropriate. American climbers have generally felt that the margin of safety should be fairly broad, and a good deal of attention has been devoted to making the sport safer, both by developing better equipment and technique and by training more competent climbers.

In dealing with various mountaineering hazards, climbers have found it convenient to distinguish between *subjective* dangers and *objective* ones. Subjective risks are those resulting from actions of the climber (such as falling off the mountain); while objective ones are the consequences of events which

Free climbing on rock.

cannot be controlled and can only be avoided (lightning strikes, for example). The distinction between these two categories of mountain perils is a crucial one because of the very important implications for safety. Thus, climbers often refer to climbs or areas with little objective danger. Yosemite Valley in California is a good example of a superb rock-climbing area with generally very low objective danger. The weather patterns are relatively stable, and the rock is mostly sound, so that natural rockfall is infrequent. Because of these and several other factors which will be mentioned elsewhere, it is possible for competent climbers to do very difficult routes in Yosemite with a minimum of real danger.

This makes the important point that difficulty and danger in mountaineering are quite distinct. A route may be very difficult, but if the objective dangers are low and adequate means of protection available, it will be quite safe for a competent party. On the other hand, a very simple climb which is subject to a lot of rockfall, to avalanches, to falling blocks of ice, or to other comparable hazards can never be really safe, no matter how strong the climbers. The old standard route on Mount Robson in the Canadian Rockies, for example, passes through a network of precariously balanced ice towers and involves rather high objective hazards. Proper timing and quick passage through dangerous sections will minimize the dangers but cannot eliminate them.

So the mountaineer is involved in the constant process of estimating and anticipating such hazards. He actively weighs his own abilities, his party, and equipment against the difficulties he may have to face, and he continuously estimates the multitude of possible problems that may arise on a climb. He must always allow adequate margins for error. Somewhere in this process is the most critical decision, which concerns the amount of danger that the individual climber and the party feel is justified on the climb they are doing. It is impossible to codify such decisions, but they are made. Most climbers are not willing to undertake climbs which necessarily involve much danger, and nearly all would agree that they are unjustifiable if the danger is due to the weakness of the party. Other questions arise on climbs involving a good deal of objective danger, such as rockfall. Such climbs tend to be undertaken much less often in America than in Europe, because most American climbers don't feel that the danger is justified. On the other hand, many climbers undertake routes at times which involve more hazards than they would normally be willing to face deliberately. Particularly on long expeditions, the participants are simply more committed to a climb; it means more to them than a mountain usually would. The balancing of ambition and danger is most difficult of all in such circumstances.

COMPETITION, ETHICS, AND AESTHETICS

As with any sport, a certain amount of competition has always been present in mountaineering. One has only to read

Climbers on the Maiden, a pinnacle near Boulder, Colorado.

the accounts of the first ascent of the Matterhorn to see competition at its ugliest. The Swiss-English party stood on the top of the mountain heaving rocks down to attract the attention of the Italian party on the other side and crow out their victory. The leader of the Italian party, for his part, had lied to Whymper shortly before in an attempt to beat him to the top.

One of the attractive things about climbing, however, is that the ideals of comradeship have been maintained over those of competition, which has generally been considered an undesirable aberration. Competition in America has become predictably more prevalent in the last few years as climbing has become more popular. One hopes it will remain within reasonable bounds, but this will depend on the attitude of climbers in general.

Climbers in every area tend to develop unwritten rules about what methods are or are not permissible on a climb. This is tricky because mountaineers in general, and American ones in particular, are an independent breed. The main justification for attitudes about how a climb should be done is that many techniques—particularly the placement of bolts in the rock—can spoil the pleasure of others doing the climb. In popular areas, the same criticism can be applied to pitons (metal spikes hammered into the rock) since repeated placement and removal ultimately changes or destroys the crack in which they are placed. These issues are discussed in more detail later; for the present, it should be sufficient to say that local etiquette on the preservation of climbs should be observed simply as a matter of courtesy.

Other attitudes toward particular climbs refer mainly to questions of style. These can safely be left to the individual climber, but it should be pointed out that more than aesthetics may be involved. If the climber finds it necessary to use a piton to stand on, for example, when it is intended simply for safety, then he is not climbing at the standard of the route. It is his own business if he wants to do the climb this way just to get up, but he should recognize that he may get into trouble farther along where an artificial foothold is not available.

THE MEANING OF THE MOUNTAINS

The mountains, rock spires, and ice cliffs of North America can provide a challenge which adds a special dimension to the climber's life, if he treats that world with respect. The mountains cannot be conquered by man, for he is only a visitor, and a rather weak and ill-adapted one; however, they can certainly be spoiled by him. Mountains are fragile in many ways. They present their challenge both to the climber's tenacity, endurance, and skill, and to his sense of restraint in using the world around him. If his methods of living in the environment and climbing there are appropriate—leaving little sign of his passage and relying on his skill rather than technological overkill—the mountains will retain both their challenge and their beauty for all the generations of men who may come in the future. If, on the other hand, the climber shows neither love nor restraint in his lust to "get" a route or a mountain, the taste of victory will be flat indeed, and its ugly fruits—beer cans, erosion, and bolts—will leave a lasting memento of his true nature.

II

Basic Mountaineering

2

LIVING IN THE MOUNTAINS

The general techniques for traveling and living in the mountains are adequately covered in books on backpacking, and the novice is referred to these for information. Most backpacking comes down to a combination of common sense and practical experience anyway, and the prospective climber is well advised to begin his career by taking as many walks in the mountains as he can. A lot of small but important skills are picked up in this way, from negotiating talus fields easily with a pack or following a trail in waning light to preparing meals efficiently. This chapter assumes that the reader is already familiar with basic backpacking and camping methods. The discussion is confined to special problems that may be faced by the mountaineer and to a few points on the care of the mountain environment.

The climber normally faces the same problems as other backpackers on at least part of his walk to the base of a climb. In many cases, the differences may be limited to the need for carrying a heavier load, since the extra weight of a rope and other equipment must be added to the pack. When climbs can be made in a day or less from reasonable campgrounds, only boots and a few other items deserve special consideration, since they may be asked to do double duty. On occasion, however, the climber may make special demands on his camping equipment and technique, and these need to be considered in choosing an outfit.

Base camps for climbs are usually placed in high meadows or near lakes around timberline. The environment is particularly fragile in spots like this, and the climber should give some attention to this fact in an effort to minimize his impact on the surroundings. His ideal should be to leave the campsite looking as though he was never there. Particularly with population pressure mounting in the backcountry, the climber should make it a rule to avoid fires at high-altitude campsites. Trees near timberline grow very slowly, and fires invariably leave very long lived scars. Although fires in camp are pleasant, they should be limited to locations well down in the timber; even there, discretion should be practiced in heavily used areas. The mountaineer should carry a stove and use it on most occasions, rather than depend on fires for cooking. This suggestion is especially appropriate for climbers, since their interests tend to concentrate wilderness use around particular lakes and meadows that are near popular climbs yet are also in the fragile subalpine and alpine life zones.

In choosing equipment, the climber should recognize that he may often have to use his gear under more rigorous and

A camp in the subalpine zone. Using a stove reduces the climbers' impact on a fragile environment.

varied conditions than the ordinary backpacker. A good mountaineering tent should be stable in high winds and suitable for
use in cold weather and snow. Single-layer-coated tents are
generally not suitable, nor are floorless models, or those which
cannot be adequately guyed for very windy conditions. The
mountaineering tent must be high-quality; a sewn-in waterproof floor is essential, and the better designs have coated
floors which run part way up the sides of the tent to prevent
leaks caused by splashing and melting snow. A tent is more
convenient to pitch, particularly in constricted places, when it
does not rely on many guy lines and tie points for its basic
stability. Extra guys should be available for use in high winds,
however. There are a number of features which are handy in
special circumstances. Snow flaps and cook holes are very helpful for snow camping. A frost liner is useful in long periods of
extremely cold weather. A light, bright color is a great psychological relief if one has to sit out a long storm in the tent. But
strength, durability, and wind stability remain the primary
considerations. A fancy frost liner and integrated fly will prove
no consolation if the tent tears up in a winter storm.

CLOTHING

Clothes for climbing and mountaineering have to be very
rugged, versatile in weather ranging from desert heat to extended drizzle to bitter cold, and as light in weight and compact as possible. While the full range of conditions may not be
met on any one trip, climbing areas do tend to present very
wide varieties of climatic problems in short periods. Climbers
with extended backpacking experience will already know a
good deal about clothing, and the books mentioned elsewhere
discuss it extensively, so only a few points will be covered here.

The outer shell garments are probably the most important
of all, although they tend to be neglected. Their function is to
deal with rain, wind, snow, and abrasion, while also trapping
an extra layer of warm, relatively still air inside. If much rain
is expected, a completely waterproof layer is essential to keep

other insulation dry. A particularly good garment for mountaineers is a cagoule, which is a very roomy anorak, large enough
so that the legs and arms can be drawn inside in a bivouac. The
roominess helps to provide extra ventilation, reducing the
problem of condensation somewhat. Rain chaps or pants can
be used for the lower part of the body. Chaps are light and
cheap and work well for rain, but the pants are useful in some
situations, such as sitting glissades on snow. Either should be
fitted to go on over boots without having to take the boots off.

Many techniques have been tried to solve the condensation problem caused by warm, moist air next to the body being
chilled against the slick surface of rain garments cooled by
outside temperatures. Most of the miracle solutions of the past
have fallen into well-deserved oblivion, but one of the latest
answers to the problem seems to help a good deal. A thin foam
layer is bonded to the coated nylon exterior and provides
enough insulation to reduce condensation considerably. The
material is still too new for much experience to be available,
but probably it will prove somewhat less durable than many of
the fabrics used in the past, and it is obviously heavier and
bulkier. Performance, however, is excellent. I spent a couple
of weeks living comfortably in a cagoule made of this material
through Alaskan rain with temperatures hovering just above
freezing—usually dreadful conditions in which to stay dry.

Other shell garments can be made in a number of ways.
In general, cotton-nylon or cotton-polyester mixtures seem to
give the best all-round performance. Pure nylon is lighter and
is satisfactory in very cold weather, but it is impossible to make
water-repellent without completely coating it. Well-designed
cottons breathe and can be made fairly water-repellent, but
are not as tough as cotton-nylon mixtures.

For general clothing, the layer system has stood the test
of time in mountaineering. Wearing a number of layers allows
for easy adjustment of insulation for hard work or resting, and
for wide temperature ranges. Wool is particularly valuable in
mountaineering, because it retains *some* insulating value
when wet, unlike most insulators. Cotton, except in shell gar-

ments, should be viewed with a jaundiced eye; cotton garments are very cold when wet and take forever to dry. Blue jeans are particularly bad except on local rock climbs in good weather.

Soft wool underwear and net underwear are popular; sometimes both are used for very cold weather. Wool net underwear is better than cotton but harder to find. The net provides small compartments of warm air for insulation; more importantly, it allows sweat to evaporate before soaking into one's clothing. Good wool underwear made these days is not itchy, and only a few people will find they are so allergic that they need cotton or synthetic fabric between the skin and the wool.

In very cold weather, when a great deal of insulation is needed and materials like wool would require garments much too heavy and bulky to be practical, down-insulated clothing comes into play. With a properly made garment, down provides more insulation for a given amount of weight and compressed bulk than anything else; for extremely cold conditions, it is still the ultimate insulating material. However, down does present problems, besides the expense. It has been overused in normal mountaineering situations, where excessive reliance can be very dangerous. Wet down is completely useless as an insulator, and it is nearly impossible to dry out under climbing conditions. In recent years there have been numerous cases where parties relied entirely on down for insulation and got into serious trouble after their clothes were soaked by cold rain. A more balanced choice of clothing will prevent such disasters. Down vests, jackets, and hoods are more useful for most mountaineering than expedition parkas, which should be reserved for extreme cold and very high altitude, or for bivouac gear when they substitute for the upper halves of down sleeping bags.

Synthetic fiber insulation has been improving every year, and although it is still not as good as down in providing maximum insulation and compressibility for a given weight of insulation, nor in recovering so well, it does have significant advantages. It does not collapse completely when wet, and most of the water can be whipped out. It is cheaper, easier to use, and simpler to clean. For insulated parkas in many mountaineering conditions, synthetics are better than down, and they have many advantages for sleeping bags for bivouacs. A good deal of care should be exercised in buying clothing using synthetic fibers, however, since poor construction methods or choice of material will easily negate the advantages.

Pockets, closures, hoods, cuffs, and the like, all need close attention when choosing clothing for climbing. Zippers that jam, buttons that tear off, snaps that don't work, and elastics that keep arms closed when one needs ventilation can be serious defects. The problems have a tendency to show up at the most awkward times. Pockets should be numerous and roomy, but they should not be placed where they will be cumbersome or have to be lifted with the leg at every step. It is convenient to have flaps for closing pockets. Hoods should be comfortable, no matter how the head is turned. Bills and wind tunnels on parka hoods are useful in rain and cold wind, but there should be provision for getting them out of the way when visibility is needed.

Lots of good climbing pants are available, but usually only at inflated prices. Surplus stores are excellent sources for wool pants at reasonable prices. Small modifications can be made when needed to adapt cuffs and pockets for mountaineering. Knickers make fine pants for climbing, giving protection to the legs while providing freedom of movement excelled only by shorts. Regular pants can be easily converted by slicing off an appropriate quantity of leg (saved for later use in patching) and adding a hem, drawstring, and plastic drawstring clamp to each side. The main disadvantage of knickers is that the high socks needed in colder weather cost twice as much as those of normal height.

It is convenient if pants will shed a reasonable amount of water. This is particularly true when cotton-polyester work pants are used for summer mountaineering. Larry Penberthy came up with the excellent solution of painting the pants with a strong silicone solution. (See the appendix for sources.)

Gaiters are very useful to keep snow and stones out of the boots and to keep the lower leg warm and dry in deep snow. Low gaiters are lighter and cheaper for the first purpose, but high ones are needed for the second. Two layers of a fabric of nylon-cotton mixture make the best gaiters for most purposes. Coated nylon tends to collect sweat inside, but in very wet, sloppy conditions it has definite advantages. For very short gaiters, or *stop-touts,* used just to keep things out of the boots, uncoated nylon cloth does very well. Specialized items such as overboots will be discussed later.

It is surprising how versatile a well-chosen mountaineering outfit is. Only a few additions or subtractions are generally needed to switch the pack from summer to winter use or to move from the Sierra Nevada to the Brooks Range.

BOOTS

The climber relies very heavily on his footwear. Along with his ice ax and rope, boots are traditional symbols of the mountaineer, and for good reason. Most climbing is done with the feet, and it is the boots which must adhere to the holds, kick the snow steps, or be strapped to the crampons. Boots provide the necessary protection when rough trails are negotiated with heavy packs. Their choice is very important not only because they are so crucial in climbing itself but because they may be relied on to protect the climber's feet from frostbite. Finally, boots are expected to put up with an almost incredible amount of abuse and to meet any number of contradictory requirements.

In choosing his boots, the climber will have to make a number of compromises. A boot cannot be equally well suited for backpacking along a trail, climbing a high-angle slab, wading an icy stream, slogging through cold powder snow, and cramponing on steep ice. The various characteristics that would best fulfill each of the many needs of the climber have to be weighed realistically and then compared with those boots actually available in which the individual can get a good fit. Fit is generally of more real importance than minor design differences, although a few really good shops have stretchers which can correct minor fitting problems.

Unless a climber is interested only in one specialized area of the sport—such as cliff climbing near the road or ski mountaineering—a pair of general-use mountaineering boots are the most basic equipment he will need. Tight-fitting, smooth-soled rock shoes are useless for general mountain travel, as are many other specialized boots. Boots intended for climbing should be very sturdy; if any snow work at all is expected, the lighter boots intended for hiking are not adequate. Soles should be heavy-duty lugged rubber, and they must be trimmed close, since soles sticking far out from the upper will make it difficult or impossible to stand on small holds. Uppers must be made of full grain leather, not suede, which cannot be rendered sufficiently waterproof. It is far preferable to choose a boot with the flesh (rough) side of the leather facing out and the grain (smooth) side in. The grain is the more water-resistant but it is also very prone to abrasion. If the grain faces out on mountain boots, it soon wears through and is lost. With the flesh out, abrasion resistance in general is improved, and the water-resisting grain is always preserved intact. The fewer the seams in the boot upper, the better, since seams always are the major points of wear and primary leakage points in a boot.

Mountaineering boots should have tongues which open enough to allow the boots to be put on without too much pain when they are frozen. If getting a boot on is a tight squeeze in a warm shop, you will find it a close relative of the iron maiden on chilly mornings at high altitude. The tongue should be gusseted at the sides to keep water and debris out. If not, make sure the tongue is at least sewn in straight.

The whole boot must be quite sturdy, and the toes and heels should be reinforced to prevent bruising. Pull loops at the back are helpful, but not essential if the boot is not too difficult to get on. Hinges of soft leather at the back of the boot should be avoided; they wear out long before the rest of the boot and are useless in properly made footwear. Lacing systems are many and not terribly important if they are sufficiently tough. It is best if the boot is fully lined with smooth glove leather. Padding inside between the two layers is common, but this should not be confused with insulation, since it does not extend to the lower part of the foot. The padding helps keep the ankle more comfortable, but it also absorbs and retains moisture, so its advantage is debatable.

The weight of the boots should be no greater than necessary to serve their purpose. Weight carried on the feet has to be lifted thousands of times for each mile of ground covered, so it is much more fatiguing than excess baggage in the pack. Good mountain boots are never light, but they need not be as heavy as many boots are. The first place to eliminate weight is above the ankle. High boots are of hardly any use for mountaineering, and the extra leather of a high upper adds a great deal of unnecessary weight. It also adds to the problem of the leather folding at the back of the ankle and rubbing against the sensitive Achilles' tendon. Around 6 inches is a good height; even a heavy winter boot does not need to be more than 8 or 9 inches high. The height should be just sufficient to give good ankle support.

Weight and discomfort can also be saved by avoiding boots that are excessively stiff. Steel shanks are commonly used to stiffen boot soles and relieve arch fatigue, and they are most desirable when such length and stiffness are appropriate. Many new climbers, however, end up in boots with long, heavy steel shanks which make the soles almost completely rigid. Such boots also usually have extra leather added for stiffness. These features are necessary to relieve fatigue in climbing long stretches of very high-angle technical ice. Unfortunately, they make the boots rather unsuitable for walking, and since the mountaineer will probably do a lot of walking during his first few years of climbing and no long stretches on very steep ice, he would certainly be better off with somewhat more flexible boots.

Probably the most difficult problem in constructing moun-

This photograph shows the difference between stiff and flexible boots. The boot above has a steel shank under the sole which aids in edging on small holds and in climbing steep ice, but makes the boot less suitable for walking or friction climbing. The more flexible boot below is more suitable for backpacking and friction climbing.

A type of double boot, designed for difficult climbing in cold weather and at high altitude. On the left is the outer boot and on the right is the inner one; the two are worn together.

tain boots is attaching the sole to the upper. This is done by first fastening the upper to a leather mid-sole, which can then be glued and screwed to the neoprene sole. The trick lies in fastening the upper to the mid-sole, which is done by one of the ways shown on the next page. The best but most difficult method is no. 3, in which the upper is folded in, and the stitching goes from the inside of the boot through the mid-sole. The advantages are many. The boot can be cut with no overhang at all to the sole, allowing excellent control on small holds. Sealing the boot against leaking water is far simpler and more effective, because the main seam does not have exposed stitches leading directly from the outside to the inside. Since the seams are not exposed, they are not subject to abrasion and wear against the rock, nor is the edge of the upper through which they are sewn. The only problem with this method is that boot manufacturers find it more difficult to accomplish.

Another method is to fold the leather outward at the bottom and stitch it directly to the mid-sole around the outside. Clearly, this is an easy way to make boots, since sewing does not have to be done in the constricted area inside the uppers. Unfortunately, it necessitates a small ledge around the outside of the boot, which is inherently undesirable in a mountain boot. With good construction, the sole can still be trimmed fairly close to the upper; but the other disadvantages cannot be overcome. This construction leaves the boot more vulnerable to leaks, because water follows the holes making the seam. Sealing has to be done more often and with less success. Even more important, both the seam and the edge which it holds are vulnerable to abrasion while climbing. Good boots made with this design use at least double rows of stitching, and a small leather strip known as a storm welt is often sewn over the fold to help reduce abrasion and leaking.

The worst type of boot construction is the Goodyear welt —a poor combination of the other methods. A strip of leather, the welt, is sewn first to the upper, so that this seam folds inside the boot; then the welt is sewn to the mid-sole along the outside. The advantages of this arrangment are considerable for

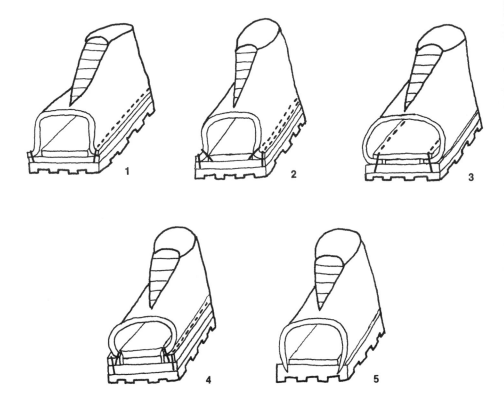

CONSTRUCTION OF BOOTS. This simplified illustration shows some of the most common ways of attaching boot uppers to soles. From left to right: 1. An outside stitched boot. The upper is stitched down directly to the mid-sole, onto which the sole is then glued. The mid-sole may be made of one or several layers of leather or rubber. The innersole is glued inside the boot. More than one row of stitching may be used. 2. Another kind of outside stitching, normally called a Norwegian welt. The upper is stitched to both the mid-sole and the innersole. Sometimes there are more than two rows of stitching, an extra innersole, and a strip of leather called a welt under the lines of stitching visible from outside the boot. Both this construction and no. 1 are used in many fine mountain boots, though the stitches are vulnerable to wear and to leakage. 3. An inside stitched boot. The innersole, upper, and mid-sole are stitched together from inside the boot, leaving the stitches protected from wear and water. There is a spacer of some kind under the innersole. Wooden pegs are sometimes used instead of stitching, and an additional innersole may be added. An excellent construction for mountain boots. May be mistaken for no. 5 (since the outsides are similar). 4. Goodyear welt construction. A strip of leather called a welt is first sewn to the upper and then to the mid-sole. It is subject to leakage, wear, and tearing, and it is generally impossible to repair. A good construction for dress shoes, but a poor one for mountain boots. May be mistaken for no. 1 or no. 2. 5. An injection molded boot. The upper is positioned in a mold while the liquid sole material is injected, so that the rubber adheres to the upper as it cures and hardens. There are no stitches or other fastenings to hold the upper and the sole together, so if the upper tears loose, the boot cannot be repaired. It is also virtually impossible to resole injection molded boots. This is a common construction for lightweight ski-touring boots, but it is not a good way to make mountaineering boots.

street shoes and nonexistent for mountain boots. The welt introduces flexibility where one does not want it, and it tends to come apart much sooner than it should, in a way that is difficult or impossible to repair.

In choosing a pair of general mountaineering boots, the first considerations should be sturdiness, sound construction, and overall suitability for mountain wear. At a minimum, the boots should be the right height, giving ankle support but not constricting the calf; the leather should be heavy and tough, preferably with the rough side out; the soles should be heavy-duty lugged neoprene (Vibram, Montagna, etc.); and the uppers should be free of seams sewn all the way through. The last feature is accomplished by designing the boot so that seams in the lining are located differently from outside seams. The boots should be fairly heavy and stiff by normal hiking standards, but the soles should not be so reinforced by steel shanks that they will remain inflexible. Other desirable features are a smooth lining, gusseted tongue, as few seams as possible in the upper, a sole cut close to the upper, and a construction using inside fastening to the mid-sole (wooden pegged fastening is best, but it is nearly unobtainable these days).

The most critical consideration, however, should be the fit. No matter how beautifully designed for climbing they may be, boots that do not fit properly will be a curse to the mountaineer. Ideally, a shop should be found which permits one to wear the boots outside when trying them on. If this is not possible, they should at least be tried in the store for some time. Properly fitting boots should be snug but comfortable when one is wearing the socks that will normally be used with them—usually one pair of heavy wool socks and one light inner pair. In particular, the heel of the foot should be held snugly, but there should be enough room for the toes to be curled. If the toes hit the front of the boot when they are jammed forward, they will be quite sore on steep downhill stretches, particularly after one's feet have swollen somewhat from a long day of walking. Some climbers are willing to pay this price to get a closer fitting boot for rock climbing, but such decisions are generally regretted.

It is very important that the boots are not too tight. Unlike some rock-climbing shoes, mountaineering boots do not usually stretch very much, and boots that are too tight are one of the main causes of frostbitten feet. The beginner should look hard for boots that feel good. Mountaineering boots will, of course, be stiffer and heavier than street shoes, but even before they are broken in, they should be comfortable. Boots that hurt even a little in the store will probably be unbearable after five or ten miles in the hills. Remember that the feet tend to swell on long hikes, and a tight fit in the shop will become painful on a long march in and agonizing on the way out.

It is a good idea to try out the boots' edging characteristics by trying to stand on some kind of small protrusion in the store —a rock in a masonry wall, the edge of a stair, a shelf, or whatever. Use a window ledge if there is nothing else—purveyors of climbing boots who do not provide suitable edges deserve no sympathy.

Take your time in buying climbing boots. Don't be rushed by the approach of the lunch hour or the problems of a clerk. Boots are the climber's trickiest and most important purchase, and you will have many painful hours to regret a hasty decision.

CARING FOR BOOTS

Boots are becoming very expensive, and there is no end in sight to the rising prices, so it behooves the impecunious climber to take care of them. Even the profligate should remember how much trouble it was to find a good pair and break them in, and he should put off the next such experience by caring for his current footwear.

Leather is made from the skin of an animal. It is as sensitive to heat as your own skin; if you keep this in mind, your boots will give you longer and happier service. Baking boots by a fire or in an oven can completely destroy them in short order. Drying boots in hot sun or over a heating vent should also be avoided. A good rule of thumb is never to subject boots to any more heat than your unprotected skin could tolerate. Besides damaging the leather, too much heat can activate the glue which holds on the soles, causing them to part company with the uppers at inconvenient times.

The second main danger to mountaineering boots is abrasion. Clearly, there is no way to eliminate wear in climbing footgear, but it is worthwhile to give some protection to the exposed seams, which are the most vulnerable places on the boots and those most frequently needing repairs. The best way to protect them is to mix up some good-quality household epoxy cement and smear it generously along all exposed seams. This treatment not only protects the line of stitching from abrasion; it also locks each stitch separately, so that a few cut threads will not cause the whole seam to open up. Many climbers use the epoxy to coat the toes of the boot too, giving some additional protection to that area, which often receives heavy wear in rock climbing.

Water is an enemy of leather, since it tends to wash out the natural oils and thus dry the leather out. Mountaineering boots should be regularly treated with waterproofing compounds, the kind and amount depending on expected conditions. Silicone-based compounds are preferable for mountaineering boots, because they have less tendency to soften the leather. Liquid treatments leave the boots free to breathe, while giving some resistance to water penetration. They are appropriate in seasons when the going is not too wet. In wetter areas and times of year, the silicone-based waxes make more sense—the more soaking one expects, the more wax one should work into the boots. The wax is absorbed best when it and the boots are warm, but heating the boots in the oven is not the answer. The wax melts just as well with the boots at room temperature, and it is far safer. The compound should be worked in with the fingers or a brush, particularly along the seams—the main leakage points. Occasionally, if the leather has been allowed to get very dry at certain points, spot treatment with boot oil may be necessary.

When boots are wet, as they frequently are, fast drying should *never* be attempted. Stuffing them loosely with newspaper will help to dry them, particularly if the paper is changed a few times. The boots should be left out in the open air, rather than packed away, until they are thoroughly dry. Boot trees are a very wise investment to prevent curling of the soles and premature retirement of the boots. External trees are best, but if the boot welt is narrow or the uppers are joined to the mid-sole internally, trees that fit inside the boots will have to be used.

Finally, make sure to repair your boots or have them repaired when they need it. If a line of stitching starts to pull out, it is much simpler to make repairs immediately, rather than wait for things to get worse. If one is so inclined, it isn't hard to make small stitching repairs at home using heavy nylon thread with a curved needle or sewing awl. In fact, one can often do a better job with such hand stitching than a shop can with a sewing machine, because with a curved hand needle you can avoid stitching through the lining.

Resoling should always be done before the rubber is worn down to the leather mid-sole. It is easy to forget this with climbing boots, because the toe often wears down to the leather while there is still plenty of rubber on the rest of the boot. Repairs involving the mid-sole become expensive or impossible, however, so get your boots resoled *before* the mid-sole is affected. Have the work done at a place experienced with mountain boots; this is not a job that can be carried out conveniently at home.

PACKS

The fashion in climbing packs seems to swing back and forth every couple of years or so between frame packs and rucksacks. The problem is that the climber would like his pack to be many things, a number of which are mutually exclusive. The contoured aluminum or magnesium frame is ideal for hauling gear along trails and open approaches on easy terrain, especially when big loads have to be carried. Unfortunately, these are not so wonderful when one is squeezing through brush, trying to look up on steep terrain, working on a rock-climbing move, skiing, or attempting to haul the pack up a cliff with a line. On reasonable walking terrain, the frame frees the body from having to lean constantly against the weight, transferring the load to the hips. On difficult terrain, it tends to do just the opposite, restricting body movement and shifting the weight to the wrong places. The frame projections are inclined to hang up on every bush or rock flake.

Many mountaineers use a frame to carry things in to a high camp, with a summit pack for use while actually climbing. This works well when the walk in is not over difficult terrain and one is returning by the same route. When these conditions aren't met, some go ahead and climb with frames, particularly in expedition climbing.

The alternative is to use some kind of large rucksack, either one that is completely frameless or one incorporating a frame. Rucksacks tend to interfere less with body movements and balance, so that they are much more pleasant to climb or ski with than frames. They are also much less prone to hang

Climber wearing a modern rucksack, designed for carrying heavy loads without hampering climbing too much. There are a number of types; this one, made by Lowe, has stiffeners that enable the wearer to transfer some load to his hips.

up on brush or rock projections. The difficulty has always been that they are far less comfortable for carrying heavy loads on the trail. Fortunately, the best modern rucksacks have incorporated some of the load-carrying capacities of frames. They will never replace frames for sheer comfort in hauling heavy weights over trails, but with reasonable loads they are quite pleasant to carry, while still retaining the climbing advantages of the rucksack. Some of them use flexible internal frames, perhaps with shoulder yokes and integrated waistbands. The best of this type is the Lowe pack, also incorporating load compressors which allow the pack's profile to be controlled, and a cross strap on the chest that leaves the arms freer for climbing and skiing.

Another approach is used in the Jensen pack, now made in versions by several manufacturers. It uses compartments to shape the pack, including a large wrap-around compartment at the bottom that forms part of a waist suspension. To be comfortable, this design has to be packed very carefully.

One other approach has the virtue of simplicity. The Forrest packs are made of very heavy and rugged material coated on both sides, with a basic sack shape and removable pockets. Padding for the back and some shaping is achieved with a stiff pad of ensolite, which can be taken out for use in bivouacs. The simple lines and rugged construction of the Forrest make it ideal for hauling up on a rope and for bivouacking. It must be packed with reasonable care, because it is frameless.

FOOD AND WATER

Preparation of food is pretty much the same for climbers as for other backpackers. Heavier meals may be indicated because of the extra exercise the climber usually gets, but this is a matter of individual metabolism. Meals should be kept relatively simple, so that excessive preparation time is not required. Plenty of extra food should always be carried by the mountaineer, in anticipation of possible emergency bivouacs and similar exigencies, and at least some of the extra food should be edible without cooking.

Stoves are necessary for cooking above timberline, and they are frequently required below that for conservation reasons. In cold weather the stove may also be needed for melting snow or ice to obtain water. The most efficient possible stove is obviously advantageous. The best currently available for small groups seems to be the new stove put out by Mountain Safety Research, which combines the advantages of very light weight with the easy lighting and rapid heating of a pumped stove. The small self-priming stoves which have been standard for years have always had the disadvantages of cumbersome ignition procedures and limited heating capacity. Small propane and butane stoves have sometimes replaced them because of easier lighting, but these are even less efficient heaters. A pumped stove using white gasoline or naphtha fuels is both easy to light and a fast heater, but the earlier models were rather heavy. The M.S.R. model is lighter than even the self-priming models because it uses the fuel can for a tank; it also has several other helpful features.

Mountaineers should pay special attention to providing sufficient water for their bodies. The combination of dry air and hard work that increases perspiration and panting tends to dehydrate the body rapidly, and one must often make a conscious effort to drink enough to replenish the supply of moisture. Dehydration will contribute to fatigue, and, in case of an accident or problems resulting from the cold, it will aggravate shock and hypothermia. Additional salt may be needed to combat profuse sweating. This can normally be provided by adding extra salt to meals, but if there is really heavy perspiration, salt tablets may be needed along with water.

In planning food and fuel one should take account of the conditions expected. More food will generally be required in cold weather, and extra fats, such as margarine, are often particularly welcome. Stew-type meals are well adapted to conditions when dehydration is a problem, particularly in cold weather and at high altitude, because some extra fluid can be gotten while eating. Fuel requirements will roughly double when water has to be melted from snow. Plenty of hot drinks should be planned in cold weather, when they are welcome both for their warmth and for replenishing the body's fluid supply.

A lightweight pressure cooker is surprisingly useful, particularly at high altitudes. Economical and concentrated dried foods like rice and beans can be used which would normally require too much time to cook. Fuel consumption is reduced considerably, because both the cooking time and the amount of water boiled away are cut down. Finally, when cooking inside a tent or snow shelter in cold weather, the condensation problem caused by water vapor from cooking is greatly reduced. A pressure cooker designed for mountaineering weighs around 3 pounds, roughly 2 pounds more than a regular pot of similar size; but on long trips the lower weight of the fuel that must be carried easily makes up the difference.

FINDING YOUR WAY

An intimate knowledge of map reading and compass work is very important for any climber who expects to spend much time in the mountains, particularly in the wilderness. Unfortunately, this art is often neglected, because mountaineers can usually navigate easily by watersheds and ridges with only a rough knowledge of the general terrain. One can travel in the mountains for years without even using a compass. However, the mountaineer is also quite likely to run up against an occasion when good compass and map work spell the difference between life and death. The only way to be ready for such circumstances is to make a practice of carrying map and compass and of knowing how to use them well.

SURVIVAL

For the mountaineer, the techniques of survival, planned bivouacs, and camping in general often tend to blend together. The experienced climber is far more likely to get into a difficult situation than the casual hiker, but he is also far more likely to be prepared for it, in terms of having both the right equipment and a good mental attitude. The proper equipment is essential for survival in bad weather at high altitude, where the mountaineer is unlikely to find boughs for a shelter, wood for a fire, or rabbits to snare. Even at lower elevations, warm clothing will be far more useful than a knowledge of edible plants. For the types of emergencies likely to be encountered in the mountains, adequate preparation is the most important asset.

Mental preparation is most important of all. People generally get into trouble in the wilderness when they do stupid things, and they rarely stay in trouble unless they continue to do more stupid things. Careful thought and observation are the best prevention and the best cure. There is no substitute for good judgment in the mountains: the ability to comprehend one's own strength, and that of one's party and equipment, and to balance these realistically against the hazards of the mountain environment. The more experience one gains, the more closely he can safely come to his limits. But the beginner who knows and respects his own limits may sometimes show better judgment than the experienced climber who is convinced he knows it all.

Special attention must be paid to the insidious effects of cold and altitude. A person beginning to suffer from the effects of hypothermia (chilling of the body core) is often quite unaware of the fact. It is important to watch for symptoms of excessive chilling in oneself and one's companions (see Chapter 18). Similarly, symptoms of acute altitude sickness should be taken very seriously and the victim brought to a lower altitude before he becomes a litter case or worse.

BASIC SURVIVAL EQUIPMENT

A number of items should always be in the mountaineer's pack, and others nearly always. By getting into the habit of carrying them, one is always prepared for trouble, and it is just this independence and self-sufficiency that is the most essential ingredient of mountaineering. Some of the items vary with the season and range of mountains. Extra clothing in summer will include raingear, while in many places in winter it will not. More extra food will be required when one is two weeks' walk from the nearest road than on a one-day climb.

Basically, however, the essentials are as simple and straightforward as the bodily needs on which they are based. My own experience over the years is that my emergency pack

Survival items: on a cagoule are, from upper left, a headlamp with extra bulb and battery, extra food, a first aid kit (packed in a watertight container), a water bottle, a map and a compass, matches, a candle, sunburn cream, lightweight sun goggles, a large plastic bag for the lower part of the body in a bivouac, a pocket knife, rain pants, extra socks, wool mittens, a wool sweater, and a balaclava helmet.

has become heavier, while my camping pack has gotten lighter, as I have learned to carry the essentials more of the time and the frills less and less.

First aid kit (see Chapter 18)	Water container
Extra food	Headlamp with extra battery
Extra clothing	and bulb
Pocket knife	Bivouac shelter
Extra matches in watertight	Map
container	Compass
Fire starter (candle, chemical	Sun cream
compound, or cigarette lighter)	Sun glasses or goggles

These items are pretty much self-explanatory, but there are a few points worth mentioning. The sun cream should be designed to cut out the strong ultra-violet component encountered at high altitude and reflected by surrounding snow. Zinc oxide creams and red veterinary petroleum are cheap and very effective. Sun protection for the eyes is also very important. Snow blindness is rarely noticed until the damage has been done, and being blind on a mountain is obviously dangerous.

The supply of extra matches is for emergencies and should be separated from the normal complement. A candle with a wick of large diameter makes a good fire starter, but many wilderness travelers prefer a butane cigarette lighter with an extension tube that can be added to direct the gas to the center of a pile of kindling. Chemical fire starters also work well.

A headlamp is far superior to a flashlight for convenience around camp if chores have to be done at night, and it is vital if one is caught at night on difficult terrain where the hands are needed for balance. Batteries should be bought several at a time and one of them tested in normal use, so that a bad batch is detected before it is relied on for an emergency. Age or exposure to considerable heat can cause batteries to deteriorate rapidly—batteries left in a closed car on a hot summer day may turn out to be practically worthless. The battery pack of the headlamp should be kept inside the clothing when in use in cold weather, since cold batteries do not perform well. If one is running short of batteries, they will last longer if the working battery and the spare are switched every twenty or thirty minutes. Alkaline cells last longer than standard (carbon-zinc) ones, perform better in cold weather, and are less affected by continuous use. Lithium cells are even better, but they are very expensive.

Probably the best bivouac shelter is a coated nylon envelope made for two or three people and allowing pooling of warmth and morale. A light color makes the inside more cheery. A roomy cagoule—the long, baggy rain parka—will serve for a one-man bivouac bag, providing the arms and feet can be drawn inside. A cheap, lightweight emergency shelter consists simply of one or two large plastic bags that the climber can get inside and seal against the weather to conserve heat and keep out cold rain. A small hole should be made for breathing. The plastic must be heavy enough so that it will not be quickly shredded in a severe wind.

3

ROUTEFINDING AND WEATHER

Routefinding is frequently the major problem to be solved in climbing a mountain—or even a small cliff. The development of real skill in this art usually requires far longer than acquiring the athletic ability to get up particular moves. In many popular climbing areas detailed guidebooks and the signs of past ascents have reduced routefinding to a matter of following a recipe. Perhaps fortunately, however, some guidebooks simply present an additional obstacle to the climber, and the route may be more obvious after he has discarded the description in disgust. Whatever the information available, no one can consider himself a well-rounded climber until he has developed at least fair skill at routefinding, if only because he may need his own skills to get him off a badly described route taken from a guidebook.

This chapter can only offer an introduction to the way that mountains are constructed. Real skill at putting together a climbing route must be acquired through study of the mountains and practice in climbing them. The experienced climber can usually be easily recognized in a group from the way he looks at a peak or a rock face—he is always standing around squinting at feasible paths, whether on major mountains or small cliffs and boulders, trying to put together the miscellaneous weaknesses into a climbing line. The game is played alike by peakbaggers, serious technical rock climbers, and boulderers, sometimes on large-scale problems and sometimes on small.

To learn routefinding, the climber must combine careful

observation with past experience. Every bit of climbing experience that one has is distilled into the making of a route: judgment of the scale and size of features; assessment of objective dangers from rockfall, avalanches, ice towers, and crevasses; guesses about steepness, the size of cracks, the difficulties of individual rock pitches, the likely condition of snow or ice; consideration of weather conditions and the equipment that will be needed; and other bits of information and judgment. The point here is that the way to learn routefinding is to get used to picking out routes and then to climb those which are within your capacity (allowing a large safety margin), measuring your estimation of the route against what you actually find. Learn as much as you can about geology and weather, about different kinds of rock and different types of snow, and about the ways people have climbed things before you. Climb on as many different kinds of rocks and mountains as you can. Sandstone slabs are quite different from granite cracks or limestone faces, and spring snow is worlds apart from glacier ice or the gullies of late summer.

MOUNTAIN GEOLOGY

Even a moderate knowledge of the climate and geology of a particular mountain or range will tell the climber a great deal about what to expect, before he ever sees a climb. If he is going to Mount Shasta in California, Popocatepetl in Mexico, or Mount Fuji in Japan—all volcanoes of relatively recent origin, and all far higher than anything else around—he could expect slopes with a fairly gentle average incline, poor-quality rock, and a good deal of permanent cover of snow and glacier ice. Recognizing that the Colorado Rockies are considerably older and more worn by the forces of erosion than Washington's North Cascades, and that the drier climate has not allowed major glaciation to take place recently in Colorado as it has in the Cascades, he will expect generally less precipitous terrain in the former, with easier descent routes on most peaks, no major glaciers, and fairly quick approaches. The Cas-

Glacially polished granite in Yosemite National Park, perfect rock for climbing.

cades are younger and more rugged, with heavy rainfall resulting in many active glaciers and steep approaches choked by vegetation.

The more the climber knows about how the mountains in which he is interested are put together, the better he will be able to anticipate conditions in a particular range and on a given route. The way that mountains are formed is extremely complex and varied, but any observant mountaineer can begin to get a feeling for the process from his first climb, particularly if visibility is good. One has merely to walk through the high Sierra to sense the awesome cutting and polishing power of glaciers. The smooth, vertical walls of Yosemite Valley attest both to the tremendous forces exerted by the glaciers and to the strength of the rock that they smoothed and polished.

Most mountain ranges are formed by upheavals in the earth's crust, by buckling and wave action. Mountains, like ripples in the water, are moving and temporary structures, although the time span involved in their uplifting is vast by human standards. Even as a mountain range or a volcano begins to rise, the forces of erosion and gravity start to tear it down. Long before a major peak or massif reaches its full height, the decision on that maximum altitude hinges on a contest between the forces pushing it up and those ripping it apart. Indeed, the form of a spire or a range is determined as the weaker layers of material are ripped away by water and ice, leaving the strongest masses of rock standing as a challenge to the climber, before they too are eventually ground back into the earth to become the building blocks for some future uplift.

The formation of a peak is thus the result of a history of the colossal forces which threw it up out of the sea and of the smaller but ultimately more powerful forces which have been wearing it away, block by block and grain by grain. The simplest to understand are pure volcanoes, which build up into great mounds from successive eruptions, sometimes miles from any other mountains. Large volcanoes often have very severe weather and glaciation, because they receive the full brunt of incoming storms. Mount Rainier is an excellent example. It is close to a soggy coast, standing 14,000 feet above the sea with no aid from high plateaux. Its self-created glaciers have carved steep walls and cirques, but it retains a characteristic volcano shape, especially from a distance.

Even volcanoes like Rainier or Shasta are formed of rock, ash, cinders, and lava of varying consistency, which will weather at different rates. The cutting action of glaciers will rapidly modify any symmetry that may initially have been present, giving the mountain its own glacial cirques and valleys, drainage systems, and ridges between them. All these features will be further modified by running and freezing water.

Most mountains have far more complex histories than volcanoes. They result from massive uplifts of thick layers of rock which were once buried deep beneath the ocean floor. A whole plateau may be lifted up without significant distortion and then eroded so that more durable sections are left as high points. The Canadian Rockies are made up largely in this way.

The various layers of rock of which they consist are clearly visible in any of the peaks, extending horizontally in essentially the same position that they were originally deposited on the bottom of the sea.

Mountains are frequently formed when a great mass of rock is pushed up from underneath, bending, breaking, and uplifting the layers on top. These upper layers may then be eroded away, leaving the underlying rock; or some of the stronger upper layers may resist erosion and remain. Alternatively, the mountains may be formed by folding of all the layers of rock under pressure from both sides and from movement of the earth's crust. Again, erosive forces will carry away the weaker layers, while the stronger ones will be left exposed longer, and will perhaps rise higher as weight is removed and uplifting forces continue. Great blocks, instead of folding, may ride up onto adjoining land when the shifting surface of the earth exerts pressure on both sides. Such a block may then have a very steep face on one side, as on the eastern escarpment of the Sierra Nevada, while the other side rises far more gently.

Most frequently, all the characteristics mentioned will be shown in some degree in any great range of mountains. There will be volcanoes here and there, sections of uplifted and eroded sedimentary sea bottoms, folds, and fault blocks, mixed perhaps with hunks of older mountain ranges. Each piece of information, aside from its intrinsic interest, is relevant to the mountaineer.

THE BUILDING BLOCKS

The rocks of which mountains are formed have a history every bit as intricate as the peaks of which they are a part, and the formation of rock is inextricably interwoven with the creation of the mountains. Many rocks are formed from molten minerals under great pressure deep under the earth's crust. The molten material may suddenly escape through a rift in the surface, cooling and oxidizing as it pours out, and mixing with debris that is carried out in the explosive eruption, finally forming one of the many types of *volcanic* rock. Cooling which is not so dramatic occurs when the molten material flows out slowly rather than explosively or when it does not actually break the surface. Slower cooling generally produces sounder rock.

Far stronger formations normally result when the molten material has cooled under pressure deep under the earth's surface, forming *plutonic* rocks, such as granite, sometimes in very thick layers. Rocks are also formed in *sedimentary* layers deposited slowly at the bottom of the sea, and gradually bonding together as a result of pressure and chemical action. Such layers may be formed from sand, resulting naturally in sandstone; from the deposit of the shells of marine animals, which forms limestone; or from mud, forming mudstone. Rock is also frequently formed by the minerals which percolating water (in which they were dissolved) deposits.

As with mountain formation, rocks are generally the result of a number of processes. Mineral-laden water may percolate through a sedimentary layer, bonding it together with deposits, or simply leaving pockets of foreign material here and there. The whole layer may then be subjected to great heat and pressure for long periods of time, transforming it into *metamorphic* rock. Some highly metamorphized rocks may be almost indistinguishable from plutonic ones.

LAYERS AND JOINTING

The consequences of these processes for the climber, though complex, are very important. The best rock climbing is usually found on plutonic and metamorphic rock, which may stand at high angles, presenting a strong challenge without the threat of crumbling at the touch. Many of the best rock-climbing regions are composed of great uplifted plutonic masses which have been first eroded by water and then scooped and polished by glaciers to form great vertical walls. Equivalent walls of volcanic or sedimentary rock present as much chal-

lenge, but they are likely to have sections that are terrifyingly
loose. In the Canadian Rockies, for example, the mountains are
composed of almost horizontal sedimentary layers, protected
for a while from erosion by a strong cap of harder rock. Some
of the layers below are quite sound, while others are very
weak. The strong layers tend to form cliffs, overhangs, and
ledges as they resist erosion. As the weaker layers are torn
apart faster, they erode out from between the harder sections,
covering the strong ledge below with a slope of dangerous
rubble, and perhaps presenting a rotten wall under the cliff or
overhang formed by the next strong layer of rock. The result
is extremely hazardous climbing, and standards on such terrain have only recently advanced significantly from those of
half a century ago. On these mountains, as on many volcanic
ones, snow and ice routes are generally preferred to avoid the
unpleasantness and danger of rotten rock.

On mountains composed of sedimentary or metamorphic
layers which are tilted, the upsloping side will usually be much
easier to climb than the downsloping side. Both ledges and
individual holds will tend to be upsloping, forming sharp
capped holds, although more loose debris may be caught on
the ledges. On the other side of the mountain both ledges and
holds will tend to be downsloping, often with overhanging
sections interspersed.

Severely tilted layers sometimes provide excellent climbing themselves. When the strata are angled steeply enough,
softer layers wear away between them, often leaving spectacular slabs or pinnacles. For example, some of the strong sandstone formations which were tilted up by the rise of the Rocky
Mountains provide excellent climbing on the east slope of the
range in Colorado, such as the Flatirons and Eldorado Springs
Canyon formations near Boulder.

Whether mountains and outcroppings are made up of layers or not, they will usually have recognizable patterns of jointing; that is, rifts from great valleys and faces to finger cracks
and minute ledges will tend to follow certain patterns, because
the weaknesses and points of stress in the rock will not be

The Flatirons above Boulder, Colorado. Stratified, sedimentary rock, these formations began as the bottom of a shallow sea, were pushed up by the rise of the Rocky Mountains, and were left standing when the softer layers around them eroded away.

random. Thus, ledges and crack systems are rarely chance formations. If one crack system peters out halfway up a cliff, there will frequently be an extension above or a parallel network not far away. A ledge dwindling away at a corner often continues around the other side. There are countless examples, but the more the climber looks at the way his mountains are put together, the more he will be able to take advantage of their natural weaknesses and strengths.

FEATURES OF THE PEAKS

The fact that the tearing-down process starts as soon as a mountain range begins to rise has important consequences for the climber. It is generally the erosive forces which create the challenges and aesthetic qualities he seeks in the mountains, and which also are responsible for most of the dangers he must overcome or avoid. Running water quickly begins to carry away weaker material from steep spots, depositing it temporarily on ledges further down the mountain or in meadows below. Stronger pieces of rock may stand out in stark pinnacles or may cap lower rotten layers on less attractive mountains.

Water can speed its destructive influence dramatically, particularly in strong rock, by freezing. On a small scale, the effect is felt in *frost wedging*. Water fills tiny cracks in the rock; when it freezes to ice, it expands and can exert tremendous splitting forces. Besides its long-term effects, this frost wedging has important immediate consequences for the climber. In many places and seasons, rockfall is to be expected from icy parts of the mountain when they are thawed by the sun or by warm air. The stones are wedged free in cold weather by expanding ice, which then holds them in place until melting occurs, when they fall. On rock which is severely affected by frost wedging, the climber should expect to find many loose blocks on ledges, ridges, and anywhere else a rock can sit.

On a larger scale, frozen water in the form of glaciers has sculptured most of the interesting climbing ranges, and in some cases is still at work. Glaciers are formed when more snow accumulates each year than melts, so that snowfields become larger and larger. Eventually they begin to slide downhill, just as water does, picking up rocks, sand, and boulders along the way. The ice and accumulated detritus grinds against the path of the glacier, wearing away more material as it goes and smoothing its path. Glaciers naturally form in watercourses, and, as they flow downhill, they move through the V-shaped valleys that have been cut by streams. Characteristically, the glacier will scoop out the bottom of the valley and smooth the sides, leaving the classic U-shaped glaciated valley. At the head of the valley, where the glacier formed, there is normally a semicircular steep, smooth cliff called a *cirque* where the ice has worn the rock down. If there were several glaciers falling over cliffs onto one another, there may be several cirques.

Most of the ranges of the contiguous United States no longer have significant glaciers. Technically, a number exist in California, Colorado, Wyoming, and so on, but they can hardly be distinguished from permanent snowfields. Large glaciers which still move very much are found primarily in the mountains of Washington and Oregon. Further north, the western mountains of Canada abound with great glaciers and icefields, as do those of Alaska. The effects of glaciation are prominent in many American ranges, however—the great rock climbs in the Sierra, in Rocky Mountain National Park in Colorado, and in the Wind River Range of Wyoming are all on walls cut by glaciers. Many of the climbing cliffs in the eastern United States are the products of more ancient glaciation. Cathedral and White Horse ledges in New Hampshire are excellent examples.

Some of the features of mountains are mentioned in the glossary.

FINDING A WAY UP

Routes up a mountain may follow any of the characteristic features—or a combination of them. Which is easiest or safest will depend on numerous factors, but certain dominant attributes are normally expected. Their effects on the climber will depend on his skill, on the nature of the range and the weather, and many other considerations.

Approaches vary a good deal, depending on the remoteness of the range, its age, and the climate. In the Sierra Nevada, the approach will generally be a pleasant backpack. Even off-trail routes will cause the climber no special difficulties, providing he avoids cliffs. Streams may require fairly long detours to find a good crossing, particularly in the spring, but brush and deadfall present only moderate obstacles, and long gentle valleys and meadows frequently allow the mountaineer to make excellent time. In the Northern Cascades or the Coast

MOUNTAIN FEATURES: A, peak; B, needle, aiguille; C, couloir; D, gully, chute; E, notch; F, saddle, col; G, pass; H, ridge; I, buttress; J, arête; K, glacier; L, moraine (medial); M, crevasses; N, hanging glacier; O, bergschrund, rimaye; P, gendarmes; Q, moraine (lateral). For more details see text and glossary.

Ranges of British Columbia, on the contrary, the approach may be more difficult than the ascent, both in terms of effort and actual difficulty. Valleys are deep and precipitous, vegetation on the floors nearly impenetrable, and slopes below snowline support steep grass and heather that may be harder to ascend and more dangerous than ice. Streams are often large and hard to cross, and the thick forest around them can make a mile-long search for a crossing take the better part of a day. Stream crossings in areas like this will often require belaying and rope techniques that are usually reserved for the cliffs above.

The *ridge* of a peak will always present the lowest average gradient of any of the possible routes up, and ridges have other advantages as well. They are essentially free from the hazards of avalanches and falling rocks sweeping down from above, and are likely to allow the mountaineer to climb above dense trees and brush sooner than would be possible on other approaches. The view is generally fine, and the route will be easier to see than from most other perspectives. Finally, ridge routes are often aesthetically very satisfying to the climber, with high airy spots and a variety of climbing problems. On the other hand, ridge routes tend to be long and exposed to the elements. The rock on the top of a ridge is often broken and severely shattered, so that trustworthy holds may be hard to come by. The continuous up and down may greatly lengthen the route, and on difficult ridges, the climbers may be repeatedly forced out onto faces on either side to bypass difficulties. If there is enough snow, there is likely to be a steep snow slope to one side, and the lee side is likely to be overhung with a shoulder of windblown snow called a *cornice.* On a corniced ridge it is frequently impossible to tell where the top of the ridge stops and the cornice starts; even when this can be discerned, there may be no good ground between a steep windward snow slope and a dangerous cornice. Finally, in case of a thunderstorm a ridge is the worst place to be on a mountain, short of the summit itself.

Faces and walls have very different advantages and disadvantages. The routes will generally be shorter and the approaches longer, and the average angle of the face will, of course, be much steeper. On the other hand, the route will probably be fairly direct, with the rock more likely to be good. The route must be carefully planned in advance, for once the climbers are on the wall their view will be so foreshortened that they are likely to lose their way unless they have carefully examined and memorized its features in advance. Climbs on big walls are often successful only after long study by the climbers from many vantage points and in many conditions of lighting and snow, each revealing different aspects and details.

Couloirs, chutes, and *gullies* present rifts in faces or ridges and generally act as the rubbish collectors for surrounding sections of the mountain, sometimes only a small section and sometimes an entire side of a great peak. They are initially formed either from weak bands of rock or from jointing, and since they also collect debris, they will often be filled with loose rock. Sometimes this piled and jammed material offers easy climbing in an otherwise difficult face. Couloirs and gullies generally retain snow and ice longer than other parts of a mountain, so they may offer a snow or ice route on a mountain that is rock everywhere else.

Routes in couloirs are tempting because they are fairly obvious avenues of progress. There seems, at least at first, to be no routefinding problem in a gully: one starts at the bottom and goes up, ending either at the top of the peak or the top of the particular feature in which the gully lies. Gullies do often form the easiest routes up the peaks, but they can be quite deceptive. To begin with, the gully will often be more gentle than the surrounding face at the bottom, but one must remember that if it is cut into the face, the altitude gain has to occur somewhere. Frequently it comes in vertical or overhanging steps part way up the chute, often worn smooth by material feeding down. Exits from gullies, both on the way up and at the top, can be very difficult or even impossible. Snow stays in a couloir because it is packed hard and protected from much sun; thus, the gully is often dark, cold, and impossible to escape. Chutes may be icy when snow elsewhere is soft, and they may be wet when other rock is dry.

Most important, gullies and couloirs are likely to be the most vulnerable places on the mountain to the hazards of falling rocks, ice, and snow. The danger involved will depend on the situation of a couloir and the soundness of the peaks around. Where the danger of rockfall is slight, a couloir may be a perfectly safe route; but a rift draining a whole loose face may be very risky even to cross and suicidal to climb. Because they are most prone to avalanches and rockfall, gully routes

Snow couloirs with cornices at the tops in Wyoming's Snowy Range provide perfect climbing when cold and hard, but warm sun could trigger the cornices, making the gullies below into death traps.

tend to be the ones where the hour and speed of climbing are most important. A gully may be safe in the early hours, before the sun hits the slopes above, while it becomes a shooting gallery an hour later.

OBSERVATION

As obvious as it may seem, the most important factor in finding a route up a mountain is observation. On the hike .or backpack in, there is a natural tendency to appreciate the beauty of the surroundings or to walk along head down, straining against the pack; in fact, one should be studying the route from as many vantage points as possible, memorizing the features of the mountain. Divergent views and varying lighting will show very different aspects. From one angle you may be able to judge the true gradient of a face, something almost impossible to tell from close up and head-on. From another situation and at a different time of day, you may be able to see a system of ledges that will provide a route. Careful attention to the relation of features on the mountain while one is at a distance can prove vital later on when one is too close to be able to see the route as a whole.

If a party is attempting a big climb a long way off, everything that will contribute to success becomes important, and study of pictures can be valuable. Those which show snow conditions at different times of the year are particularly useful, not only because the snow may provide a route, but because it reveals many details of the mountain that are otherwise not apparent. Snow will show up ledges and gullies that may be nearly invisible or might otherwise be mistaken for rock bands or water streaks. Snow may also tell one a good deal about the angle of a face, since it will rarely rest for long on anything steeper than 45 degrees. Permanent snow and ice will stay in steep gullies, and glaciers and snowfields in precipitous cirques on the mountain; but seasonal snow in large quantities will avalanche off steep faces.

ON THE MOUNTAIN

The final test in routefinding occurs on the mountain. Things are always a bit different from what might be expected by even the most skillful mountaineer—that is what renders the ascent of a new route, or an old one with no description or guide, a particular challenge. Making a route go requires climbing skill, insight into the structure of the mountain, and sometimes audacity in pushing unlikely possibilities.

It is important to remember when one is climbing that eventually it will be time to go down. Looking back along the way is as vital as inspecting the ground ahead. It can be surprisingly easy to lose the way, even on difficult rock, because things look very different going down. Even if the party plans to take a different route off, it should be able to reverse the ascent in case of bad weather or unexpected difficulties. This means taking note of features where the way might be confusing— remembering which gully or ledge one came up onto a ridge. Cairns sometimes need to be left to mark the take-off from a plateau or snowfield. On some mountains it may be necessary to take compass bearings or leave wands to mark the return, particularly on snow routes when fog or storms may come in. Wands are usually light bamboo sticks that can be bought in garden shops; they can be made more visible with bright plastic strips tied to the top.

WEATHER

Mountain weather, which is notoriously fickle, is critical to the climber and mountaineer. The backpacker may get wet if he misjudges a thunderstorm; the climber risks electrocution. Bad weather poses one of the inescapable dangers of climbing. The mountaineer can try to avoid it and to minimize the consequences if he is caught by surprise, but it is impossible to eliminate its dangers from the sport.

Every range of mountains has its own weather patterns,

and the better the climber learns them, the better chance he will have of staying comfortable, making successful climbs, and avoiding predictable dangers. The most general statement one can make about mountain weather is that it is only predictable to a limited degree. In any of the major mountain regions of North America, cold rain and snow can occur at any time of the year. The mountain traveler who is not prepared to survive in such conditions with rain gear, wool clothing, and the like, is not unlucky when he gets caught; he's merely a fool whose time has come. The mountains are deceptive, because the weather can change so quickly from baking hot to bone-chilling cold; but they are consistently deceptive—people are caught unprepared and killed every year. The reasonably prudent mountaineer carries his survival gear whenever he goes high.

The *hypothermia syndrome* should be known and studied by every mountain walker. Cold weather and chilling wind, particularly wet cold which robs clothing of its insulation, saps the body of its warmth. Exhaustion, dehydration, and insufficient food will all speed the process. As the victim's body is chilled, he loses his good judgment; he is rarely aware of what is happening, and he frequently does the wrong thing. Eventually, he becomes completely irrational, often stumbles and hurts himself, and finally passes out and dies. Unless the prospective hypothermia victim stops the heat loss and increases heat production at an early stage, he becomes unable to help himself and will die unless someone intervenes and warms him up.

Hypothermia is by far the most common weather-related cause of mountain accidents and deaths, and many tragedies which are attributed to other causes are caused at the root by hypothermia—the fall or the error in judgment that result from a numbed mind. Fundamentally, however, hypothermia is caused by lack of preparation. Beyond repeating that it is important to be prepared and alert, there is little one can say.

Storms coming in can present the climber with a host of other problems, and to the degree possible he should stay aware of them when he climbs. Freezing rain can coat rocks with a thin film of ice called *verglas,* making climbing difficult or impossible. Besides chilling the climber, hard rain can sometimes cause formerly safe snow to become so heavy that it is quickly ready to avalanche. Reduced visibility makes routefinding difficult. Snow or rain can cut the range of sight dramatically. The worst of all is a whiteout, caused by thick fog rolling in over a snowfield or glacier and so reducing visibility that one can scarcely tell up from down.

Heat can also cause problems for the climber. In desert regions and in some rock-climbing areas, the hot sun can ennervate the climber and drain the moisture from him very quickly. More than one party has found itself in real trouble on big climbs in Yosemite Valley when caught with inadequate water in the hot summer months. In spring in the high country, the winter snows commonly avalanche after being softened by the sun, so that an early climb must be planned to avoid avalanche danger.

ELECTRICAL STORMS

Probably the most feared of mountain hazards are lightning storms, mainly because they can develop so quickly, and because the only preventive measure is to be somewhere else when one hits. Thunderstorms frequently occur when major fronts move over the peaks, but they are also caused by the peaks themselves when warm air rises from the sun-heated mountainsides. In many ranges, afternoon thunderstorms are so common in summer that climbers simply have to plan to be off the summits and on their way down by noon. The electrical charges which are released by thunderbolts tend to concentrate on peaks, pinnacles, and ridges, so these are clearly the places to be avoided. When a strike occurs, however, the charge on the mountain is dissipated by currents which run along the ground, and many reported lightning strikes are actually cases of people who are in the path of a ground current. The ground currents are strongest near the strike points.

Clearly, the appropriate action if a lightning storm is

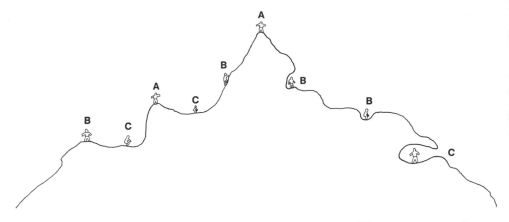

RELATIVE DANGER FROM LIGHTNING: A, suicidal; B, dangerous; C, relatively safe.

threatening is to get off the mountain. If a line of thunderheads (big, dark cumulus clouds, particularly mushroom- or anvil-shaped ones) is approaching, and especially if one is forming over the mountain on which you are standing, it is only wise to get off. A good eye to the weather will prevent most close encounters, which are generally caused when a party is so intent on climbing that people pay no attention to the sky. Unfortunately there are times when people are caught, despite their care. A thunderhead can sometimes form out of a cloudless sky in the space of fifteen or twenty minutes. There are also times when a party will emerge on the summit at the same time that a storm system arrives from the other side. Those, as they say, are the breaks of the game; one can always take up Ping-Pong instead.

If a thunderstorm does threaten, there are a few precautionary measures that can be taken—sometimes. The illustration shows the best and the worst places to be. The most important thing the climber can do is try to find a place of relative safety. The discharging electrical currents stay on the surface of the mountain, and they will follow the line of least resistance. You should assume a position which ensures that that line does not pass through you. The feet should be close together on the ground, and hands should not touch the rock. It is particularly important not to let the body bridge gaps over which a spark might jump, since a current between the hands and feet or the two hands will pass through the heart. It is not important whether or not one has metal hardware, even though it may buzz with static discharge. Squatting on pack or rope helps to insulate the body from the ground. Crack systems are often carriers of current, and so are wet ropes. If a spot is so precarious that the climbers need to be tied to the rope, it is at least best to have the anchor at the feet if possible; if it is above, on a rock wall, current may travel through the feet and up the rope. Obviously, climbers high on a wall can do little in a thunderstorm except try to keep their hands off the rock. Rappelling off on a rope can be very hazardous, since the current is quite likely to follow the rope.

It is often difficult to decide on the safest course to follow when lightning threatens a party on an exposed route. Ground currents much too weak to kill by themselves can still cause muscles to jerk violently, knocking climbers off even easy terrain. Placing protection, as discussed in Chapter 8, will help prevent this sort of hazard from being fatal, but it will also slow the party, and speed in getting off dangerous terrain is often the most important consideration during an electrical storm.

SCRAMBLING
ON ROCK AND SNOW

Scrambling is the general term to describe climbing which requires using the hands occasionally, but where the difficulties and dangers are not sufficient to require a rope. Naturally the term is rather flexible, since both the conditions of a climb and the people doing it vary a good deal.

Easy scrambling is merely an extension of the techniques used in walking on rough ground. Proficiency depends mostly on experience. Negotiating talus blocks or willow clumps simply requires confidence, a sense of balance, and a practiced eye.

As slopes become steeper and the hands come more into play, the beginner should concentrate on keeping his weight over his feet and letting the legs do the work, with his hands reserved for balance. Your arms aren't strong enough to pull you up the mountain, and they will tend to throw you off balance if you try to use them that way. Keeping the arms low and the weight on the feet will conserve a lot of energy.

Good technique on scrambling terrain can teach the novice the form he will need on more difficult climbs. All the same kinds of holds are used. Learn where the boot will stick—how steep the rock can be, how slick, how wet, or how slimy. Practice edging the boot on small holds, finding out how to use them most effectively. Try wedging the boots in cracks in various directions—many excellent holds can be found this way. Use short steps on small holds rather than straining awkwardly to reach big ledges.

It is very important to get into the habit of testing all holds

Climbing on easy scrambling terrain on Crestone Needle in Colorado's Sangre de Cristo Range.

as well as inspecting them visually. This does not really take a significant amount of time. With handholds, one simply gives a yank or jiggle before trusting one's weight to the hand. Footholds can be tested with a kick. Movement or a hollow sound should indicate special caution, although loose holds may often be strong enough for use in some directions.

Rhythm and balance are the two most important things to

learn in scrambling, and they will stand in good stead in more difficult climbing. Moving with a regular rhythm rather than jerky start-and-stop movements conserves energy and encourages good climbing style. Smooth movements ultimately get one up a climb far faster than jerky spurts of speed.

Climbing in balance serves to make the legs do the work, and thus prevents the arms from tiring too quickly. Equally important, the body then stands away from the slope, so that one can see what is above. If the climber leans in toward the slope, he cannot see what he is doing. Leaning in is an instinctive reaction if things get a little steep, but it is usually a bad idea. Clutching the rock brings the weight inside the feet and tends to push them off the rock or snow, so that one becomes less rather than more secure.

CLIMBING ON SNOW

Snow climbing is at least as varied as rock work, but it is quite different, because the snow cover is always changing. The same slope may be an easy scramble in the morning and turn into an icy ramp or an avalanche trap in the afternoon. Thus the climber must be constantly aware of the changing nature of the climb. These factors and the proper use of the ice ax and crampons are discussed in later chapters, but the beginner should be very wary of venturing out on snow unless he knows what he is doing. Snow slopes often provide the most straightforward avenues to the peaks, but they can be traps for the unprepared and the unwary.

On the simplest snow, a slope can be climbed by simply kicking steps. Particularly in the spring, the snow is often soft enough so that the foot can easily kick a platform, yet firm enough to hold the body's weight. This is commonly the case when recent snowfall has been wet, when the sun or warm air has softened the surface, or when a hard wind or sun crust is thin enough for holes to be kicked in it.

When steps can be kicked, easy progress can be made up snow ranging from a mild gradient to very steep slopes. In fact, when the snow is in this condition, the beginner's problem is more likely to be his ability to get out of his depth rather than overcoming actual obstacles. It is important to remember that even on slopes where steps can easily be kicked, loss of balance or a broken step can send one plummeting downward. If the slope is short and has a good runout, this may be of no importance; otherwise, it is prudent to have some way of stopping. Belaying with a rope or self-arrest with an ice ax are the techniques used, and they are discussed elsewhere in the book. It is also important to stay off slopes where one is not sure of the absence of avalanche hazard, both on the climb up and during the return journey.

Balance is even more important on snow than on rock. Except on extreme climbs, with which the novice is not concerned, all the climbing is done with the feet. The hands and ax, when they are used at all, are strictly for balance. If the climber leans into the slope for comfort, he will be pushing outward on his steps, and they may break out. Snow is frequently very strong under compressive loads, but with an outward push or pull it is generally quite weak.

Ascent may either proceed diagonally up a slope, with the whole boot or most of the edge in contact with the snow at each step, or one may kick straight up, in which case only the toe will penetrate in harder snow. This direct approach is generally more strenuous but faster, and frequently one alternates to rest different muscles in the legs.

The leader does much more work in this sort of climbing, so the lead should normally be changed frequently. When he tires, the first man can merely step aside and let the line pass him, dropping to the back so that the party keeps moving during the switch. This allows each person to lead as long as he can and gives him a short rest while the others pass. Naturally, individual strength will vary, but the load should generally be shared. A self-styled hard man who works himself to exhaustion can be more of a liability on a mountain than a weaker person who knows his limitations. In snow climbing, as elsewhere, it is usually best if the party keeps going at a steady pace. This proves faster than spurting along and then stopping for long periods to recover.

Normally the leader kicks steps just large enough to support his own weight, and succeeding members make the steps larger. The situation varies with the snow, but merely stepping into the holes made by the leader often breaks them out and spoils the party rhythm.

Descending snow slopes by step-kicking is quite easy, since the weight of the body can be used to provide the force of penetration. One simply plunges down on the heel, stiff-legged, hence the terms *plunge step* and *heeling down.* Again, the key is keeping the body upright with the weight over the feet. This is psychologically harder in descending, because one can see the slope below and instinctively tends to lean back into the slope. In fact, sitting back will cause the heel to break out, so that the sense of security provided by shying back is very false.

It cannot be overemphasized that it is easy to get into trouble on even moderate snow slopes. Before venturing onto snow, the climber must be sure that he will be safe from the dangers of slips and from avalanche hazard, both on the ascent and on the return journey.

THE LIMITS OF SCRAMBLING

The expert climber is likely to consider scrambling on climbs where no beginner should be without a rope. With more skill and experience the seasoned mountaineer will have a fairly precise knowledge of his own abilities and the difficulties that the peaks present. On severe climbs there are also situations where the delays required by roped climbing may present more danger than the possibility of a slip. But the beginner is nearly always foolish to take chances; where the consequences of a fall would be serious, he should not proceed without proper protective measures.

The limits of scrambling should thus be set by danger rather than difficulty. The two may be related, but they often are not. One may occasionally make quite difficult moves on a scramble, surmounting an 8-foot cliff over a broad, grassy ledge, for example. As long as the consequences of a slip would not be more serious than a wounded ego, difficulty is not important. On the other hand, easy climbs may be unjustified without the use of a rope. If a pulled-out hold or a falling rock would plunge the climber off a high precipice, he is not on safe ground for scrambling. A classic example is walking on flat glaciers that are active enough to have crevasses. The difficulty involved may be no greater than walking along a trail, but in certain snow conditions unroped climbers risk death should they break through a snow bridge.

Scrambling ascents provide the best training ground for beginners to learn all the skills associated with mountaineering and climbing, but it is important to remain cautious, particularly when one is unsure of the mountain or one's own abilities. With trustworthy and experienced leaders, the novice can undertake much more difficult climbs, but he should always exercise his own judgment as well, both in order to learn and in order to maintain safety. If the climber is not sure he can make a move safely, he should not hesitate to say so. Just as important, he should learn always to weigh the multitude of factors that might indicate turning back on a climb: the time, the weather, the strength of each person and of the party as a whole, the difficulties and dangers on the climb, problems that might arise on the descent, the possibility of becoming lost on the route, and the equipment carried by the party and by each member. Clearly, the same party would have to turn back sooner under the threat of a storm if one of the members had brought only light clothing.

A FEW GENERAL RULES

Accident reports show several recurrent patterns that are well worth keeping in mind. Although most of the rules that they indicate would seem to be obvious, the repetition of the same mistakes, often by competent parties, indicates that considerable care is sometimes needed to avoid doing silly things.

The first rule of survival is to *carry adequate equipment* for any conditions one might reasonably expect to encounter. Heading the list are suitable clothing and the survival items mentioned in Chapter 2. Sunny days in the mountains are so pleasant that one is tempted to go off on a climb with only light clothing on the assumption that one will be down early, anyway. This may work on many occasions, but it has been the cause of a number of deaths and harrowing experiences. Weather changes quickly in the high country, and accidents can overtake the most experienced and cautious climbers. The margin of difference between an unfortunate incident and a disaster is generally the clothing and other survival items carried by the individual or the party. The same general rule applies to technical equipment, which should be carried for the worst conditions that might occur. If avalanche conditions in the afternoon might require the party to rope down on rock rather than returning by the easy snow slope used on the ascent, for example, prudence would dictate carrying a rope and whatever other equipment might be needed.

It is also simple common sense to *turn back soon enough.* Clearly, this is a matter of judgment, but problems usually arise not because people don't realize that they should head down, but because they allow their desire for an ascent to override their common sense. The easiest way to handle this is to discuss the problem early in the day on a one-day climb and set a reasonable turn-around time suitable for the route. If the party is not really prepared for a night out, time must be allowed to get down those sections that it would be unreasonable to descend in the dark. Subtracted from the hour of darkness, perhaps with extra allowance for the unforeseen, this will give the latest possible time to head back. The same principles apply on multi-day ventures, except that wider latitude should be given for error. Once food runs out, efficiency will start to go down, and there is always the possibility of a storm which will greatly complicate a retreat.

In a difficult situation, *don't let the party separate.* Accident reports are replete with examples of groups which have multiplied their troubles by carelessly allowing some members to split off under the pressure of an emergency or an impulse. If a climbing party is lost, it is clearly not very smart to allow two factions to follow their intuition off on different paths. Again, it is very poor tactics to leave one exhausted person alone on a route while the rest go on to the summit, since the effect on his condition and morale of being left sitting alone in the cold may cause him to wander off. The rule here does not preclude ever separating, but climbers should recognize that the effects of altitude, fatigue, and cold have the insidious consequence of impeding judgment without the victim's being aware of the fact. For this reason, any impulse to split up under strain should be resisted.

Finally, *don't get in over your head.* Anyone who climbs for very long will find plenty of situations to test his mettle without looking for trouble. Both the beginner and the ambitious hotshot should be particularly wary of this temptation. Besides the danger of having one's climbing career nipped in the bud, there are matters of style and aesthetics involved here. In some popular climbing areas, the growth of competition has pushed people into attempting routes far beyond their current capacities, hence the increase in rescue operations and accidents. The serious climber is looking for a challenge that will push his own abilities to the utmost and test them in a crucible where self-reliance is assumed. The point is clearly lost if he develops the attitude that the rescue squad will come up and bail him out if he blows it.

III

Protecting Yourself and Your Companions

5

ARRESTS ON SNOW

As slopes become more continuously steep, scrambling becomes more dangerous, because a slip could lead to a long fall, probably with fatal consequences. In such circumstances the many devices used for protection are called into use. The most basic of these for the general mountaineer is *self-arrest* —the use of the ice ax to stop a slip on snow or sometimes ice.

On snow, the climber is particularly vulnerable to slips. Even on relatively easy slopes, steps may break out and precipitate him into a sudden downhill slide, which is uncontrollable without proper use of an ice ax. Many moderate snow slopes make very fast slides indeed, and the rocks at the bottom can provide a most uncomfortable means of stopping.

In self-arrest, the falling climber uses the pick of his ice ax as a brake on the snow or ice to stop unwelcome downward progress. The most critical fact about self-arrest is that it is not enough to know how to do it. *Self-arrest must be practiced until it is instinctive and reflexive.* Undoubtedly, there are lucky climbers who have managed to arrest a dangerous fall effectively after simply reading a book, but there are many others who have not been so fortunate. Successful arrests on soft snow can lull one into thinking the technique is easy, but things happen very fast after a tumble on steep hard snow or ice, and the reaction must be equally fast and very well executed to be effective.

Practice in arrests is also essential because the climber must know when they will work and when other kinds of protection are required. Accurate assessments of the effective-

79

ness of an arrest on a particular slope and of the distance that would be required to stop are crucial if a reasonable margin of safety is to be maintained. Only practical experience with arrests on many kinds of snow and ice will allow the climber to make such an assessments.

THE SELF-ARREST

The method of self-arrest is quite simple in principle. The ax is held across the trunk of the body. One hand grasps the head of the ax, the fingers gripping over the top and the thumb around the adze, so that when the hand is held in front of the shoulder the pick sticks straight out. The other hand holds the ax near the spike, controlling the angle and keeping the spike in a safe place down near the hip, where it cannot gouge its owner. In this *arrest position* the pick will dig into the snow if the climber falls forward, and, if he raises his rear into the air, his weight will come onto his toes and the pick of the ax, digging them into the snow and stopping the fall. The arrest position normally means that the ax is held in this way, the head at shoulder level, and the body of the climber is jacknifed slightly above the snow, so that the toes and the ax head dig into the snow. In a properly executed arrest there is also a tendency for one's face to dig into the snow.

Since falls are rarely planned and may start in any direction, one must learn to arrest from various positions. The most common slip on snow is also the easiest to arrest. It occurs when a step breaks out on the ascent, and the climber begins to slide on his stomach, feet first. From here he simply needs to get the ax in position and bend at the waist to be in arrest position. With a little practice this can be done so quickly that a slip can usually be stopped almost as soon as it starts.

After some practice in this position on an easy slope, work should be done on more subtle variations. Digging the ax and toes in as quickly as possible is ideal to stop a slip immediately, and it is appropriate in soft snow. On hard, steep snow it may be necessary to exercise a little restraint, learning to dig the

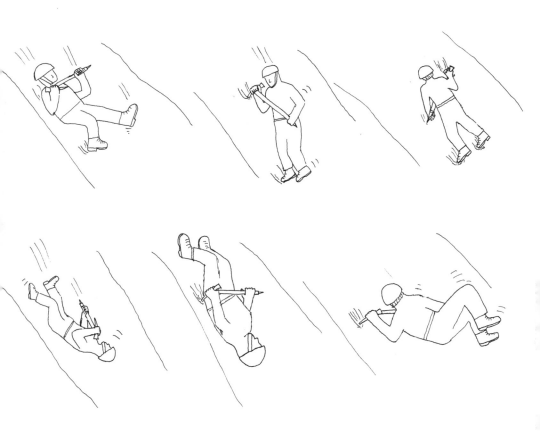

ARRESTS FROM SLIDES ON THE BACK.

Upper series, left to right: The climber slips while facing out, thus sliding on his back. He must *not* dig in his heels if he is traveling at all rapidly, lest he flip over. In the center, he is rolling *toward the pick* of his ax; rolling the other way could tear the ax from his hands. At the far right he has rolled into normal arrest position, and once the pick is biting well he can dig in his toes. The left hand is close to the spike to keep it from catching the snow or injuring the climber.

Lower series, left to right. The climber has fallen backwards and is picking up speed upside-down. The right arm is held straight down (in relation to the climber's body), and the left hand pivots the pick around to dig into the snow just past the hip. As soon as the pick digs into the snow (center), the whole body can be pivoted around it. The climber pivots (right), tucking his knees to speed the turn, and goes into normal arrest position.

pick in quickly but without jabbing, that is, applying the pressure and turning the pick into the slope so that it does not dig in so quickly as to be ripped out of the hands. Considerable practice may be needed to acquire the necessary finesse to make a quick arrest without risking the loss of the ax, particularly for those who have weak arms and hands. To avoid somersaults, the ax head should be dug in before the toes if much speed has been picked up.

Because the arrest can be applied so quickly, arrests from a head-uphill, face-down position are easy to learn and rapidly become tame. One should practice applying them after allowing a slide to start for a little while and then move on to the trickier problems. The next difficulty is arresting a slip on one's back or seat with the feet downhill. The procedure is to bring the ax into position first and then to *roll toward the head* of the ax onto the stomach. This brings one into normal arrest position, and the method already learned can be applied. Since more time will be required, arrests from this position often have to overcome greater body momentum. It is important to roll toward the head of the ax; if you roll to the spike side, the spike is liable to catch in the snow and rip the ax out of your hands.

The next problem arises from pitching face-forward down the slope. As usual, getting the ax into position comes first. Next, the body must be turned around so that the feet are headed downhill. This is done by digging the pick of the ax into the snow; the toes should not be dug in at this point. The momentum of the legs, hips, and trunk will turn them around the dragging pick, after which normal arrest can be used to stop. In very soft snow the pick has less drag, and some scrambling may be necessary to get the legs around quickly. On faster snow, after a little experience has been acquired, the novice will find that the turn can be speeded up somewhat by tucking his legs as they go around.

The most difficult to arrest is the backward fall, when the sliding climber is speeding downward on his back, head first. There are two techniques for arresting this kind of fall. The first is to get the ax in position and to roll onto the stomach toward the pick, head still downhill. Then pressure on the pick can be used to swing the legs around as in the previous type of fall. Once the legs are headed downhill, normal arrest technique can be applied. This method is satisfactory for moderate slopes that are not too hard, but as the snow gets faster, its inadequacy begins to show. On hard, steep snow I feel it is just too slow to be safe. Difficult arrests must be applied quickly if they are to work at all, because it does not take long to gain enough speed to be hurtling downward, bounding this way and that. Arrests in such circumstances may be accomplished by luck, but they cannot be relied on.

A faster method to arrest from the backward, head-first fall is accomplished by grabbing the ax as usual, reaching up, and plunging the pick into the snow beside the hip. (The pick must go in on the same side of the body as the hand controlling the head of the ax.) The drag of the pick then effectively gives the hand a grip on the snow, and the legs are flipped downhill, traveling half under the torso and half around to the side. The body ends up in the normal arrest position, head upslope and face down into the snow. This maneuver can be accomplished very quickly, but practice is definitely required.

PRACTICING SELF-ARREST

Beginners should plan at least one full day to learn the rudiments of self-arrest, remembering that effective arrests require drilling. It is a lot more fun to do arrest practice in large groups, since by its nature it tends to be a wet, cold, and dull activity. One should dress warmly, and waterproof shell clothing is a good idea. A change of clothes is often welcome at the end of the day. Gloves or mittens are mandatory, if only to protect the hands from abrasion.

The best practice area is a large bowl, ranging in slope from steep at the top to a gentle runoff at the bottom. Practice areas should be free from avalanche risk, protruding rocks, or other hazards anywhere in the runoff path. It is much more convenient if the slope has a good runout so that an uncontrolled slide to the bottom would not be dangerous. Otherwise, beginners will have to be belayed with ropes during practice, involving quite a few experienced climbers and much more time.

Students should begin by practicing falling in place in arrest position and continue through progressive stages of difficulty, starting with arrests in each position on gentle slopes and working up to arrests from long slides on steeper slopes. At a minimum, the student should be able to stop any of the common falls on slopes of moderate speed.

Climbers should aim to keep improving their arrest skills. Periodic practice is advisable anyway, if only to keep one's current abilities sharpened so that they are available when needed. First practice sessions are generally held on relatively soft spring snow, and there is no substitute for getting out later and honing one's skill on steep, hard stuff. There is a big difference! If a climber cannot get out on regular practice sessions, he should at least take time for some practice occasionally on a climb.

Once the basic techniques of arrest have been mastered, it is also worthwhile to go on to practice with a pack, again running through the entire sequence on various slopes. Ambidexterity, arrest with crampons, and group arrest, all of which are discussed below, also need practice before one can rely on them in real climbing situations.

THE ICE AX

The ice ax, along with boots and rope, is one of the traditional symbols of the mountaineer, and rightly so. It has many uses, but the most basic one is self-arrest. With the proper technique, an ice ax makes many snow climbs possible without the use of the rope. On some terrain, particularly on glaciers, ice ax arrest provides the main means of security even when the rope is used. Once the beginner has had some practice in arresting methods, he will realize how critical the ax is in many situations. Without it, the climber is helpless after a slip on the most trivial snow slopes, but with it arrest can often be accomplished on rather dangerous chutes.

Because of all this, some care should go into choosing an ice ax. This piece of equipment was rather neglected for many years by the more intelligent innovators in the field, but recently a number of important new designs have appeared. Since they are recent, there is still a good deal of controversy about them.

Perhaps the first thing to consider here is the use to which the ax will be put. A lot of the debate that has raged over axes is really rather silly. Ice axes are used in widely varying situations, and any ax will be a compromise, more suited to some uses than others. Thus, for climbing on big, snowy mountains, for probing on glaciers, for use on winter climbs when deep powder snow may cover more consolidated layers on moderate slopes, and in various other circumstances, an ax with a longer handle is most desirable. On the other hand, for extreme climbs on steep ice and hard snow, a short ax is far more convenient. Hence, arguing over whether a short or long ax is better makes little sense—it depends on what kind of climbing is contemplated. The same sort of controversy can rage between the advocates of different lengths of short ax. For the French technique of ice and snow climbing, an ax around 27 inches is excellent; but those using front-pointing methods generally prefer an even shorter ax. This is simply one example of special requirements and features.

The beginner is not likely to be doing extensive front-pointing on 75-degree ice for a couple of years, and he should concentrate on the general mountaineering features that will fulfill his needs. This does not mean that he will have to get an ax that is completely unsuited to difficult ice climbing. Many general-use axes made today are more suited to technical climbing than anything manufactured a few years ago.

Axes for general mountaineering use are generally chosen with shafts long enough to reach the ground when the head is held in the hand. While this has proven to be a good length, it is not at all critical. A slightly longer ax will serve well enough, and many climbers prefer a somewhat shorter one. The shorter length will not serve as a good walking stick for balance, but it will get in the way less in rock climbing and will be more suitable on steep climbs. Less experienced climbers should stick with an ax at least 27 inches long, and preferably somewhat longer. Short axes have some serious disadvantages on general snow climbs. Those who insist on starting with a short ax should consider getting one with an extension, so that the handle can be made longer.

Metal shafts have definite advantages over wood. Wooden shafts are weaker, less uniform, and can rot and deteriorate with age. Laminated wooden shafts are more uniform in strength, but they are still weaker than metal and will weaken with age. If an ax is going to be used only on steep ice this may not be important, since all belays would be from pitons or ice screws; but for other uses, including the approaches to those same steep ice climbs, I feel that wooden shafts are dangerously obsolete. Even the commendable tests which are now being done at Recreational Equipment are not adequate to assure the safety of wooden shafts; they do not test at the tangs, where most wooden axes break, and deterioration is still a problem.

There are two more points of importance in ice ax design. The first is the hooking angle. Most older axes had a pick which stuck almost straight out from the shaft. Both arrests and climbing on steep snow are easier if the pick hooks down at a considerable angle. The precise droop is more important to the ice climber than the general mountaineer, but the angle between the end of the pick and the shaft should be 75 degrees or less. This hooking angle makes the pick tend to dig into the snow and is important on difficult arrests.

A second point is what Larry Penberthy has called "positive clearance." This feature is not important for climbing or for arrests in soft or moderately hard snow; it is very important in difficult arrests on ice and hard snow. I have done some testing of axes on difficult arrests and found that in icy conditions, positive clearance of the pick often made the difference between loss of control and successful arrest.

Some modifications can be made on existing axes. A good shop can often increase the droop of the pick. There is no problem in arrest with axes that have pointed picks or positive clearance, but those with a chisel tip with negative clearance, such as the Chouinard and SMC, have to be filed to get positive clearance and maximum arrest effectiveness. Again, this is of no importance on very steep technical ice, but it is very important in arrest. (See the illustration on page 297.)

Ice ax design is discussed in detail in Chapter 12, which considers features for chopping steps, French technique, clawing, and the like; but a few recommendations can be summarized here.

Anyone planning to use his ax for general climbing who does not expect much use on extreme ice pitches should get an ax of moderate length, 28 inches or longer. Metal shafts are desirable for arrest, and for belaying they are essential. All-metal axes are made by SMC, Interalp, M.S.R., and others. Ice ax belays are tenuous enough without the additional danger of a broken shaft. If maximum arrest capability on climbs of moderate difficulty is desired, positive clearance in the pick is very important. A good hooking angle is helpful both for arrests and for more difficult climbing. Climbers who plan to use their axes exclusively on moderate snow climbs—that is, do not expect to cut steps or claw on ice—may want to consider M.S.R.'s aluminum-headed ax to save weight.

ADDITIONAL POINTERS ON ARREST

When the ax is being held in the arrest position in case of a fall, the wrist loop can be used to back up the strength of the hand by passing it over the ax head and around the wrist. While this is an excellent precaution, arrests should also be practiced using the strength of the hand alone, because when the ax is used for climbing, it is not always being held in arrest position.

Students relying on arrest for safety should carry the ax in arrest position, or at least grip the head for an arrest. Considerably more practice is needed to be able to shift the ax from some climbing positions and get into arrest without dropping it. Beginners should also get into the habit of using the wrist loop or sling for safety. A dropped ax on steep terrain can leave the climber in real trouble.

It is essential to become ambidextrous in arrest techniques. If a climber can arrest equally well with either hand he can carry the ax on either side, leaving him much freer to use the ax for balance and climbing.

Gloves or mittens should be worn whenever it is likely to be necessary to arrest, particularly on hard snow. Granular snow is very abrasive.

When the climber begins to use crampons, he must retrain himself for arrest, particularly if crampons with protruding front points are chosen. If he digs them in before a fall is controlled by the ax, he will probably be flipped into the air in a backward somersault. The climber wearing crampons has to retrain himself to keep his feet clear of the snow at the beginning of the arrest and to use his toes gingerly afterwards.

It is also worthwhile to practice *group arrests* once the basic arrest methods have been mastered. Group arrests are useful in certain limited circumstances, such as glacier travel. Two, three, or four climbers are roped together, so that if one climber slips and is unable to arrest his fall, the others can stop him. Anyone slipping immediately shouts "Falling," and the entire rope team falls into arrest position. This method of protection may be very useful on a snowy glacier, where if one member falls into an unseen crevasse the others can stop his fall by going into arrest. The rope team is allowed to move all at once without time-consuming belays. The method also has limited utility on slopes where ice runnels or other short irregularities might make it difficult for one person to arrest, while the others would be able to arrest easily in good snow. A good deal of caution should be exercised in depending on team arrest, however, since in most circumstances when one is reluctant to rely on individual arrests, group arrest would be no better. Team arrest members have the advantage of advance warning if the falling climber shouts immediately, but they have the disadvantage of the sudden tug on the rope. There have been too many cases of teams alternately yanking each other out all the way down a mountain.

For practice, the team should find a steep slope with a good runout. Lengths of rope between climbers should not be too long—perhaps 50 feet. A few coils of slack should be carried by the second and third men, but none by the leader. Large amounts of slack should not be allowed to develop, since they will merely ensure a harder jerk on the arresting climber. When one person shouts "Falling," the others should immediately drop to arrest. In training sessions the falling member should not arrest, allowing the others to do the work. As the team gains proficiency, one member should be able to arrest the whole team. In real climbing situations everyone goes into arrest and stays there until it is clear that the whole team is secure.

6

THE USE OF THE ROPE

When the climber starts to venture into really airy places, he finally begins to taste the stuff that distinguishes his sport completely. In passing indisputably out of the realm of hiking and backpacking, he also enters the areas of inherent danger, where his safety margin depends wholly on care and specialized techniques. Scrambling in the mountains also presents a number of dangers, but they are incidental. Once the mountaineer begins to climb on steep rock and snow, he must develop an altogether different attitude. To maintain a reasonable margin of safety he relies heavily on equipment as well as on himself. The single most important piece of equipment is the rope.

It is appropriate that the rope has always been the badge of the climber and mountaineer. Without it, each climber is essentially alone. A companion may provide moral support, but if one member of a party should slip, there is nothing his friends can possibly do to stop him from falling off a cliff or into a crevasse. They may be able to pick up the pieces afterward, but this is the limit of the assistance they can render.

The rope is thus much more than a tool to the climber. It is the instrument which ties the members of the party together figuratively as well as physically. In serious climbing, a mountaineer is likely to put his life in the hands of his companion dozens of times in a day—he does this through the rope. When climbers tie into opposite ends of a rope, they are tying their fates together, at least for a time.

Proper use of the rope is a subtle art with many facets.

This chapter discusses some of the most basic techniques. They are essential if the rope is to be an instrument of safety rather than a suicide pact.

HOW ROPES ARE MADE

Although rope can be made of many materials, nylon has become universally accepted for the construction of climbing ropes because of its strength, durability, and elasticity. Other materials have some advantages for special functions in climbing, and they will be discussed elsewhere; but for general-purpose climbing ropes, nylon's supremacy has so far gone unchallenged.

Mountaineering ropes are constructed in one of two ways. *Laid* ropes are twisted from three large strands, each of which is itself made up from a number of twisted yarns. The yarns are twisted from smaller yarns which are composed of twisted nylon fibers. In a new rope, these fibers are continuous, running the entire length of the rope. Mountaineering ropes are known as "hard-lay" or "mountaineering-lay," which means they are stiffer than similar ropes made for other purposes, such as boating. The most common rope of this type which is currently available is Goldline, made by Plymouth Cordage.

The other main type of climbing rope is the *kernmantel.* As with laid ropes, the nylon filaments are continuous throughout the rope, but they are braided into one or more inner ropes, forming the core or *kern,* and this core is covered by an outer braided sheath or *mantel.* Ropes of this construction are also commonly known as *Perlon* ropes, Perlon being a European trade name for nylon. Nearly all kernmantel ropes sold to climbers are made in Europe.

There are advantages and disadvantages to each of these types. Laid ropes are significantly cheaper than kernmantel ones, because the twisting process is less expensive than braiding. But each of the fibers in a twisted rope may appear on the rope surface one or more times in the full length and may be cut by abrasive wear. Most of the fibers in the kernmantel rope

The two main types of climbing rope: a kernmantel rope (above) and a laid rope (below).

are protected inside the sheath, and are thus not subject to abrasion. On the other hand, kernmantel also has several structural disadvantages. The core fibers cannot be examined after an accident involving possible damage to the rope. And in certain types of stress, the core can slip inside the sheath.

The greatest advantage of a kernmantel rope is its excellent handling qualities. It has far less tendency to kink than a laid rope and is less prone to stiffen excessively when wet. It is generally much nicer to work with. The smooth outer surface is a big help on difficult climbs, since it does not build up so much friction when threaded through various pieces of climbing hardware.

There is good reason to believe that kernmantel ropes are more prone to cutting than laid ones, although more research is needed on this subject. This is an important feature in mountaineering ropes, because there is always a possibility that a falling climber's rope will saw across a rough edge of rock. A kernmantel rope will definitely wear out much faster than a laid one under conditions of severe abrasion, as in rescue work.

The final important difference between the major types of

rope is their stretch under body weight. This feature is not necessarily important to the average climber; but on severe climbs, the second man often climbs the rope to save time and energy, and excessive stretch under body weight is then a great disadvantage. For this reason, kernmantel ropes which are made in Europe are designed to stretch as little as possible under body weight. They begin to stretch significantly under heavier loads. Laid ropes stretch much more under body weight, and they tend to untwist slightly, so that a climber hanging free will spin.

CHOOSING A CLIMBING ROPE

The beginner is probably best advised to avoid buying a rope until he has to. If his early climbs are done with experienced people, he may be able to delay the purchase for some time, giving him longer to form an intelligent opinion of his individual needs. Eventually he will want his own, at least for local practice climbing. The first choice is in rope construction. Some of the advantages and disadvantages of laid and kernmantel ropes have been mentioned. Laid ropes are much cheaper, stand up better under severe use, can be checked easily for damage, and are probably more resistant to cutting. Kernmantel ropes handle much better, have less tendency to kink, and may last longer under moderate use. Most kernmantel ropes stretch far less under body weight, and none of them untwists when one is hanging on the end. Some of the new belaying methods should not be used with laid ropes because untwisting may produce kinks and jam the belay.

Kernmantel ropes have become far more popular than laid ropes in the past few years. This has been true partly because of their very real advantages and partly because of fashion. The rope drag problem with laid ropes makes them less suitable for difficult climbs, so the best climbers naturally prefer kernmantel ropes. Since the best climbers prefer them, so do most others.

The novice should give careful consideration to his real

needs before going out and spending a lot of money for a rope. Especially in early practice, the disadvantages of a laid rope are not too significant. Even much later, the advantages sometimes are persuasive.

For general climbing, 7/16-inch and 11-mm diameter ropes have become standard. These are large enough to have sufficient reserve strength even with all the weakening factors (discussed later in the chapter) operating on the rope. They are also large enough to give a good grip. Bigger ropes become unmanageably heavy, and smaller ones do not have the reserve strength, resistance to cutting, and grip that are needed in many situations. Smaller diameter ropes are preferred for some special applications which will be discussed later. It should be noted in this connection that the common 9-mm Perlon ropes are recommended only for *double* use in any high-angle climbing. This technique has never gained much acceptance in North America, but in Europe many climbers prefer to climb with two ropes running between the climbers, and 9-mm ropes with the UIAA *(Union Internationale des Associations d'Alpinisme)* approval are intended for this double use, not as normal single climbing ropes.

Finally, the climber must choose a suitable length of rope for climbing. Several factors are involved. Obviously, the longer the rope, the heavier it will be, and the more weight has to be carried into the climbing area. A rope that is too long is also more of a nuisance to handle than a shorter rope. The extra length makes for more kinks, more possibility of snagging, and more rope to be pulled up by a leader who has gone a shorter distance.

The standard lengths of rope in this country are 120 feet, 150 feet, and 165 feet. One should adhere to the standard lengths for the simple reason that when climbs are established, the descriptions and any fixed hardware on the route will use standard rope lengths. The standard mountaineering length for many years was 120 feet, so most older climbs can easily be accomplished with ropes that size. This is a good length for general mountaineering, and it fits in well with current methods of protection. However, 150 feet has been normal for rock climbing in the past decade, and the climber using 120-foot ropes is likely to find that he will run into a lot of difficulties if he tries to repeat climbs done with 150-foot ropes. The 165-foot ropes have some advantages for climbs on big walls, but most climbers are likely to find they are not worth the extra weight and trouble.

Shorter ropes have advantages for local practice and for carrying to remote climbs where only very short sections require a rope. For such purposes, lengths of 60 and 100 feet are often used.

SLINGS AND OTHER ROPE USES

Rope and webbing are used for numerous purposes in climbing besides tying the climbers together. Most importantly, short lengths called *slings* are used frequently to attach the climbers or the rope to the mountain. A number of these slings are commonly carried by each climber. Their use will be discussed in more detail elsewhere. They are generally made of nylon webbing or rope of the same type as climbing rope. Each has certain advantages. Webbing is cheaper, has less stretch, holds knots well, is comfortable in applications where it bears directly on the body, and will sometimes slip through constricted cracks that are too tight for inserting a rope. On the other hand, it is more easily cut and more subject to severe weakening by normal wear and abrasion.

KNOTS

Rope handling is the stock in trade of the climber, whether he is a mountaineer or a technical rock climber. There is simply no substitute for a basic competence in using ropes and slings. No matter how athletic a rock gymnast one may be, he will not get up a hard move if he gets his rope jammed. No matter how fast one can climb, inept rope handling will slow down progress on a big route to a crawl. Finally, the beginner is likely to find that many experienced climbers will be patient through almost anything else, but not with improper knot tying.

Knots are only one part of the art of handling a rope properly, but they are a vital part. A climber's life can depend at any time on his own knots. It is always a good idea to master more knots, but it is much more important to know the basic ones well.

There are many knots which can be useful to climbers which are not shown here, and the interested reader will find references listed at the back of the book for additional study. Some specialized ones are also shown elsewhere in the book. Those shown on the following pages have proved particularly useful and should form a basic repertoire. The climber should be wary of adopting novel knots without thorough testing.

There are several important characteristics for climbing knots. They should be relatively easy to tie, since the climber has to tie a lot of knots, often under adverse circumstances. They should be strong; that is, they should weaken the rope as little as possible, and they should retain their shape under strain. Some knots weaken the rope more than others, and many knots simply collapse under strain. For many climbing purposes, it is important that knots are not too difficult to untie after heavy loading; many knots are not suitable because they jam under a load. In other applications jamming may not be important, but the possibility of the knot's working itself loose would be very disturbing indeed.

The knots presented here are widely used and versatile for climbing situations. The general rule for tying climbing knots is that they should be secured by having the free ends tied off with overhands, sometimes with several. Great care must always be taken to secure knots tied in nylon, and they should also be inspected frequently, particularly if they are subject to alternate tension and slack that will tend to work them loose. Nylon rope does not hold knots very well, and they can often untie themselves with remarkable facility. Thus, all knots should be pulled tight and secured, unless they are tied

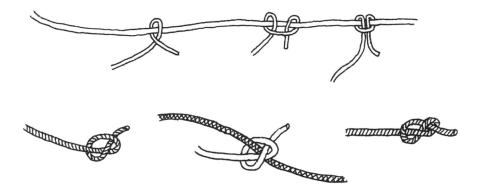

KNOT SERIES

1. BASIC KNOT FIGURES AND SAFETIES. Above are half-hitches, often used for utility knots and safeties. They are always used at least in pairs. At the left is a single half-hitch; in the center a second has been added, inverted in direction from the first; and at the right both have been tightened.

   Below left is a basic overhand knot, which has many climbing uses. In the center it is shown being used as a safety. Below right is a basic figure-eight knot, which is made like an overhand but with an extra turn around the main (standing) part of the rope. The figure-eight has many climbing uses but is not often used as a safety. Most climbing knots must *always* use one of these safeties or the half-grapevine safety. The safety must be pulled tight and must have enough extra line protruding to prevent its working loose.

2. HALF-GRAPEVINE SAFETY. This knot is a bit more difficult to learn than the safeties in the first illustration, but it is much more secure. It is the best safety to use in most situations.

in the middle of a rope. Knots tied in webbing or rope for permanent slings are often left unsecured by extra overhands to reduce the amount of sling material. If this practice is followed, one must be careful to jam the knots very tight, preferably by standing in a hanging sling and jumping. Even so, the ends should not be too short, or they may be pulled through by severe strain. Webbing holds knots better than rope.

In learning knots, there is no substitute for practice. Once you know them well, try some variations. Tie them with your eyes closed, and try a few behind your back. You might finish off in a dark, cold shower before congratulating yourself that you really know your knots. Some climbing situations can approach just these conditions.

One other point which might be mentioned here is that there are several ways of tying certain knots, as well as various shortcuts. The beginner will be well advised to stick to one method for quite a while. Trying a second way before knots are completely mastered is usually confusing later on.

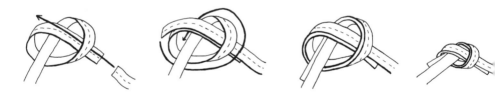

KNOTS USED TO TIE TWO LINES TOGETHER

3.   RING BEND (water knot, overhand bend). This is a strong and simple knot, easy to recognize. It is most commonly used to tie slings in webbing. For this purpose many climbers put a lot of weight on the knot to tighten it and then do not use a safety. The knot should habitually be checked before use, and if it is tied in rope it must be safetied. It is tied by making an overhand in one end, then following the curve back in the reverse direction with the other end. Be sure the knot is neat, so that you can tell whether it is tied correctly. Jams after heavy loading.

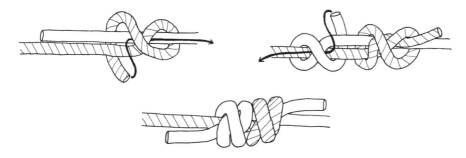

4. GRAPEVINE. An excellent knot for tying slings in rope. It is strong, and if it is pulled tight it can be used without a safety. Once learned it is easily recognized in rope. Most climbers do not use it in webbing even though it is strong, because it is so sloppy that it is difficult to tell whether it is tied correctly. It jams after heavy loading.

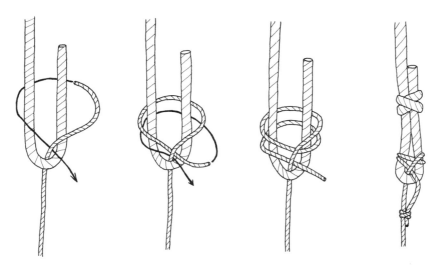

5. DOUBLE SHEETBEND. A very strong knot for joining ropes. It is the knot of choice when ropes of different size must be joined, and in this case, the smaller rope must be the one that makes the double turn around the bight of the larger rope. With ropes of equal size, it is immaterial which rope forms the double turn. The double sheetbend is also the best knot to use if the rope will be heavily loaded, because it can be untied even after such loading, unlike the preceding two joining knots.

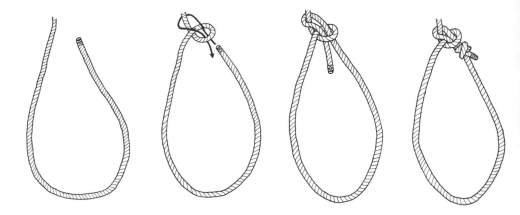

KNOTS USED TO TIE INTO THE END OF A ROPE

6. BOWLINE. The traditional climber's knot, and one that should be known perfectly. Its characteristic form is easily recognizable. The free end must be safetied. It can be tied around the waist or through a harness.

7. HIGH-STRENGTH BOWLINE. This knot is more complicated to tie than a regular bowline, but it has the virtue of not coming untied accidentally. It can be used without a safety, but it is a good idea to use one anyway. The initial small loop is made (left) as with a bowline. This is doubled, the free end is passed through as with a bowline, and then the end is passed through again before the knot is tightened. The author's favorite tie-in. Easily untied after heavy loading.

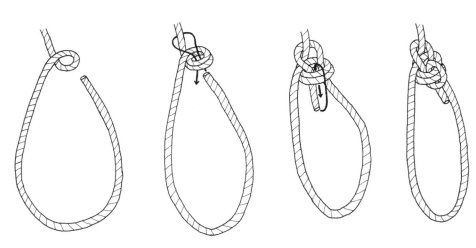

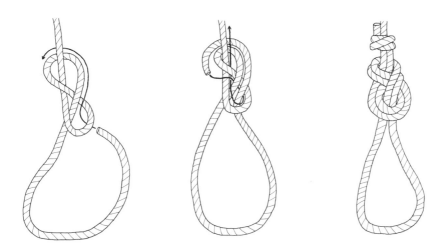

8.	FIGURE-EIGHT ON A BIGHT. The most popular tie-in, it is easy to tie and does not come undone readily. It is commonly used without a safety, but it is best to use one, since some tests have indicated that if the loop itself is pulled apart, as it would be if clipped into a belay anchor, it is not good for full strength unless the knot is safetied. Can jam under heavy loading. This knot can be tied in a different way (see knot 12), but to tie it through a harness, this method must be used. A simple figure-eight is tied in the rope, the free end is passed through the harness, and it is then fed back through the knot in reverse.

9.	BOWLINE-ON-A-COIL. This knot can be used to provide a more comfortable tie-in than a single bowline if a harness is not carried, as on routes which have only minor roped climbing. It is also useful for shortening the rope. The knot must enclose *all* the coils around the waist, or it will be deadly in a fall. The safety is best tied around a single strand, so that it will be less likely to come undone.

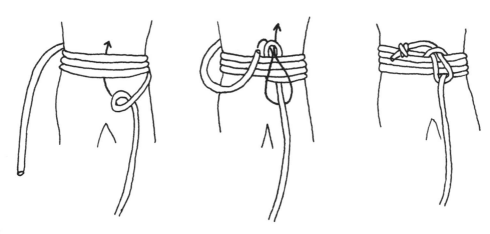

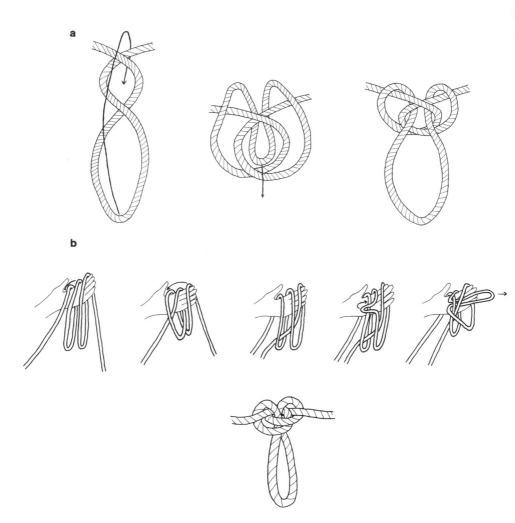

KNOTS FOR TYING INTO THE MIDDLE OF A ROPE

10. BUTTERFLY. Two methods are shown for tying this knot. Experiment to find out which suits you best, and then learn that way thoroughly. This is a very strong knot and it is the traditional method for tying into the middle of a rope with a waist loop. It is worth knowing for a number of reasons, but it cannot be used with a harness unless it is clipped in with a carabiner, a bad practice. I prefer knot 11 for this purpose. The butterfly is good for making loops in the middle of a rope with minimum loss of strength. It is useful to make

a belay loop for the ice ax in glacier travel, to tie a heavy load into the rope in glacier travel, and to isolate a damaged section of rope. Note carefully the drawing of the finished knot, at the bottom. Each wing of the "butterfly," formed after the knot is pulled tight, goes around one side of the standing rope and then over and around the loop. If this form does not appear, the knot is incorrectly tied.

11. BOWLINE TIED WITH A BIGHT. This is a simple middleman knot to learn, because it is nothing more than a standard bowline tied into a loop pulled out in the middle of the rope. It can be used to tie into a harness or to provide two loops around the waist. It is difficult to safety in the normal way because of the doubled rope, but a carabiner can be used to safety it as shown. This knot can also be used to provide a three-loop harness by pulling the loop (through which the carabiner is clipped) further through and adjusting one loop to fit the waist and two to fit the legs.

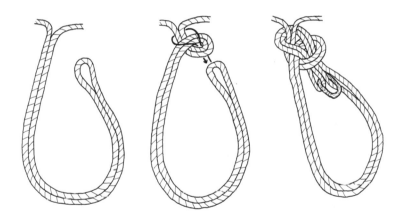

KNOTS FOR TYING THE ROPE INTO AN ANCHOR

12. FIGURE-EIGHT ON A BIGHT. This is a foolproof knot to use for clipping into an anchor. It is the same knot as number 8, but tied in the middle of a rope by a quick and easy method. An overhand can

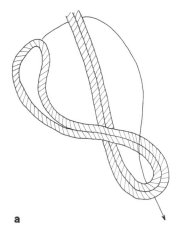

a   b

be tied instead of the figure-eight, but it is weaker and will jam more quickly under stress. The only disadvantage of this knot for clipping into an anchor is that it is difficult to adjust for a belayer changing his position. This knot is also used by some for tying into the middle of a rope. It cannot be tied through a harness.

BELOW AND OPPOSITE

13. CLOVE HITCH. Below is a clove hitch used in the traditional manner for holding a rope on a post. The clove hitch is used by many climbers for tying into an anchor. Clipped into a carabiner, it jams well under tension, and it can be adjusted easily, so a belayer can clip into it and then readily tighten or loosen his anchor as he gets into a belaying position. At top, opposite, a rapid method of tying the hitch for this purpose is shown. Care must be taken that the clove hitch cannot shift around on a carabiner and open the gate. Beginners should use a locking carabiner or two regular ones with the gates reversed to prevent this.

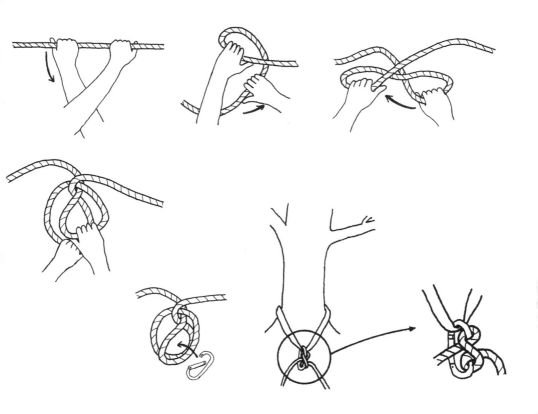

14. BELAYER'S HITCH. This knot is preferred by some to the clove hitch, because it requires less care to prevent its slipping around and opening a carabiner gate. It is a bit harder to adjust.

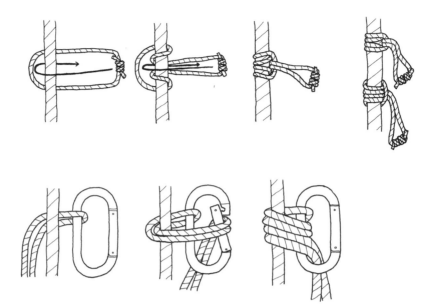

RATCHET KNOTS (USED FOR CLIMBING ROPES AND SIMILAR PURPOSES)

15. PRUSIK KNOT (top). This is the traditional ratchet knot. It requires only a sling of small-diameter rope and should be known perfectly by every climber. Suitable prusik slings should normally be carried in an accessible place. As shown, the loop is passed twice through itself around the larger-diameter rope. When pulled tight it will not slip, but when loosened it will. At the right, the knot is shown tied in both directions. It is easily tied one-handed. Tests should be made with the prusik slings you carry on the rope you are using, since gripping power varies. In difficult situations, an extra turn or two can be taken with the sling to increase friction. The prusik sling *must* be of smaller diameter than the rope on which it is tied.

BACHMAN KNOT (bottom). This is a useful variation of the prusik using a carabiner for a handle to loosen and move the knot. It is very easy to tie, and with many (but not all) combinations of sling and rope it has as much or more friction as the prusik. When it works and when the carabiners are available, it is much easier to use for climbing a rope. As with the prusik, more turns can be taken for more friction. The two turns shown in the drawing are a minimum. The Bachman sometimes works with soft webbing.

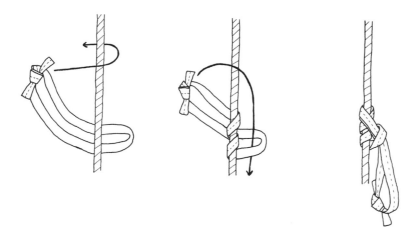

16. HEDDEN KNOT. This is a ratchet knot that generally works when tied with webbing, whereas the others cannot be relied on for this purpose. Since webbing slings are often carried while climbing, this is a worthwhile knot to know. Softer webbing generally works better. More wraps do not usually increase the effectiveness of the Hedden knot. It must be tied in the direction shown, with the loop coming from a wrap at the upper part of the rope.

17. TIED HARNESS. A good climbing harness can be tied from 1-inch webbing in the manner shown on the next page. Twenty-five to thirty feet of webbing are normally used. Tie one loop in the center of the webbing with an overhand knot. (This puts the middle of the harness slightly off center, a feature that most people prefer, since the harness knot is then out of the way of the tie-in.) Adjust the size of this loop to fit snugly around the top of the thigh, wearing normal climbing clothes. Tie another loop of the same size about 6 inches away from the first. Put the loops on the legs, and wrap the ends around the waist in opposite directions as shown. After going around the back, each end goes once through the nearest leg loop, to help keep the loops from sliding down. The ends are wrapped several times around the waist until the remainder is a convenient length. Tie the harness with a ring bend, and safety both ends. (The safeties are not shown for clarity.) Tie the climbing rope through all the loops, including the section between the leg loops. There are many variations of this harness. It is adequate

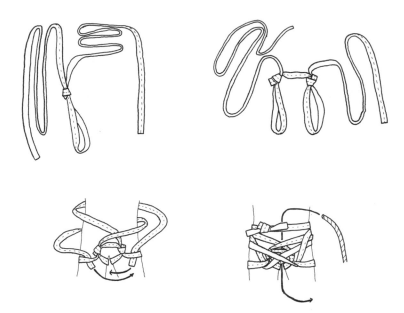

for rock climbing, but a chest tie-in is also needed when climbing with a heavy pack, particularly when carrying loads across a glacier.

18. A SIMPLE WAY TO EQUALIZE LOADS (opposite). It is often necessary to distribute possible loads between several anchors, to prevent a large shock from coming completely on one anchor at a time, breaking them in turn, or to use the anchors more effectively. Several elaborate methods are used, particularly for rescues, but in normal climbing situations, the one shown here is effective and practical. In the first drawings (a), the method used is WRONG. A sling has been clipped to both anchors, and the climbing rope is then clipped over the sling. The load is equalized and pulls directly on the anchors, but if one anchor pulls out, the carabiner used to attach the rope may slip right off, as shown.

The bottom drawings (b) show the RIGHT way to equalize the load. The sling connecting the nuts is given a half-twist, and the carabiner is clipped over the intersection of the X formed. If one anchor pulls out, the carabiner is locked in as shown. The same method can be used with more than two anchors by forming additional half-twists between each pair.

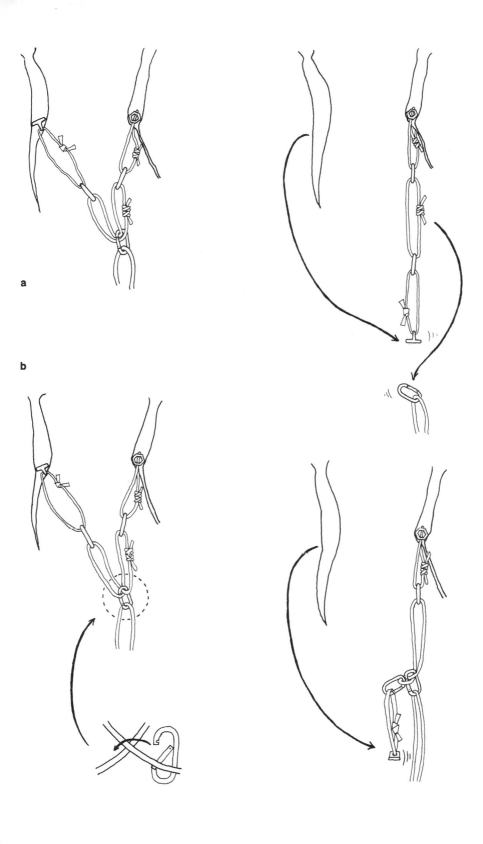

a

b

CARING FOR ROPES AND SLINGS

There are a few characteristics of nylon rope and webbing with which the novice should be familiar from the very beginning. Nylon is very strong and resistant to attack by rot and mildew, but quite vulnerable in some other ways. It is quickly weakened by abrasion, and, more importantly, *it is much more prone to wear and cutting when under tension.* A rope under the weight of a falling climber, for example, will cut very easily if it is allowed to run over a sharp edge. The main consequence is that climbers have to be very careful to avoid such situations. A minor result is that kernmantel ropes tend to abrade less in normal use than laid ones, because the sheath is normally not load-bearing and is thus under less tension. Laid ropes wear rapidly at first, forming a fuzzy outer surface; but later this outer fuzz, which is no longer under tension, tends to protect the rest of the rope from further abrasion.

Great care must be taken to prevent damage to a rope and to detect any which has taken place. One should never step on a rope. If there are any sharp rocks about, the rope can be cut even when it is not under tension. Furthermore, particles of dirt can be ground into the rope which will cut the fibers later as it twists back and forth. One should avoid getting the rope dirty whenever possible, for the same reason. When it does get dirty, it should be washed in warm (not hot) water with a mild soap or detergent; a washing machine does the job well. It should then be hung out to dry thoroughly before storing. If a rope is hit by a rock or stepped on, it should be immediately inspected for damage. A laid rope can be twisted open to check for hidden damage. With a kernmantel rope, one has to feel carefully for any dents or irregularities that might signify internal cutting. A damaged section can be temporarily isolated with a butterfly knot, but once the rope is no longer immediately needed the cut should be finished with a knife.

Nylon is easily damaged by heat, so a rope should never be left where it might be hit by sparks or otherwise exposed to hot objects. In this same connection, it is very important for climbers to understand the effects of nylon rubbing against nylon. The friction of nylon surfaces against one another is relatively high, and considerable heat is generated; so, if a rope runs against a nylon sling, a good deal of heat results. Part of the heat is dissipated along the running rope, and no section will pick up enough to cause a problem. The heat that goes into the sling, however, is all concentrated on one small area, and this area can rapidly heat to the point where nylon begins to soften and fuse. The softened nylon is quickly abraded off, and a deeper layer of the sling is then exposed and cut in its turn. Climbers should be extremely careful to *avoid situations where a nylon rope would run against any slings or fixed sections of the rope.* This is a hazard insufficiently appreciated by many climbers and one that can be very dangerous.

Nylon is also vulnerable to ultra-violet radiation, and climbers should be aware of the fact even though the consequences are far less important than some of those mentioned earlier. A climbing rope will not be significantly weakened by ultra-violet radiation in normal use, but it obviously should not be stored for long periods in bright sunlight. The main caution here, however, has to do with slings left on peaks and spires by other parties. Climbers, being an impecunious lot, are frequently tempted to use old slings left by other parties for descent. This practice should be scrupulously avoided because of ultra-violet and other weathering effects. Nylon slings frequently look bright and new for years of exposure, but their strength is another matter.

Obviously, climbing ropes and slings should be kept away from paints, chemicals, solvents, and the like. Although gasoline and motor oil seem to have little effect, prudence would seem to dictate distrust of any ropes and slings that have been in contact with any chemically active substance.

A new rope should have the ends melted first to prevent unraveling, then taped, whipped, or dipped in lacquer or urethane paint to further strengthen the end. Before cutting sling material or rope, it is best to tape the spot to be cut, slicing through the taped section and then melting the ends. Great care should be used with lacquer, which partly dissolves the nylon fibers and fuses them, to ensure that none gets on the working part of the rope. Sling material usually has a shorter working life than a rope, so that fusing the ends with a match is sufficient to preserve them.

It is desirable to mark a rope in the center and at a spot 20 or 30 feet from each end. With laid ropes this can be done with Rit dye for ten minutes at a temperature of 150°F. The same method can be used with kernmantel ropes unless they are too dark for the dye to show well. Another good method for kernmantel ropes is simply to stitch some thread into the sheath, using a color that shows well. Thread whipping can be used on laid ropes for marking, but there is some danger that a loose end of thread will catch in climbing hardware, so if this method is chosen, the thread should be a weak cotton that will break easily.

COILING THE ROPE

There are many ways to coil a rope, but the ones shown here have the virtues of simplicity and speed, both in coiling and readying the rope for use. Whatever method is used, the rope should first be arranged so that it will feed readily into the hands. Usually this is done by starting at one end and feeding the rope into a pile on the ground and then starting to coil from the end on the top of the pile. In actual climbing, the rope is usually piled this way already.

ROPE COILING. A useful standard method of rope coiling is shown at top, opposite. An end is left hanging, and then loops are draped on one hand, each loop formed by a length of rope a little less than the width of the arms spread out. Normally a half-twist is given to each new loop so that it hangs without twists, but some climbers advocate allowing kernmantel ropes to form figure-eights to prevent the core from twisting inside the sheath. Practice doing this until you can coil a rope quickly and neatly. The finish shown is effective and can be done or undone quickly. The end left dangling is brought up to the top of the coil and turned back on itself. The remaining

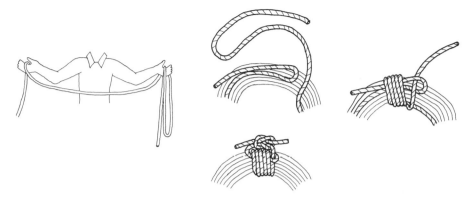

end is wrapped around the coil at this doubled portion, beginning from the open end of the loop and moving toward the closed end. At least four wraps are needed, but more than seven or eight are tiresome. When two feet or so of the end are left, pass it through the eye of the loop as shown, pull the free end of the loop tight, and tie the two ends with a square knot.

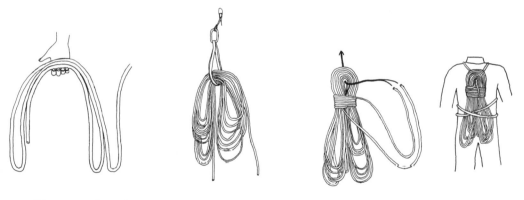

The second method of coiling shown is useful in specialized situations. It was invented by Ray Jardine and presented several years ago in *Summit Magazine*. The rope is laid back and forth across the hand, beginning with loops on each side made with the full reach of both arms, the loops gradually getting smaller. This "lap coil" can be laid across the lap or hung up with a sling as shown, and it is useful for belaying on big walls. One end of the rope can be wrapped around the top of the doubled coil as shown, and then both ends can be passed through the top eye to form a backpack that is very easy to carry, even over a small pack.

BREAKING IN A NEW ROPE

Kernmantel ropes handle very nicely when they are purchased, whereas laid ropes have a great tendency to form kinks and snarls until they have been used a few times. The handling characteristics of a new laid rope can be greatly improved by doing three or four carabiner brake rappels the full length of the single rope. (This technique is described later in the book. It should not be attempted by beginners until they have thoroughly mastered rappelling methods and safety measures.)

BELAYING

Belaying is easily the most important skill the climber needs to master. It is the means used by the second member of the team to handle the rope so that he can hold the climber in case of a fall. Belaying is a complex subject, and many techniques are used. As with most climbing skills, it can only be mastered by practice. Drilling is absolutely vital in developing good belaying techniques. In many other facets of climbing, mistakes are permissible, but in modern American climbing the security of the team ultimately rests on the belayer. Although the climber may never fall, it is the belayer who provides the margin of safety in case he does. The whole point of the rope is to provide a margin of security by ensuring that the consequences of a fall are not too serious. If a belay is insecure it is worse than useless, because it provides a false sense of security to the climber, thus impairing his judgment of the real situation.

Different sorts of belays are used to provide security in different circumstances. The simplest belay is the *upper belay* or *top rope.* It is used by a belayer sitting on top of a cliff, on a ledge, or whatever, above the person who is climbing. Obviously, this belay provides maximum security. The belayer takes in rope as the climber comes up to him. There are never

A belay from above, using a sitting belay position, the most stable of the various belay positions. The belayer is tied in from above and behind, with the anchor in line with the direction in which the force of a fall would come. The gloved right hand is the holding, or braking, hand; the left hand is the feeling hand. The rope is clipped in at the belayer's waist so that it cannot possibly ride up or down. This position would not be secure if the belayer were not tied into an anchor.

more than a few feet of slack rope, so the climber cannot fall far, and the force which must be held by the belayer is never much greater than the weight of the climber. This belay provides maximum security and is the one used for practice climbing on local rocks and cliffs. The novice should get plenty of practice with it before going on to more difficult belays.

ANCHORS

The first step in setting up any belay is to find an appropriate *anchor;* this is equally true whether one is on top of a 30-foot local boulder or in the middle of a 3000-foot face. One of the arts that the beginner can start to learn in his first belaying session is that of finding and using anchors. The anchor is used to tie the belayer—and through him, the climber —to the cliff or mountain. *The anchor must be absolutely solid.* It can be a tree, a large rock flake or boulder, a hole in the rock through which a sling can be passed, or one of the artificial anchors discussed in the next chapter (nuts, pitons, bolts). Large trees are excellent, but one should be cautious of smaller trees and dead ones, particularly when they are growing in precarious spots. The principles of belaying rest on the assumption that the anchor used cannot be pulled loose by any force that might be exerted on it, even if the climber falls and pulls his belayer from position. Although the forces generated in top-rope situations are not great, the beginner should make it a rule from the start to use only very strong anchors. The forces that can be generated in falls under more difficult circumstances are very large indeed.

Careful inspection of rock flakes and horns to make sure they are firmly attached should become a habit. The forces of erosion eventually break off all such projections; make sure that the process is not already well along when you arrive. Never assume that just because someone else has used an anchor, it is safe. A good bit of the art of climbing consists of developing the habit of checking and rechecking everything.

Besides being secure, the anchor should be fairly close to

the line that will be followed by the climber. Draw a mental picture of the rope running straight from the potential anchor to the climber. If the climber began to go hand-over-hand up the rope, would the location of the anchor cause him to take a great swing? If so, the anchor is not properly placed; it should be as close as possible to straight above. It should also not be too far behind the spot where the belayer will sit, because the longer the anchoring rope is, the more it will stretch.

The normal position for the belayer is seated on the ground, tied to the anchor directly behind him, with the rope running out in front, passing around his hips and between his legs. The belayer should always be in the direct line from the place where the climber would fall to the anchor. If he is out of line, the pull of the falling climber will tend to yank him into line and out of his belay position.

In picking a suitable spot, the belayer should try to find a seat that will allow him to resist the pull of a fall, ideally a depression, with places to brace the feet when his legs are spread apart so the rope to the climber runs between them. This position gives the belayer a very stable triangular stance. Many variations are possible, and after a little practice and thought the beginner will begin to spot the good ones. If the belayer sits on the edge of a good depression and the rope goes directly down to the climber between the belayer's legs, this tends to pull the belayer into his seat. The ideal belay position is one that is strong enough to hold a fall without the anchor, but which also has a good anchor as a back-up.

Once the site and anchor have been found, the belayer ties in and gets into position. There are several common ways to tie into an anchor, and the novice should practice a number of variations. Sometimes one is more suitable, sometimes another. As with all rope-handling situations, practice is the key to real competence. Slow and inept rigging of belays and use of the rope is usually the main problem for inexperienced climbers on their first big climb.

Assuming that there are two climbers, one will be tied into each end of the rope. Even with top-rope climbing this is a good habit, since it will always be the way the two would be roped on a longer climb. One good method of tying the belayer in is simply to take a bight of the climbing rope and tie it to the anchor, leaving just enough rope between the belayer and the anchor to give a taut line. This also anchors the end of the line going to the climber, so that on a long climb he would be stopped at the end of the rope even if the belay failed. This is often the quickest and best way to set up a belay. It has the virtue of simplicity and requires no extra equipment. Its only defect in normal situations is that a section of the climbing rope is tied up in the belay, so it is not available to the leader if he should need to go a little farther. For top-rope climbing, naturally, this difficulty does not arise, and the method is useful under many conditions.

Another common method of tying in is to use a sling of

An upper belay that is easy to set up and requires no extra equipment. The belayer has looped her end of the climbing rope around a rock projection, moved to a good position, and secured the free end from the projection to the harness with a clove hitch to a carabiner. This system makes adjustment of the anchor rope very easy. Note that the belayer is anchored from both sides, so it makes no difference which hand is used for braking.

Using the same belay position with a different type of tie-in. In this case a figure eight knot is tied and looped over the projection. Adjustment of the anchor rope is slower and more complicated, though tying off a fallen climber would be easier. If the belayer is using a harness, as in the photograph, it is important that the pull come on the same side as the anchor rope. Here the belayer's left hand is her braking hand; the pull of a fall would come on her right side, turning her against the tie-in. If she belayed from the other side, the force of a fall might spin her around and the belay might fail.

webbing or rope around the anchor. This sling is then either attached directly to the climber's waist loop or, if the belay spot is farther from the anchor, may be attached to a loop tied in the climbing rope at an appropriate length from the belayer. Since slings are usually carried already tied in loops, they are normally attached to the rope by clipping the two together with a *carabiner*. This is an elongated oval ring with a spring-loaded gate, so that ropes and slings can easily be attached to one another. (Carabiners are discussed in detail in Chapter 8.) It is important when tying into a belay anchor to use a sling that is strong enough to provide a good safety margin. Lightweight slings are often carried for various purposes in climbing, but the belayer should remember that the belay must not fail. As a general rule of thumb, slings for the belay should be 1-inch webbing, or rope which is 9 mm or ⅜ of an inch in diameter.

When artificial anchors such as pitons, nuts, or bolts are used, the belayer may attach himself directly to them with a carabiner or sling, or he may be hooked in through the climbing rope. For a belay it is usually prudent to use at least two artificial anchors; even the most experienced climbers are sometimes fooled by a piton which seems secure but turns out to be weak. The belay is a bad place to take chances. All the cautions which are discussed in the next two chapters on placement, testing, and load-sharing with artificial anchors are even more important in setting up belays.

Another method of utilizing the rock projection anchor. Here a sling is put over the horn and is clipped to a figure eight knot tied in the climbing rope. The comments in the preceding example regarding the direction in which the belayer would be turned apply here.

Even with natural anchors it is often a good idea to use more than one, especially if you are using a rock flake or a tree that is not so large that one could confidently swear it was "bombproof." You can tie in separately to the different anchors or use a load-sharing system like that shown on page 109. Whatever the system devised, it is important that when force is applied, the line from the anchors will run directly through the belayer to the falling climber, so that the rope handler will not be pulled from his position.

When rigging a belay, remember how easily nylon can be cut under tension. Watch for sharp edges, and don't run ropes or slings over them without first padding possible abrasion points. This can be done with a sweater or a pack. Use padding to avoid nylon-on-nylon contact whenever possible, because of the melting problem. If the belay rope runs over a sharp edge going from the belayer to the climber, it *must* be padded.

When carabiners are used in rigging a belay, they must be inspected carefully to see that they will not be pushed open in case of a fall. Gates should be positioned away from any rock surfaces or rigging that might open them. Strain should come *along* the carabiner, never *across* it.

One very important rule which is often neglected is that *the belaying rope must never run tightly across the anchor rope or sling.* Remember the melt-abrade phenomenon with nylon. A climbing rope under the tension of a climber's weight can cut through an anchor sling like a hot knife through butter. If the anchor sling or rope is abraded through, the belay will quite likely fail, so this danger is very real indeed. If the position of the anchor rope and the belay line is such that this problem might occur, a sweater or some other piece of clothing can be used to protect the anchor line. Several carabiners can be used to clip the climber in at the back, with the rope running through one of them, but this is rather awkward to set up. This problem can also be solved by using one of the belaying devices discussed in the next chapter.

Once the belay has been set up, the belayer gets into position and brings the climber up. Unless one can learn under experienced tutelage, however, all the actions should be practiced carefully until they have been mastered before they are ever tried in a place where failure could result in injury. The motions of belaying can be practiced as well in one's backyard as on a cliff. The main trick is learning to take in and pay out rope without ever releasing the braking hand from the rope.

A few of the many mistakes that can be made in setting up a belay. Ungloved hands can sustain severe rope burns, which may be disabling to the belayer, even if a fall is stopped. The rope here runs over the anchor sling and might well cut it in case of a fall. The belayer, in a position where she might be thrown, has no helmet, and could hit her head and lose the belay.

The basic principles of belaying are fairly simple. The belayer is seated and firmly anchored from behind. The rope passes around his body and is lightly held on both sides. The hand holding the rope going to the climber is the *feeling hand*. With it one pulls in the rope and feels the progress of the climber if he is not visible. The hand grasping the rope after it passes around the body is the *holding hand* or *braking hand*. By passing the rope around the torso, a good deal of friction is obtained if the braking hand clamps down on the rope, and quite a bit of force can be held even by a person who does not have an extremely strong grip. By throwing the holding hand further around the body as it grasps the rope, even more force can be held. Almost 360 degrees of wrap can be achieved by throwing the hand either across the front of the waist or down over the thigh.

The belayer must wear gloves. This is vital. Falls can generally be held with an upper belay without gloves, though even here some nasty blisters can sometimes result. However, the novice should remember that he is practicing for more difficult belaying situations, and it is all too easy to get sloppy about wearing gloves while belaying. Serious accidents have resulted from this mistake, and even some deaths. Part of the energy of the fall is absorbed by the heat of friction of the belayer's hands. If the palms are bare, a severe fall will burn them badly and often tear them to shreds. Even if the fall is stopped, thc belayer has become an invalid when he may need to help the climber who has just fallen. Gloves with leather palms arc not essential, but they last longer.

The motions of the hands when taking in rope are shown in the accompanying illustrations. They are really quite simple, but they *do* need to be practiced. The common mistake of crossing hands, so that the holding hand temporarily leaves the rope, is nearly impossible to avoid without training oneself carefully. If the climber should fall when this occurs, the mistake could be disastrous. The feeling hand, having no friction wrap to help it, cannot possibly hold a fall; and even if by sheer luck one manages to grasp the rope again with the holding

The basic sequence in belaying: the right (gloved) hand is the braking hand and must not leave the rope. The anchor is a very strong nut behind the belayer. The sling around the boulder is a back-up anchor, though the belayer would be pulled several feet from her position before the back-up stopped her. Here the feeling hand is forward, and the brake hand is as far back as it should go.

Taking in rope. The feeling hand pulls back, feeding rope around the belayer's back, and the braking hand goes forward, taking up the slack.

The feeling hand is then moved forward, sliding along the rope until the fingers can hold the rope *in front* of the braking hand.

The braking hand can now be moved back without ever leaving the rope. Thus, if a fall occurred at any time during the sequence, the braking hand would be on the rope, ready to stop it.

Taking in rope again, the feeling hand pulling the rope back and the braking hand pulling it forward.

Wrong. The common beginner's mistake is to grasp the rope with the feeling hand *behind* the braking hand, so that the braking hand must temporarily leave the rope to pass the feeling hand. If a fall occurs at this time, the belayer would be helpless to stop it. In this photo the belayer's left hand is her braking hand, and the right one, which is holding the ropes, is her feeling hand.

Holding a fall. The braking hand is thrown as far around the waist as possible to increase available friction. The braking hand can also be thrown down between the thighs, wrapping the rope partway around the leg.

hand, the climber will have fallen some way in the meantime.

The belayer must keep himself aware of what the climber is doing. He has to keep slack from developing between himself and the climber, but without pulling against the climber and possibly dislodging him from his holds. The belayer should also keep himself informed of where the climber is and where the pull on the rope would come if the climber fell. This can change even in top-rope climbing. A short move by the climber can bring the rope around a knob or flake which would act as a pulley and thus completely redirect the direction the rope would yank in a fall. Such a move could thus turn the belay suddenly from a very good to a very poor (or completely useless) one. Every belayer must train himself to be constantly aware of such possibilities, which tend to become more complex at more difficult levels of climbing.

SIGNALS

Every climbing team should have a set of clearly understood and well-defined signals. There are a number of systems; as long as everyone knows *exactly* which ones are being used and what they mean, it makes little difference which are used.

It is important to note that it is easy to become careless about such matters, however, and very dangerous. Don't be misled when you see an experienced climbing team which is apparently casual about signals; they may be sloppy or they may simply have been climbing together long enough to have established a private but well-understood set of conventions. One often gets into situations in climbing where it is hard for people to hear one another at precisely the time when fatigue and danger combine to trap the unwary. A rigidly followed series of signals should be established and followed invariably to prevent the possibility of fatal misunderstandings.

The following signals and their meanings are suggested because they are in wide use in the United States. The signals marked with an asterisk should be used *every* time a pitch is climbed with a belay.

Climber: **BELAY ON?** (Asking whether the belayer is anchored and ready.)

*Belayer: **ON BELAY!** (Affirming that he is in position and holding the rope. From the instant he calls "On belay," the belayer must be ready to hold a fall. The climber's life is in his hands until he gets permission to take the belay off.)

Climber: **READY TO TEST** (Indicating the climber would like to test the belay by pulling on the rope. Generally used in practice, but often helpful for both parties to find out which way the rope will pull and to confirm the strength of the belay.)

Belayer: **TEST** (Confirmation. Go ahead and test.)

Climber: **TESTING** (As he puts weight on the rope.)

Climber: **READY TO CLIMB** (Useful on longer climbs when the climber has several tasks to perform after he is put on belay before he actually starts moving. This indicates to the belayer that he should be ready to take in rope.)

Belayer: **CLIMB**	(Indicating the climber may proceed; the belayer is ready to take up the rope.)
Climber: **CLIMBING**	(I'm on my way.)
Climber: **SLACK!**	(Tells the belayer to let out rope. It is often important not to confuse this signal with the next one, both of which are pretty universal in American climbing. Thus the climber should not say, "Give me some rope!" since if only the last word is heard, the belayer is liable to haul it up instead.)
Climber: **UP ROPE! or ROPE!**	(Pull in the rope; I have too much slack. As for "slack," "Take in the slack!" is an ill-advised substitute.)
Climber: **TENSION!**	(Pull in on the rope as hard as you can, and hold it.)
Climber: **FALLING!**	(With a descending note. This signal often degenerates into a surprised yelp, but it should be attempted, since giving the belayer a spit-second's extra notice may save both parties a good deal of grief.)
*Climber: **OFF BELAY**	(Giving the belayer permission to take him off; once the climber has said it, he is on his own. Some care should be exercised by belayer and climber both at the beginning and end of the pitch not to jump the gun. If the belay position is a dangerous spot, the climber should not go off belay until he is tied in to the anchor.)
*Belayer: **BELAY OFF**	(Confirming that the climber had better take care of himself from that point on.)

To be worthwhile, all these signals must be memorized and practiced until they are second nature.

ROPE SIGNALS

Rope signals are hardly ever needed in top-rope climbing, but later on the climber will find occasions when they are important. In general mountaineering it is not uncommon to encounter situations where the climbers cannot hear one another because of wind or because they are separated by a rib of rock. Even on small rock formations, wind or the sound of a river in spring flood may make communication by voice impossible. A previously agreed-on set of rope signals will render such circumstances far safer. There are no commonly accepted rope signals, but the following set is suggested. The rope between the climbers must be reasonably taut for the signals to be felt.

ON BELAY:	The upper man, when he is anchored and ready, *jerks the rope twice.* The second man acknowledges the signal by *jerking twice.*
READY TO CLIMB:	When the second is ready, he signals by again *jerking the rope twice.* The belayer above *jerks the rope twice* to acknowledge.
UP ROPE:	If too much slack accumulates, the climber *jerks three times.* In this case the only response needed is to take in the slack.
TENSION:	The climber needing tension *jerks three times and pulls steadily on the rope.* Acknowledgment is to pull up any slack and hold the rope taut.
SLACK:	The climber *jerks the rope once and then pulls steadily.* The belayer pays out rope until the pull is no longer felt.

In all cases, the signal should be repeated until the proper response comes.

TOP-ROPE PRACTICE AND BOULDERING

Whether he has instruction or not, the novice should get out as often as possible with someone else at his own level for practice in climbing and belaying on local boulders or short cliffs. A lot can be learned simply by working on hard problems near the ground, and for this one does not even need a companion. Long traverses a few feet above the ground on boulders or at the bases of cliffs are excellent training. The art of doing very difficult pitches which are relatively close to the ground has even developed into a specialized sport, known as *bouldering.* The really skilled boulderer can move on holds that are scarcely credible, and a special rating system has been developed which is briefly explained later in the book.

For the purposes of this chapter, however, bouldering is mentioned mainly for its usefulness in training. It is helpful to do as many belayed climbs of a rope length or less as possible, sharing equally in the belaying and climbing. This enables the novice to develop confidence in the belay, to practice climbing with a certain amount of air below his feet, and to improve his belaying skills. Belays should be practiced under supervision before they are trusted, or they should be worked on extensively, and tested, under circumstances where the consequences of failure would be insignificant. Some of the testing at least should be unexpected.

Beginners should get some practice on rock pitches which are too hard for them, and should practice pushing to their limits. One only learns just what those limits are by falling. By repeated attempts one pushes the limits and also pinpoints them more precisely. It is important to push to the limit, however, not just to give up and fall. The conditioning and information gained in days of top-rope practice will be priceless to the climber later on. Once a pitch is mastered climbing up, one should repeat it going down. Downclimbing is a separate valuable art.

Novices should also practice going up and down easier pitches. Strength and technical ability are learned by pushing one's limits, but steadiness and rhythm are best acquired on longer and easier stuff. Remember to practice using balance, and relying whenever possible on the legs and feet, making

small steps rather than long reaches, looking ahead and planning moves in advance, testing holds before relying on them,
and maintaining an easy rhythm on the rock.

One should try to find as many different kinds of belaying
and climbing situations as possible on local rocks. To become
a well-rounded climber it is necessary to practice on the types
of problems one finds most difficult.

MULTI-PITCH CLIMBING

We now come to the meat of the subject—the use of the
rope for protection on longer climbs which are too steep and
hazardous to be climbed safely without it. Such climbing
should be approached with great caution by the beginner. This
is the point in climbing where one should obtain competent
instruction if at all possible. In any real climb where there is
no way to set up a top rope, someone has to go first, to *lead* the
rope. For the second man, many long climbs are not too different from a number of practice climbs piled one on top of the
other; but for the leader, there is a world of difference.

By far the simplest and safest way to learn to lead is to go
as a second on as many climbs as possible with a competent
leader. A much slower and more hazardous method is very
gingerly to work up from easier climbs to more difficult ones.
The only way to do this with a modicum of safety is always to
climb way below one's limit in order to have a good margin for
error. Naturally, this is not the fastest way to acquire great
technical proficiency. On the other hand, as long as one *does*
stay within one's limits, it is a good way to become a very
strong and solid climber, because one acquires much more
experience by taking responsibility for one's own safety.

Multi-pitch climbing naturally falls into many categories
of difficulty. Rating systems, which are designed to describe
roughly the difficulties that may be encountered on a particular climb, are discussed in Chapter 10. Here some methods of
roped protection will be discussed which are applicable on

relatively simple climbs. A great deal of caution should be exercised in evaluating a climb, however. One should never trust anyone else's estimate of difficulties very far.

EASY ROPED CLIMBING

The simplest roped climbing is that which is encountered on scrambling routes which get just a little *too* airy. Many moderate mountaineering climbs include short sections which are not difficult, but where the consequences of a slip would be very serious indeed. It is prudent to rope up in such places; in fact, this kind of climbing is excellent training once one is well versed in the art of belaying on local rocks. Usually the sections of the climb which require a rope are relatively short, so some experience can be acquired without unduly delaying the climb.

Setting up a belay on a mountain is not much different from setting it up on a practice, except that you will have to pay far more attention to the problems of direction. In choosing an anchor and belay position and in actually belaying, the belayer must keep an eye constantly on the situation and calculate where the climber would fall and which way the rope would run. To take an example which occurs quite frequently, if a climber is working his way along a sharp ridge, the pull may come from directions 180 degrees apart, depending on which way he falls. Such problems must be anticipated from the beginning, since all the possible directions of pull have to be taken into account when the anchor is set up. If the climber goes upward, and the rope runs over a knob or the trunk of a tree, then a fall would make the knob or tree act as a pulley. If the belayer below were anchored to a flake, the resulting upward pull might pull the belayer from position, unhook the loop from the flake, and so destroy the belay.

Thus, anticipation is one of the keys to belaying on multi-pitch climbs. It is also important to have practiced holding falls developing more force than the simple body weight of the climber. A leader who is being belayed to surmount a short cliff near a drop, if he fell at the top of that cliff would fall on past the belayer, going twice the length of the rope he had out, and then some distance farther while the belay and rope stretch absorbed the force of the fall. Practice in holding hard falls, which is discussed in the next chapter, is very helpful in giving the belayer a clear idea of the enormous forces involved.

Mention of these problems also shows the difficulties which arise in roped climbing on steep terrain. As a practical matter, the rope alone can be used to provide security on short sections which are steep and difficult; as a security device when the ground is steep enough so that one might fall a long way in case of a slip, but where it would be a sliding fall, with no great momentum developed; or where the terrain itself is not hard, but the possibility of falling off a lower cliff exists. Clearly, however, if the leader is climbing a steep cliff above his belayer, with 100 feet of rope out, and he falls, the belay will be useless. If the cliff is less than vertical, he will bounce on all sorts of projections in the 200-foot fall before the rope begins to come taut, and quite possibly be killed even before the belay begins to take effect. If the cliff is vertical enough or smooth enough that he falls freely, then the force developed might be too great to be held by the belayer or the rope, or to be borne by the climber's body. Thus, on steep and sustained climbs, the problem of protecting the leader becomes more complex, and this is the subject of the next two chapters.

7

BELAYING THE LEADER

The problem presented in the last chapter, that of protecting the leader, is faced on any long, steep climb, even one which is not particularly difficult. A leader on a relatively vertical face, a hundred feet above his belayer with nothing between them but the rope, is in practically the same position as the solo climber—a minor slip would probably mean death, despite the strength and elasticity of modern ropes, the effectiveness of a good belay, and the love of his guardian angel. Most climbers are not willing to take such severe risks very often, and quite rightly. If the climb is also very difficult, then with this sort of protection it would be too hazardous for most climbers to consider the risks justified.

If, however, the leader could step sideways over a tree and proceed upward, then if he fell, he would drop only down to the tree and then the same distance below it before the rope came taut between him and his belayer. The tree would form an intermediate *running belay,* and the critical distance would be the one between the leader and the tree rather than the one between him and his belayer.

The technique which is used to safeguard the leader on a steep climb is for him to employ a number of such running belays to provide protection as he works his way upward. Whenever the consequences of a slip begin to look too dreadful, the leader looks for ways to attach his rope to the mountain which will work to stop a fall in the same way the tree trunk would.

RUNNING BELAYS

The tree trunk in the example just given acts like a crude pulley. The climber can continue to climb above it without significant interference, since the rope runs freely over the trunk. If he falls, the belayer holds the other end of the rope, which passes over the tree and holds the climber dangling below it. The length of the fall is twice the distance the leader had gone above the tree, plus a certain amount of rope stretch and line which passed through the belayer's hands while he was stopping the fall. Tying the rope to the tree would not have worked. The rope has to be free to slide, even though it is attached at a certain point to the cliff.

The device which is normally used to provide a running belay in climbing is the *carabiner* or *snap link*, an oval or D-shaped ring of metal with a spring-loaded gate. The rope can be easily inserted, even in the awkward situations often encountered in climbing, and will then slide freely through the 'biner. If the carabiner can be attached in some way to the cliff or mountain, a running belay has been provided. The technique of protection consists largely of learning ways to attach the rope to the mountain.

A few points about carabiners should be made before we go on to discuss belaying and placing protection. The first is that carabiners are designed to provide *running* belays. Every time the rope goes through a carabiner (or around a tree trunk), it is dragged by friction; and the more sharp the bend made, the more friction. Each time the rope is run through another carabiner, more drag is put on it. So the rope must be clipped through in a way which causes as little friction as possible. This point will be discussed in more detail in the next chapter. For the moment it is sufficient to note that the rope must be clipped into the carabiner in the direction that will allow it to run most freely after the climber has passed and climbed on. It is worth practicing this technique on home ground, if possible, since until one learns to visualize the direction things will go, the rope is frequently clipped in the wrong way round. The importance of clipping properly is clear if you visualize the unpleasant consequences of having the rope jam at an awkward moment.

Since a carabiner is made with a spring-gate in one side, it is also important to place it so that the gate will not be forced open in case of a fall. Even if the rope does not come out, the carabiner loses half its strength if strain comes on it when the gate is open. The effect of a fall should be carefully visualized when the snap link is placed, whether in setting up a belay or leading a pitch. The normal rule for running belays is that the gate should be directed *down and out;* that is, the gate should be on the outside, with the opening end down.

CARABINER STRENGTH AND ORIENTATION

Carabiners are not all equally strong. Fortunately, dealers in climbing equipment are again becoming responsible in reporting equipment strength. It was once standard practice in the United States to include this information in catalogues. Anyone offering carabiners for sale should have some test results, and the climber should be wary of carabiners for which he cannot get them; a few types have appeared that have been notoriously weak.

A carabiner is strongest when loaded along its major axis with the gate closed; that is, the stress comes along the length of the carabiner. Modern oval carabiners generally have a major axis strength of 2500 or 3000 pounds with the gate closed, but only about 1500 pounds with the gate open. Minor axis strength—that is, across the carabiner—may be under 1500 pounds. D-shaped carabiners generally have a much higher major axis strength, open and closed, with closed-gate strength ranging from 4000 pounds up, and open-gate tests exceeding 2000 pounds. Minor axis strength is generally under 2000 pounds. These figures are given here as indications of what should be expected. Strength should be checked before purchasing carabiners.

The main reason for discussing carabiner strength at this

Some carabiners. From left are a standard aluminum alloy oval, the stronger "D," and a modified "D." On the right are two ovals under load, the left one correctly loaded along the long axis and the right one incorrectly loaded across the much weaker short axis.

point is to indicate the danger of placing carabiners in ways which could allow strain to be applied in unusual directions. Some snap links which test at around 7000 pounds when they are properly oriented will still break at less than 2000 under cross-loading. Loads of 2000 pounds can be developed fairly easily in a leader fall.

THE PROBLEM OF BELAYING THE LEADER

The brief discussion above of running belays should give the beginner some idea of the problems involved in holding a leader fall. With a top-rope belay, the belayer is never required to hold a force much more than the weight of the climber, because no more than a few feet of slack can develop. Furthermore, the direction from which the force is likely to come is usually pretty easy to determine, and it doesn't normally change much as the climber comes up the pitch.

But when the novice goes on his first *continuous climb* on steep rock, the situation is drastically changed. Suppose, for example, that the leader has climbed up to a ledge a rope length above the ground and brought the second up. The second then ties into the anchor and prepares to belay the leader. If the leader climbs up around 8 feet and falls off before setting up a running belay, he may fall right past the ledge and the belayer. The force that the belayer would then have to absorb if the rope did not slip, even after the rope has taken up some of the energy of the fall, would probably be over 2000 pounds. This would depend on the weight of the leader and on other factors, of course, but it is a far cry from the small forces involved in a top-rope belay.

In addition to the increased loads involved, the belay has become much more complicated. Continuing the previous example, let us suppose that the unhurt leader climbs back up, clips into the running belay where he had fallen, climbs on up several feet, and falls again. A large force will once more be put on the belayer, but instead of yanking him down, the force will pull him up toward the running belay. If he is sitting in an alcove, this could easily bang his head against a rock shelf above, knocking him unconscious and causing him to release his hold on the rope. If the belay anchor is a sling looped over a rock flake, the force of the fall could lift the belayer and the sling, pulling him right off the ledge and eliminating the belay.

Let us introduce one final problem before turning to the solutions. In either of the previous two falls, suppose that the second manages to belay properly and to catch the fall, but that instead of being unhurt and able to climb back up, the leader is injured and his weight is hanging at the end of the rope. With the full weight of the leader suspended around his waist, the second is not likely to be able to do very much except sit and hold the rope. In order to assist his companion or take any other action, he must somehow tie off the rope so that he can release himself from the weight.

The first problem mentioned is one that was discussed in the previous chapter; all aspects of the belay have to be strong enough to withstand high-impact loads, and at practice sessions, the student has to get experience in holding high loads, not just body weight. Anchors have to be strong, and the lines must be tight and run straight, so that the force of a fall will not tend to pull the belayer out of position. Again, it should be stressed that gloves are essential to hold leader falls without burning the hands severely.

MAKING ANCHORS NON-DIRECTIONAL

The simplest way to solve the problem of falls exerting forces on the belay which may come from different directions is to make the anchor strong against a pull from any of the possible directions. In continuous climbing, this is usually most easily done by the person first setting up the belay. If he knows that the same belay point will have to serve both for the upper belay he has to give and for the lower belay that will follow, it is faster to arrange an anchor that will hold any kind of pull.

There are many possibilities for arranging such a belay, and each demands a creative mind in the climber. A tree with a cinched sling may offer an easy solution. A sling threaded through a hole in the rock will work equally well, regardless of the direction of pull. Separate anchors can be set up, one good for a downward pull and one for an upward one. Sometimes it is better for anchors to be opposed, with the sling from one passing through that to the other, so that the resulting force, regardless of direction, just pulls both anchors tighter.

Another possibility is to set up a running belay in front of the belayer, so that whatever the direction of pull on the rope, the force on the belayer is always toward the running belay, enabling him to use a flake or some other anchor behind him that may only be strong for a pull in one direction. Whatever method or combination of methods is chosen, the critical ingredient is a careful analysis by the belayer of the direction and magnitude of the forces involved.

One other point that must be considered is the fact that in the case of a strong upward pull, the belayer will be completely dependent on his anchor to keep from being lifted out of position. Sitting upper belays are often strong enough to hold considerable forces without relying on the anchor. A well-chosen upper belay stance may become stronger as the rope pulls down on the belayer. When the pull is up, however, obviously the belayer will be pulled off his stance as soon as the force is greater than his own weight, unless the anchor restrains him.

THE BELAY

With a solid anchor, suitable for any of the directions from which a pull might come, the second is ready to belay. The most common belay is the *sitting hip belay* shown in the previous chapter. The belayer is anchored at the waist; he runs the rope going to the other climber around his waist; the hand on the side of the rope leading to the climber is the feeling hand and the opposite one the holding hand. *The holding hand must never leave the rope while the belay is on.* In case of a fall, some of the force is immediately absorbed by the rope; the bodies of the climber and the belayer absorb some more as the rope cuts into them; and the rest goes into heat of friction as the rope is pulled around the belayer's waist and through his hand. It is because of this friction that gloves are so important. *In general, the belayer should clamp down with the holding hand as soon as he knows of the fall, stopping it as quickly as possible,* and voluntarily letting rope run through his hand only if he feels some part of the belay system failing. The more quickly the fall is stopped, the less likely the climber is to hit a ledge or other projection below, perhaps injuring himself severely.

The principle of stopping the fall as quickly as possible relies on modern climbing ropes and harnesses, which are unlikely to break under the strain and are elastic enough so that they will not put too high an impact force on the falling

climber's body. The principle of belaying which was long ad-
vocated in North America to prevent rope breakage and excessive impact was the *dynamic belay,* in which the belayer deliberately allows some of the rope to slide through his hands,
braking the speed of the fall more gradually.

Actually, all the belays commonly used in North American
climbing are dynamic, because of the energy-absorbing properties of the rope, because of the give in the belayer's body and
the anchor, and because some rope will slide through the
hands even when the rope is held tight. The *deliberate* dynamic belay is not usually desirable, however, since the falling
climber may be injured by projections in falling the additional
unnecessary distance. In some kinds of climbing, when really
strong anchors are not available, it is sometimes better to give
an intentional dynamic belay, allowing rope to slip through the
braking hand, and stopping the fall gradually, to prevent tearing out the protection and causing the climber to fall farther.
In difficult direct aid climbing and high-angle ice climbing, this
is frequently the case. Ice ax belays on snow are also usually
dynamic to prevent pulling the ax out. Dynamic belays, to be
given properly, must be carefully practiced in advance, because the braking hand must use varying pressure depending
on the friction that has already built up as the rope passes
through a series of carabiners. In the great majority of cases,
however, the belayer simply clamps down on the rope as hard
as he can, ignoring theoretical considerations.

The position taken by the belayer will vary a good deal,
since the sitting belay is not always possible. If the belayer has
to stand, the rope should still pass over the hips for a belay from
above, and just under the buttocks for a belay from below.
Regardless of his stance, the belayer must take care that the
pull of the rope could not slide it up or down on his body to
a position where he could not control it. Probably the simplest
way to manage this is to run the rope around the waist and
then clip it to the waist loop on each side with a carabiner,
making it impossible for the rope either to ride down under
the hips or up onto the back. This practice makes changes

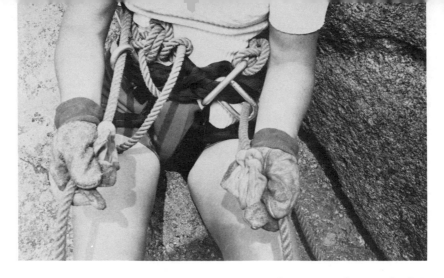

A method of keeping the belay rope from riding up or down, which is particularly useful when the direction from which the pull would come changes during the belay, as with many belays of leaders. The belay rope is clipped to the belayer's harness on both sides. (The tie-in in this case is the climbing rope tied to the harness at the front, going back around the belayer's right side, around the anchor, and coming back around the belayer's left side, where it is attached to a locking carabiner with a clove hitch.)

unnecessary when a climber goes by, shifting the belay from an upper to a lower one. Although clipping the rope in is not always necessary, it should be done whenever there is doubt. This has the additional advantage of making it much harder to lose the belay completely.

USING NUTS FOR ANCHORS

Various natural anchors were discussed in the last chapter. Trees, flakes, boulders, holes in the rock, and similar natural anchors are to be preferred when available, because they are reliable, quick to use, and require a minimum of extra equipment to be carried by the climber. One common natural anchor is the *chockstone,* a rock which has wedged into a constriction in a crack. Some chockstones are jammed rather insecurely and are quite unsuitable as anchors, but others are very solid and make ideal belays. Such anchors are often directional and must be inspected carefully; since the chockstone has fallen into position, there is normally at least one direction in which it can be easily dislodged, unless it is very large. As with any directional belay, care should be exercised to ensure that the force of a fall would not loosen the anchor. Chock-

An example of a good but limited belay point, a climbing rope tied into a figure eight loop and hooked on a nubbin. This would be a strong belay, as long as the force would come down on the nubbin; otherwise it would be worthless.

stones should obviously not be relied on if they rest only on narrow points of rock and the crack becomes larger below, if they are made of rotten or easily fractured rock, or if they are perched unstably so that they could rotate out.

The corollary, given a narrowing crack and a rock of the right size, is to make the rock into a chockstone by putting it in the crack. Several years back, English cliff climbers began going a step further by carrying pocketfuls of stones to drop in cracks and tie off with slings. The next stage was to carry small machine nuts to chock into the cracks, with slings passed through the center holes. For some time, ethics demanded that only nuts found lying about could be used, presumably because these formed part of the natural landscape. This particular restriction naturally did not last long, and stocks of store-bought nuts made their way into British cracks. Finally, of course, came the development of dozens of kinds of *chocks* and *nuts* specially made for climbing.

Nuts now range in size from the tiniest slivers of metal to those designed to span 8-inch jam cracks. The smallest sizes are not suitable for belay anchors. Some of the many imaginative placements of chocks are discussed in later chapters. Only the basics are covered here.

The principle used in all nut placements is somehow to get the nut into a relatively wide opening in a crack or hollow and to arrange it so that any pull on it will tend to jam it into a narrower, more constricted section of the crack. A sling is normally tied around a natural chockstone, but manufactured nuts are strung with nylon webbing, rope, or wire cable. The strongest material that will fit through the holes should be used, up to 1-inch webbing, 9-mm or ⅜-inch rope, or ³⁄₁₆-inch steel cable. With smaller nuts, the largest rope or webbing that can be forced through the holes is generally strongest, although a slightly smaller size may sometimes be desirable for other reasons.

Nuts can be strung with either rope or webbing, each of which has certain advantages. Webbing can be worked through narrower constrictions, so it sometimes makes possible placements that could not be made with a nut strung with rope. Webbing is also more flexible and less likely to displace the nut. On the other hand, rope will wear better and is less subject to cutting, and the extra stiffness is sometimes helpful in jiggling a nut into position. I tend to carry most nuts on webbing, with a few on rope, thus mixing the advantages.

Nuts should normally be carried on full-length slings, made of around 3½–5 feet of sling material. A short sling will not work in all nut placements and also tends to jiggle the nut loose in many positions unless a regular sling is added to lengthen it. Nuts that are strung with wire are occasionally useful, because the wire can be used as an inserter in some difficult placements; as a rule, however, they tend to be worked loose more easily. Wired nuts are used frequently in direct aid climbing, and nuts that are too small to be threaded with a sling of adequate size are wired. Most climbers on regular routes carry a few wired nuts, but rely primarily on those threaded with webbing or rope.

In placing a nut for a belay anchor, the direction of pull is the first consideration. Sometimes a placement can be found that is essentially non-directional. There may be a long hollow at the back of a belay ledge, with only a narrow crack for an opening; if a large nut can be slotted into this cavity at one end and worked down to the belay point, a bombproof anchor for a pull in any direction may be possible. More often, however, the nut will only be good for one direction of pull, and it will have to be treated like any other directional anchor. A second nut can be used for another direction, two or more nuts can be opposed, a nut and a sling over a flake can be opposed, and so on. Some examples are shown on pages 145 and 146.

Any nut placement must be examined critically not only for directional stability but for strength as well. For its strength, the nut depends on being wider than the constriction of the rock in the direction of pull. If only a couple of small nubbins of rock provide the resistance to movement, the nut cannot be very strong. If only two points of aluminum on the nut are being held by the rock, it will have little strength. If the climber has simply jiggled the nut around in the back of a crack until it jammed, with no idea whether it is being held by the body of the rock or by a rotten grain, he is courting disaster.

Even if it is perfectly placed, a nut is no stronger than the sling with which it is threaded. As a rule, only nuts threaded with 1-inch webbing, 9-mm kernmantel, or ⅜-inch laid rope

A large nut in use for a belay which is very strong in vertical pull. The flake behind which the nut is placed is not detached and will not move. A new sling is very important if reliance is being placed on a single anchor, since worn slings can be unexpectedly weak. Here, two oval carabiners with the gates on opposite sides have been used for safety, so that the belay cannot be weakened by a gate accidentally pushing open.

A belay anchor using two nuts, a Chouinard stopper on the left and a Forrest copperhead on the right. With the line of pull at this belay spot, either placement would be secure by itself, so the nuts are independent anchors. But they also reinforce one another, each improving the other placement, and together they make a non-directional anchor.

Nuts in opposition: the sling of the wedge on the left goes through that of the hexagonal nut on the right. The belayer clips into this sling for an anchor which is non-directional. Note that the two nuts form a single anchor, since if either fails there is no back-up. For a belay anchor it is best to have another separate back-up.

should be trusted for a belay. Several smaller nuts with a load-sharing sling may be used. Single artificial anchors like nuts should also not usually be relied on, unless they are in such a position that they are absolutely bombproof. More often, even if a nut seems very strong, it should be backed up with a second equally good one before being relied on for a belay anchor.

Some nuts are shaped in such a way that they can be placed in a "camming" position, so that pulling on the sling tends to rotate the nut and lock it more tightly. Forrest's Titons and Chouinard's Hexentrics can be placed this way. Camming placements can be used effectively in relatively parallel-sided cracks. They are also very useful for horizontal cracks. Careful analysis of each camming placement is necessary before too much trust is placed in it, as with all anchors.

More suggestions on nut placements will be found in the next chapter.

PITON ANCHORS

The standard artificial anchors for many years in North America were *pitons*—metal wedges which are driven into cracks in the rock with hammers, and which can exert tremendous forces within the crack due to the wedging action, forces which resist dislodging of the properly placed piton. Good piton placement requires care and thought, just as the use of nuts and slings does, although pitons allow a slightly more simple-minded approach, because their safety is not quite so dependent on the direction of pull and because no solidly placed piton can be jiggled loose as a sling or a nut can.

Pitons—also known as *pegs, pins,* and *iron*—should be avoided whenever possible, and most of the time it is possible. Driving and removing them is noisy and unaesthetic. Pitons and hammers are heavier than chocks and don't last as long. Most important, repeated driving and removal of pitons will destroy the cracks in which they are placed. In some climbing areas pitons are *fixed* at certain points, so that additional ones need not be driven and removed. This is a good answer to the problem of degradation of cracks, but climbers should inspect such fixed pins carefully, because pitons can be loosened by weathering or become brittle by remaining in the same position, under pressure, for long periods. There should generally be more fixed pins for a belay spot than would be placed by a single climber, providing additional back-up should one piton weaken. Fixed pins can be tested as described below, if one carries a hammer.

Pitons come in an assortment of shapes and sizes, designed to fit a wide range of cracks. The very thinnest ones—knife-blades, rurps, and crack tacks—are designed for use in direct aid, and will be discussed in a later chapter. Next in order of size are the *horizontals,* which have varying forms, all with the plane of the carabiner hole, or eye, perpendicular to the blade. These used to be distinguished from *verticals,* which have the eye and blade in the same plane but which are rarely seen now, because it was found that horizontals work better in both horizontal and vertical cracks.

Horizontal pitons are made in both soft iron and highly tempered chrome-molybdenum (chromolly) steel, as well as in some steels of medium hardness. The softer pitons are reasonably strong, work better in a few kinds of rotten rock, and are cheaper. They cannot be reused many times, because they

Pitons. In the upper row at the left are several soft iron horizontals, which are weaker than chromolly ones, but are cheaper and scar the rock less. The rings that are included with one of the horizontals and the (black) angle piton to their right are welded, and their strength is not always uniform. At the right in the top row are two bong-bongs, or large angles. In the lower row are a rurp, a crack tack, a thin and a thick knifeblade, eight Lost Arrows, a Leeper Z-section, and angles measuring ½″, ⅝″, ¾″ (standard angle), 1″, and 1¼″.

deform too much when pounded back and forth. Since they are cheap and difficult to remove they are frequently used for fixed pins, as they are less likely to be taken home by scavengers.

Chromolly pitons were developed in America, and the best ones are still made here. They are stronger than other pitons, and, more important, they can be driven and removed dozens of times. On the big wall climbs for which they were originally designed, this allowed a selection of moderate size to serve throughout a climb requiring hundreds of individual piton placements. Removal of chromolly pitons is very damaging to cracks, particularly when it is done repeatedly on popular climbs.

The ethics of piton placement have varied somewhat with

time and climbing area, but the general American attitude for many years was that each climber should leave the route as "natural" as possible for the next party. In line with this view, everyone was supposed to remove his pitons when possible, unless the result would be too destructive. At a time when there were few climbers this made a lot of sense, but as the climbing community grew, the destructive effect of repeated placement and removal of chromolly pins began to be inescapably obvious in popular climbing areas.

The modern American ethic of *clean climbing* largely follows the model set a number of years ago by the British. On most climbs in most areas, responsible climbers do not even carry pitons, but rely on nuts and slings. Where pitons seem necessary in popular areas, the climbs may be "established," with fixed pins put in where nuts will not do or where pitons seem desirable on easy climbs to protect the inexperienced.

The climber should start using nuts and slings for protection from the time he begins the sport. Pitons are discussed here because they still have some place in certain kinds of climbing, particularly in winter mountaineering, and because if a climber places or uses fixed pins he should be aware of the essentials of piton placement.

The crack in which a peg is placed has to be inspected, just

Placing a piton. Selection of a proper piton and crack is the most important step. Here an angle is being placed in a horizontal crack. When inserted by hand, one-half to two-thirds of the usable blade length should go into the crack. The sides of the crack should not be rotten, and the crack must be deep enough for the piton to be driven in without bottoming.

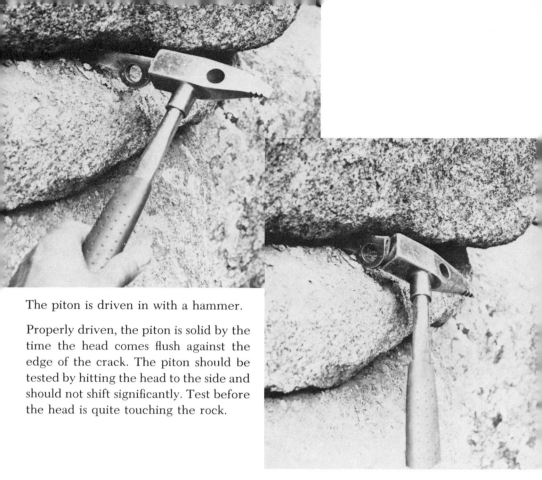

The piton is driven in with a hammer.

Properly driven, the piton is solid by the time the head comes flush against the edge of the crack. The piton should be tested by hitting the head to the side and should not shift significantly. Test before the head is quite touching the rock.

After testing, the pin is hit once or twice more to re-solidify it. If the tip or the head of the piton is already against really solid rock, further beating will just vibrate the pin and tend to loosen it. Note that much more practice is needed to judge when a piton is good than to tell a good nut or sling. One should never rely on untested, old, fixed pins.

as with a nut. If it runs behind a loose block, driving a wedge in will serve only to knock the block off onto your head. If the sides are rotten, the piton will be weak. If the crack is flaring and shallow, a good placement will be difficult—nuts may work better. As always, look for a decent nut or sling placement before driving a pin.

As a general rule you should be able to push half or two-thirds of the piton's length into the crack before starting to hammer. The piton should fit the crack, having a similar taper. It must be reasonably hard to drive; if a few light hammer blows knock the pin all the way in, it will be weak.

The choice of piton and the place to drive it are the most important factors in good placement. Look at the crack and the pin with the same eye you use to find ways to slot nuts. A locally wider spot in the crack will enable the peg to resist shifting. A good horizontal placement will tend to resist a downward pull without relying heavily on the wedged strength of the piton, whereas a pin in a parallel-sided vertical crack will be wholly dependent on wedging to resist rotating out with a downward pull. Horizontal placements are generally better than vertical, unless projections will keep the vertically placed peg from rotating.

For larger cracks than those accommodating horizontals, there are various types of angle pitons, and there is some overlapping between the smaller angles and the larger horizontals. The well-designed Leeper Z-sections are in the same size range as some horizontals and small angles. Some standard piton placements are shown in the illustrations.

In addition to the information you get about the strength of a piton by looking at its positioning before and after placement, you can tell a great deal by the way it goes in. The sound gives some guide, with a ringing of rising pitch being the traditional good indicator. Actually, there are plenty of good pins that don't ring well and some bad ones that sound wonderful. This is only one sign. If you drive a piton into a smooth-sided vertical crack, it can ring like a bell and rotate out under a force of a few hundred pounds. But the sound *will* tell you

A good horizontal piton, driven properly, with the eye against the rock and with an oval carabiner clipped in correctly.

Wrong. The same piton in the same placement, but driven in upside down, allowing much more leverage to develop.

Wrong. A thicker horizontal driven into the same crack will not go in all the way, and the carabiner clipped into the eye will exert tremendous leverage in case of a fall.

Marginal. If the thicker horizontal had to be used, tying it off like this would give much better protection. The tie-off is with girth-hitched ¾″ webbing.

Poor. A horizontal which is well-driven in a vertical crack; however, the crack is of uniform width below the piton, and a few hundred pounds of force might rotate the pin out.

Good. Placements in vertical cracks are never as strong as good horizontal positionings, but this type of vertical placement is fairly good. This Leeper is in the same crack as the piton in the preceding photo, about a foot away. The crack constricts above and below the piton, and the eye of the piton is against the rock, all features tending to resist rotation. Note that if the crack opened wider above the piton, the placement would be weak. In general, placements in vertical cracks must be chosen with much more care than those in horizontal ones.

Bad. This angle is placed upside down and in such a way that a great deal of leverage would increase the effective force acting to break it or pull it from the crack.

Good. A properly placed angle with a "D" carabiner clipped in.

Good. A baby angle placed in a pocket in a vertical crack.

some things. If you have a nice rising ring, and all of a sudden the sound goes "thunk," you have split something off or hit bottom, either of which is bad. Pounding on a bottoming pin loosens it. It is also important to watch the crack as you are driving to see if it widens.

An ideal placement will bring the eye flush with the edge of the crack, but pounding after the head of the piton is against the rock will tend to loosen the pin. When the piton is almost in, hit the head sideways to judge how strong the piton is, then knock it in a little more. Don't stop pounding too soon for fear of "overdriving." Pitons can be overdriven, but until you have a feel for what is just right, it is far better to err on the side of overdriving than the other way. Angles are easier to overdrive than horizontals. (Overdriving means hammering a piton in so solidly that it cannot be removed without risking breaking off the head.)

If a piton that is not driven in all the way has to be used, the regular carabiner hole should not be employed. Instead, the pins should be tied off as close to the rock as possible with webbing of adequate strength. If necessary, a carabiner can be clipped in to prevent the tie-off from accidentally slipping over the head of the piton. A piton is normally tied off by attaching a loop of webbing to it with a girth hitch or an overhand slip knot, in order to reduce leverage. The technique is illustrated on page 154 and in Chapter 13.

For a belay anchor, at least two *good* pitons should be used. Pitons are harder to judge than nuts, even for an expert who has placed thousands, and hopefully that kind of expertise will be getting rarer as pitons are replaced more and more with clean protection. In any case, one can always be fooled, so at least two pins, preferably with a load-sharing anchor, should be used. It is vital to remember that no guarantee of reliability is attached to fixed pins left on a route.

BOLTS

Overuse of bolts is pernicious, because they permanently deface the rock in which they are placed. Nevertheless, most climbers have felt that their use is occasionally justified to make safe climbing on some routes possible, where no other protection could be placed, or to provide belay or rappel anchors on popular routes for various purposes: to stem destruction by repeated placement and removal of pitons, to provide a wider margin of safety for beginners, and so on. Local customs and careful consideration by the community of experienced local climbers are the best guides to placing bolts in particular areas. In some climbing regions, bolts are hardly used at all. In others, bolting is generally restricted to isolated spots or sections which connect up otherwise fine routes and therefore justify bolt placement. In still other places, there is generally no protection possible except for bolts, and their reasonable use has been accepted as standard practice.

Bolts are discussed further in Chapter 13. No more will be said here about ethics except that no novice or climber new to a particular area should take it upon himself to place bolts until he has discussed the matter with a number of local climbers or become familiar enough with the area to understand the local feeling and tradition. In particular, it is rarely justifiable to place a bolt on an established route, except to replace an old one that is rotting out. In this case it is best to pull the bolt and fill in the old hole with a mixture of epoxy and sand matching the color of the rock.

If they are placed at all, bolts should be put in well, so that others can trust them and will not feel impelled to drill more holes in the rock. Again, discussion with experienced local climbers is the best guide to the type of bolt that works well in a particular kind of rock. Most bolts are designed to fit into holes drilled with a standard fluted percussion drill, which is fitted into a holder and rotated while the holder is struck with a hammer. A short rubber tube is used to blow rock dust from the hole and the drill often has to be sharpened or replaced several times while drilling a hole. It is important to drill the hole deep enough so the bolt will not bottom out, causing it to loosen as it is driven in or allowing leverage at the surface. Different kinds of bolts require different depths, however, and one must check to find out the method of drilling that provides maximum holding power. The proper size drill is also essential; different types of bolts of the same size require slightly different-sized holes because of the varying methods used to exert force inside the hole. Finally, it is important to drill straight into the rock. Jiggling and vibration of the drill will result in an oversize hole that will not allow the bolt to develop maximum strength.

For most types of rock, a *self-drilling* bolt works well. It has cutting teeth so that the bolt itself can be used to drill the hole. After drilling, an expanding insert is placed at the bottom of the hole and the bolt is driven onto it. A hanger is then attached with forged alloy steel cap screw. A holder for drilling the hole can easily be made from a section of aluminum rod and a stud with the same thread as the bolt. In hard rock, the cutting teeth of self-drilling bolts may dull before the hole is finished, and a second bolt may have to be used to complete the hole.

With any type of bolt, hangers, nuts, and screws should be left in place, so that subsequent parties will not be forced to put in new bolts for lack of the proper type and size of hanger. For belay stances, two bolts should normally be placed if the stance is insecure. Bolts of ¼ × 1½ inches will serve in strong rock, but longer bolts of larger diameter may be required in areas with weak rock. In poor-quality desert sandstone and some other very soft rock, the best bolts are angle pitons driven into holes about two-thirds to three-quarters their diameter.

Obviously, bolt placement requires careful attention. The line of pull should come at right angles to the bolt, rather than out on it. A hanger has to be placed so that it cannot become a lever to pull the bolt out. The rock into which the bolt is placed must be strong; a bolt in a loose block or a rotten or cracked surface is poor security. The bolt should be placed at least a foot from the nearest crack or other bolt, to prevent fracturing. In some regions, it has been found helpful to pour epoxy in the top of the bolt hole to retard weathering. There is something to be said for painting bolts and hangers an inconspicuous color.

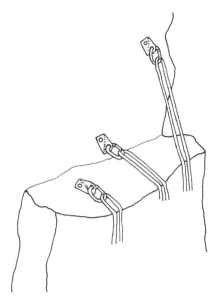

BOLT PLACEMENTS. The type of hanger shown is the most commonly used today (the Leeper). It is very strong as long as the force is applied parallel to the surface of the rock, but it can act as a lever with an outward force. The placement on the left might be quite good, if there is enough solid rock around the bolt and the block is not loose, but the sharp angle of the rope over the rock edge may need to be padded and might cause the rope to hang up if this placement is for a rappel. The center placement is BAD; it has the same problems as the one to the left and puts dangerous leverage on the bolt. The placement to the right is best in most circumstances; it reduces rope drag for a rappel, and it is above where the belayer would sit if the ledge were used for a belay.

A bolt anchor. There are many types. This one is a Leeper hanger on a 2" long ⅜" Star Dryvin bolt. Even more than with pitons, it is difficult to judge the reliability of a bolt one has not placed personally, though a well-placed bolt in good rock is a very strong anchor. Bolts permanently deface the rock in which they are placed, so they should only be placed by experienced climbers familiar with the ethics of the area in which they are climbing.

This section has been deliberately brief. Some mention of bolts is necessary even for beginners, since novices have to be cautious about bad bolts and to understand the basics of their placement. More extensive discussion is not necessary, however, since beginners should *never* place bolts. Bolt kits have their place on certain climbs and in certain emergencies, but they are not needed in the first couple of years of a climbing career.

ADDITIONAL BELAYING NOTES

The belayer is the rope handler as well, which is one of the reasons that good belaying requires practice. Belaying from below, he has to keep paying out rope smoothly, without getting things snarled, so that he does not hamper the leader. He must feel the progress of the climber above without pulling him off the rock.

When two climbers of equal ability do a route together, they normally alternate leads, so the belay does not have to be changed and the correct end of the rope is at the top of the pile made by the belayer. If one climber is doing all the leads, however, the pile has to be turned over when the belay is changed, so that the leader's end comes off the top. Otherwise, the rope will soon snarl.

When belaying from above on a steep climb, there is often a problem in managing the rope. In most cases it is bad policy to allow the rope to dangle down the face, because it can become jammed in some inaccessible spot below. This and similar snags in many situations, particularly on traverses, have to be watched for. There may also be places where the rope has to be flipped over a knob or other obstruction to provide better protection or to avoid snagging. The belayer must be particularly watchful when the climber is above him until the leader places protection. If a leader with no running belay crosses behind the belayer and falls, the rope will be pulled out from behind the belayer's back with disastrous results if he has not prepared for this possibility.

HANGING BELAYS

On many steep and difficult routes, adequate belay stances are separated by more than a rope length, so belaying has to be done suspended from one's anchors. Actually, there are a whole range of transition situations. Best are adequate sitting positions that provide enough stability to hold a fall without even putting a strain on the anchors. Poor sitting belays on sloping ledges, and standing belays around the hips, could absorb a fraction of the force of a fall before it came onto the anchors. Finally, there are stances where the belayer's weight rests on his anchors, whether or not he has a place to put his feet.

Hanging belays are not likely to be encountered by the beginner, and some experience in complicated kinds of rope handling is necessary to avoid dangerous mistakes. As usual, the belayer must pass the rope around his body in such a way that it is impossible for it to slip up or down. Using carabiners to clip the rope to the harness is an effective method. To be certain of the direction from which the force of a fall would come, the rope will often pass through a carabiner attached to an anchor as soon as it leaves the belayer, so that the direction of pull will be the same whether the leader has put in additional protection or not.

Since even more weight and reliance is being put on the anchors in a hanging belay, it is vital that such anchors are secure. Two good bolts or three good nuts or pitons should be considered standard, although fewer anchors may be adequate if they are bombproof, and more will be necessary if they are doubtful. Self-discipline is necessary, because it is easy to become overconfident and to place too much faith in equipment; single bolts, for example, will work nearly all the time, but only one failure is required to kill you and your partner.

A hanging belay is likely to be a confused mass of hardware, slings, and ropes. It is important to work out methods of being as systematic and orderly as possible, both to promote speed and to prevent accidents. In a rat's nest of slings, nuts,

pitons, and carabiners, it is easy to make a mistake and clip or unclip the wrong thing. Double-check every move before making it. Work hard to avoid rope jams. Don't allow confused stackings of carabiners, which can cause cross-loading on the gates, opening gates, or leverage on anchors.

The comfort of the belayer depends on equipment and on the belay. Since climbing on very steep terrain is often time-consuming and the belayer's attention to the belay is essential, some effort should be made in the beginning to make his position as comfortable as possible and to satisfy any bodily needs before starting to belay. Many harnesses are relatively comfortable to sit in while belaying, and one can rig the aid slings for standing. A specially made belay seat is often used for the purpose, but it is strictly a place for the belayer to rest his posterior, not part of the anchoring system.

BELAYING BRAKES, PLATES, LINKS, AND HITCHES

In many belays it is helpful to use a friction device rather than the customary round-the-waist turn. Such devices have been in use in Europe for some time and are becoming increasingly common in the United States. They have many important advantages, especially on big wall climbs and in winter. Many climbers now use them almost exclusively, but they can be dangerous when used improperly.

The general principle in all these methods and devices is that the rope must make several sharp bends as it is passed through; if the belayer pulls on the free side of the rope, the bends become sharper, and a great deal of friction results. Some of the devices and methods used are discussed below, but since they are all employed in pretty much the same way, their general use will be discussed first.

OPPOSITE

A hanging belay, or belay in slings, this one on the Maiden. The climber above is belaying his second up.

A belaying device often greatly simplifies rope-handling problems. The device is normally clipped to the front of the climbing harness, and the rope passes in and out in a small area immediately in front of the belayer. With some experience, the rope is easy to feed. The possibility of the climbing rope running across the belay sling or of its riding up or down on the belayer is avoided. The holding hand serves mainly to pull the rope over, and does not have to provide as much of the belaying force, so there are important advantages for belaying in winter, when it is difficult to get enough friction on a snowy rope with heavy gloves, and for weaker climbers belaying heavy leaders. In summer when light clothing is being worn, painful rope burns across the back are avoided, and the strength of a belay is not affected by the pain threshold of the belayer. The belay device keeps the rope in position, and the

Sticht belay plate in use. The belayer's right hand is the braking hand, and her left is the feeling hand. The rope goes through the plate, through a locking carabiner clipped into the belayer's harness, and back out through the plate. The short length of parachute cord prevents the plate from riding out or being lost. The laid rope in use is sufficiently broken in so that excessive kinking will not occur. The belayer's anchor is not visible in the picture.

Holding a fall with a Sticht plate. The braking hand pulls the rope to the side, which presses the plate against the carabiner, creating a large amount of friction and allowing the fall to be held fairly easily. Although belay plates have a number of advantages, they also present considerable problems, which are discussed in the text.

belay is not completely lost if the belayer momentarily loses control of the rope—a particular advantage on difficult climbs when one may have to belay for hours, with attendant risks of boredom or drowsiness in the belayer. It is easy to tie off the climber. Belaying can often be done with one hand, sometimes allowing the belayer to sort gear or eat safely while working.

There are a number of disadvantages to belay devices, however. To begin with, it is difficult to control the restraint of the belay. With a normal sitting belay, the belayer should try as much as possible to use the seat of his pants and body bracing to catch the fall, using the anchors as a back-up. Even if he is pulled against the anchor, his body will have absorbed much of the impact force, reducing the strain on the anchors and thus the chance of failure. Even when the rope is held as tightly as possible in a conventional belay, it will slip a good deal, resulting in a more dynamic belay. By their nature, belaying devices result in less dynamic belays, higher impact forces throughout the belay chain, and a consequent higher risk of the failure of some link.

Misuse of belay devices can result in even more serious problems. As a general rule, they should not be attached directly to the anchor, but should be on the front of the harness or waist loop. In this way, the belayer can absorb at least some of the impact force before it is transferred to the anchor. Even in a hanging belay, the body and the tie-in will take up some of the impact; whereas if the belay device is fixed to the anchor, the full shock force will be transmitted directly to it, greatly increasing the risk of failure.

Belay devices should not be used at all until the beginner has completely mastered the conventional types of belay. This should be so if only in the interests of simplicity, to prevent the climber from being dependent on equipment. More important, using the belay devices safely and effectively requires a good deal of manipulative skill with the rope and "feel" for the belay, which are best acquired through conventional practice.

Any belay device requires considerable practice with the rope with which it will be employed. Some ropes are stiffer than others, some twist more than others, and such handling factors can make a considerable difference to the safe operation of any belay device. These cautions are especially important if one is using laid ropes, which tend to be stiffer and to twist and kink more than kernmantel ones. A belay device should never be used with a new laid rope, because of the kinking problem. It should be carefully tested with any other laid rope to be sure that there is not excessive kinking before use in real climbing situations.

Sticht belay plates. These are the original belaying devices of the current group. There are several types: the standard plate for a single 11-mm rope; double-slotted models for either 9- or 11-mm sizes, which can be used in the conventional way, for double rope technique, or for double-strand rappels; and plates with one slot for 11-mm ropes and one for 9-mm ones.

The Sticht plate is normally used in conjunction with a locking carabiner fixed to the harness or waist loop. A piece of parachute cord goes through the small holes in the plate and is attached to the carabiner, preventing loss and keeping the plate from riding too far away from the body. A bight of the climbing rope is passed through the Sticht plate and clipped into the carabiner, which is then locked shut for safety. As long as the rope is fed directly in and out of the plate, the device can easily be kept at a distance from the 'biner and will feed smoothly. In case of a fall, the belaying hand pulls the rope over away from the plate, the device slides up against the carabiner, and the resulting cinch brakes the fall.

The Sticht plate is fairly simple to use with practice. Gloves should be worn as with any belay, although they are not quite so important as with conventional belaying. Keeping the plate from jamming up by itself requires a little practice. The belayer must be careful that there is ample room for his holding hand to move over to the braking position; in a cramped belay spot, this can be overlooked. He must also be watchful for kinks in the rope; they will not pass through the plate and will cause more trouble than with a conventional belay. When tying off a climber, a simple knot will hold in the plate.

M.S.R. belay links. The M.S.R. link is just a cheaper, simplified version of the Sticht plate, using an aluminum oval ring, like a chain link, for belaying with ropes of 11 mm or so. The link is used exactly like a Sticht plate, the only significant difference being that holes are not provided for the auxiliary cord.

Lowe rings. The Lowe ring is made from a descending ring and a short loop of swaged cable. It is used in roughly the same way as the two devices already discussed, except that it is intended for use with two carabiners instead of one. Thus, regular oval 'biners can be used, with gates reversed for safety.

Munter hitch. This is a knot which can be tied around a locking carabiner that provides friction like the other devices discussed. The hitch is shown on page 168. Belaying is done in the same way as with the Sticht plate. The hitch reverses under

A Lowe belay ring works on the same principle as the Sticht plate. Two oval carabiners with gates reversed are used instead of a locking 'biner.

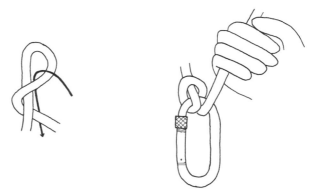

MUNTER HITCH. To tie the hitch, simply make a full twist in the rope and clip a locking carabiner through as shown. Friction from the hand causes the hitch to tighten. It will reverse when pulled, unless the narrow end of a D carabiner jams it.

tension; hence if one is taking in rope and the climber falls, the hitch will turn over so that it is correctly oriented. Practice with the rope that will be used is essential with the Munter hitch, because ease of handling is quite dependent on rope stiffness. Stiff laid ropes tend to cause too much friction for the rope to be conveniently paid out or taken in. A carabiner with a fairly smooth curve is best for this; D-shaped carabiners tend to jam the knot, so that it doesn't turn over easily enough. Tests with the Munter hitch have shown it to be safe, even though it relies on nylon-against-nylon friction, because none of the rope is stationary and so heat is not concentrated in one place. Some climbers object to the knot because of this reliance, however.

8

LEADING

Leading is the real crux of climbing; and like climbing itself, there is no cheap and easy way to learn how to lead a rope. Only by practicing in gradually more difficult situations can one become a competent leader. There is no special scheme for learning to lead, any more than there is a formula for becoming a competent mountaineer. Probably the best and fastest way is to second a number of routes with a strong climber, learning and pushing one's own limits, strengthening muscles and refining balance, and learning where one's own margin of safety is on many kinds of climbs. At the same time, while removing the nuts, slings, and other anchors that the leader has placed for his protection—"cleaning the pitch"— the second can study his placements. Finally, he can start to lead his own climbs, working at a level of difficulty well below the climbs he has seconded confidently, and thus acquiring the special refinements of judgment that are necessary to lead safely.

A number of climbers not fortunate enough to be able to learn this way begin leading climbs when they are still relatively inexperienced. It is important to recognize how dangerous this learning process can be. Although there are plenty of scary situations encountered in climbing second on the rope, one is usually fairly safe. Seconding on pitches involving long traverses can occasionally be even more difficult for the second than the leader, but such situations are uncommon, particularly with a good leader. Until one has done a reasonable number of leads, it is hard to realize how much trickier leading a pitch is than seconding it. The moves that have to be made are the same (assuming one does not fall), but the leader must rely on his own skill and what protection he can place for safety, while the second can generally depend on the rope if he should happen to misjudge. The leader needs to have a far more precise idea of just what he can do, and he needs the experience and inner reserve to do it even when he is frightened. If he manages to lead out 40 feet past his last protection and reaches a thin move before he can get a sling on a nubbin, he has somehow to make that move not by lunging but in control.

For the climber learning to lead, a few pieces of advice may be worthwhile, but the most important is to be careful about getting in over your head. Climbing holds plenty of thrills and potential dangers without inviting a serious accident. The best climbs as a start for leading are those you have seconded in good control. Moreover, try to think back and remember whether there was plenty of protection available on the climb. The actual difficulty of making the moves is not the only factor determining how hard it will be to lead a pitch, particularly for a beginner. The availability of adequate protection, especially at the difficult spots, is even more important.

If you can't do your first leads on climbs you have been up before, try to pick your route by the same criteria. Use a guidebook, talk to some local climbers, or examine the route very carefully. Choose something you are sure is well within your abilities, and find out as much as you can about the ease of protecting the climb. If you can find a climber familiar with the area, ask about the protection. Get any clues you can from a guidebook. If you are looking at a route with no description available, pick something that looks well broken up, where there seem to be flakes for slings and cracks for nuts. Don't try your first lead on a smooth slab with only the barest hint of cracks for 500 feet.

LEADER PROTECTION

The essential principle of a running belay was mentioned in the last chapter; it is not particularly complicated. The leader finds some firm way of attaching to the mountain: a tree growing in a crack; a solid block over which to loop a sling; a crack in which a nut can be jammed securely or a piton driven; a bolt placed by an earlier ascent party; or one of the means discussed in later chapters for anchoring to snow or ice. He attaches the rope to this anchor by means of a snap link either attached directly to the anchor or connected to it by a sling. So long as all the elements of this anchor are strong enough, the belay has been extended up to the level of the anchor.

While the principle of the running belay is simple enough, in practice protecting the leader is a good deal more complicated. For one thing, a rope leader who relies primarily on equipment for safety will probably come to grief sooner or later. Skill, self-control, and a knowledge of his own limits are the leader's first line of defense.

The logical extension of this is that when leading a pitch, a climber needs to retain an overall understanding of his situation—the reliability of the belay and of the protection points below, the difficulty of the climbing, how well he is moving, the objective dangers and the reliability of the holds, the distance down to the last anchor and the length to be covered before reaching the next, the dangers of a fall in a particular spot, the possibilities for the next belay stance, and so on.

Since the essential ingredient is the ability to match one's own capabilities against the difficulties presented by the climb, nobody can learn to lead from this book or any other. Most of this chapter will be devoted to the techniques of placing protection.

Each anchor which is placed by the leader for a running belay is put in separately; but it is very important to keep them all in mind. The whole system of protection developed can be either greater or less than the sum of its parts, and the result is crucial to the climber. For example, the leader may place a very strong sling over a large and solid flake. Suppose he comes to a difficult move 10 feet up from the flake, and sees a good protection point above but only a poor crack where he is. He might want to put a small nut in the crack, strong enough only for a very short fall, but adequate to protect the hard move. He is depending on the sling below for his major protection and the placement above after it is reached. The nut in between is part of the system, a good idea if it does not interfere with the other parts. However, it might interfere with those parts, and the leader has to keep this in mind. The extra rope drag caused by clipping into the nut might be excessive, or the angle of the rope once it is clipped to the nut might pull the sling off the flake below, thus sacrificing a really good protection point for a very dubious one. The leader must always think of each anchor as a link in the whole chain of protection he is building up.

Finally, before going on to discuss specific placement techniques, it seems well to remind the beginner that mountains were not designed by the writers of climbing books. Systematic as the job of protecting a pitch may sound, reality is rarely so tidy. There are climbs where very little protection exists and others where a good deal of imagination is required to make use of the features available. Climbing would be a dull sport if conveniently placed and absolutely secure eye bolts were found every 10 feet. Discovering reasonable protection is quite often the most difficult part of mountaineering or rock climbing.

Runners Although the carabiner provides the link that allows the rope to run properly, it must still be attached to the mountain. One of the simplest and most desirable ways to do this is to use a *sling* or *runner*, which is made of rope or nylon webbing. Runners can be looped around trees and flakes, hooked over knobs and nubbins, threaded through holes or behind chockstones in cracks. Properly placed, they are very strong. They require only moderate effort to place and remove, are versatile and fairly cheap, and they do not mar the rock. Because of all these advantages, runners are generally the most desirable way to protect a climb.

Runners can and should be carried in a variety of lengths.

These are naturally rather arbitrary. A useful standard length can be made from 5 or 6 feet of sling material. Longer slings, which are carried double, require about 9 or 10 feet, and triple-length ones approximately 12 or 13 feet. Most slings are made up permanently and are carried around the neck, sometimes in front, sometimes over the shoulder. Slings can either be knotted or, in the case of webbing, they may be sewn. There are advantages to both rope and webbing runners, and arguments for both sewn and knotted webbing.

Rope slings are more resistant to cuts than those made of webbing, and they are much less subject to weakening by abrasion. Their stiffness sometimes makes placement simpler, when a projection is difficult to reach. On the other hand, webbing holds knots better, can often be worked into placements where rope slings would not fit, may have less tendency to jiggle off a placement because it is more flexible, and can be sewn for additional strength.

When permanent slings are tied, the knots used should be very secure. Knots can be jammed by suspending the sling and jumping in it after they have been tightened as much as possible by hand. The ring bend is a favorite knot for slings, and it is quite safe if it is pulled really tight, with a couple of inches left in each end so that the ends cannot be pulled through under strain. If it is not pulled really tight, overhands should be used to secure the knot, and it should be checked frequently. A double sheetbend is a very strong knot for slings, but it can work loose rather easily. In permanent slings, these knots can be easily secured after pulling them tight by sewing down the ends to the rest of the sling. Not much sewing is needed, since the only function of the stitches is to prevent the knot from working loose. This method is more secure, less bulky, and uses much less sling material than tying off the knots with overhands. A very secure knot for tying rope slings is the double fisherman's or grapevine. This has the advantage that when pulled tight by hand it will not work loose and does not require safety overhands, but it does use a lot of rope.

Sewn webbing slings are stronger than knotted ones, pro-

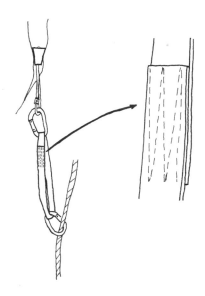

SEWING JOINTS IN WEBBING. At the left is a loop of webbing used for protection which is sewn rather than tied. This gives a stronger joint (the full strength of the webbing) and has some other advantages. The detail on the right shows the general pattern for sewing such a joint, developed by Cal Magnussen and presented in *Off Belay Magazine*, October 1972. The zigzag running lengthwise is the best pattern, but many more passes are needed than shown. With no. 24 polyester thread, overlap the ends of the webbing 4 inches for home sewing, use 10 stitches to the inch, and make 24 passes for 1-inch webbing and 12 passes for 9/16-inch or 3/4-inch.

viding the job is properly done. Knotted slings should not be assumed to have more strength than the single-strand strength of the material, since even though they are used double, the knot greatly reduces the strength. Sewn webbing slings are somewhat stronger and also more compact, which can be useful in certain placements. The sewing patterns shown were developed in tests by Cal Magnusson, Quality Control Engineer for Recreational Equipment in Seattle, and published in *Off Belay* (October 1972). Slings which are sewn should be inspected frequently for abrasion. Since the strength of the sling is entirely dependent on the exposed stitching, any wear should be treated as a major cut. This is especially important with commercially sewn slings, which are usually sewn in such a way that the stitching protrudes from the surface and is thus particularly subject to wear.

All webbing slings should be retired as soon as they begin to look worn. Unlike rope, webbing has a large percentage of fibers exposed at any point and is weakened significantly by wear which does not look too severe. Ropes are usually stronger than they look, while webbing is usually weaker.

A selection of various types, sizes, and lengths of slings is usually most versatile. One or two that are tied loosely enough to be undone can be helpful in some situations, such as threading through a small hole.

PLACING RUNNERS

All protection systems have to be looked at as a whole, so the art of placing individual runners is only part of the technique of protecting a climb with them. A particular sling not only provides protection for a portion of the climb; it adds friction, directs the rope, and in directing the rope may hold another runner in place or pull it off. Thus, each device must be considered in all the ways it influences safety and the climb generally.

The best runners provide anchors that are *non-directional.* They will stay put and resist a pull no matter which direction it comes from. Slings looped around large trees or big boulders and those passed through holes in the rock are examples. Such runners are ideal because they will stay put regardless of the pull of the rope and because they will help to hold a fall even if unforeseen circumstances cause the force to come from an unexpected direction.

Every possible anchor must be looked at with a jaundiced eye. Is it really solid, or does it only appear to be? Is that great flake connected to bedrock, or is it undercut by cracks so that it is just perched on the cliff? A protection point that will be pulled off onto your head after you have fallen is not what you are looking for. Besides the physical danger that might be presented if a fall pulls such an anchor off, poor anchors can present the psychological danger of inducing wholly unjustified confidence. A poor anchor may be better than none if you fall, but not if reliance on it was what let you persuade yourself to risk the fall.

Most runners are good only in some directions. A sling draped over a flake or cinched onto a small rock projection is far more common than the more desirable non-directional anchors. The main art of placing such runners is not in setting them so that they are adequate when you put them on, but rather in getting them to stay there after you are 10 feet farther up. It can be very disconcerting indeed to place a sling on a horn, climb up to the difficult wall above, and when halfway across look down and see the runner and its carabiner sliding down the rope toward your belayer.

The most important trick in making good placements is to visualize all the forces that will be placed on the runner as you continue. How secure is it? Will it stay on the horn if it is lifted a foot? Two feet? Where does the route go from that runner? If you traverse across the rope, you will be pulling against the sling in a different way than if you went straight up or traversed in the other direction. Most slings will be stable when pulled in some ways, but will come off quite easily when tugged from another direction. To keep the sling in place, you must anticipate how the rope will pull as you go up to the next protection point, how its direction will change when another anchor is placed, and where the force of a fall would come at any time along the way. Finally, the problem of rope drag has to be considered. The more in line the anchors are, the less drag will be produced; if the rope jags back and forth across the pitch, the drag may become impossible long before the next stance is reached.

There are several ways to prevent a sling from being dislodged. The easiest and often most effective is simply to use a long sling or a couple of slings fastened together. Since the runner will droop a long way below the point over which it is looped, it will be much less likely to come off. Beginners are often reluctant to use a long enough sling, because it will mean a longer fall, but of course a much longer tumble would result if the sling came off altogether. Clipping into the sling with two or more carabiners in a chain is often useful, because movements of the rope will not be transferred to the sling so easily. A few steel carabiners can be helpful for clipping into slings that are looped over small flakes. The extra weight of the steel 'biner makes the rope less likely to lift the lower part of the sling.

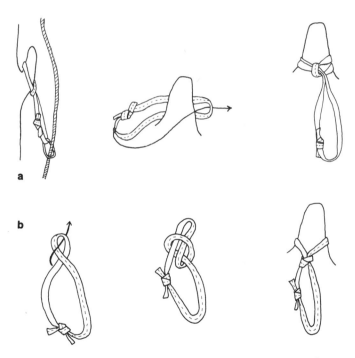

SLINGS ON NUBBINS. Two ways are shown of cinching a sling on a horn or other object. (They can be used to tie off pitons.) The first *(a)* is called a girth hitch. The second method of cinching shown *(b)* results in an overhand knot tied in one side of the sling to form a slip knot around the other side.

A climber placing a sling for protection on harder moves above. If a fall should occur, the carabiner on the sling will act as a pulley, and the force on the belayer will come from above.

One final trick for getting a runner to stay on a projection is to cinch it. A girth hitch can be used, but I have often found that an overhand works better; it can be tied in a prepared sling very quickly.

Finally, the climber should not neglect the possibility of placing a sling solely for the purpose of improving others. A runner can be hooked on a downward-pointing flake to anchor one which is looped over an upward-facing projection. A sling can be used to make the rope follow a particular path so that drag will be reduced or so that other slings will not be dislodged by the climber's movements or by a fall.

NUTS

Nuts are commonly used along with slings to protect rock-climbing leads. Generally speaking, a reasonable selection of slings and nuts will serve to safeguard the climb adequately, and they have the added attraction that they are "clean" protection devices—they do not damage the rock when placed or removed. This advantage is twofold, because clean protection is easier to place and remove, allowing the climbers to move faster and with a more natural feeling.

The basic nut placement is in some crack or other opening which is wide enough to allow the nut to be inserted at one spot, but narrows in the direction of pull, constricting sufficiently to prevent the nut from pulling through. The basics are simple enough, but it often requires a good deal of wit and imagination to devise placements that will work to protect the climber in case of a fall.

A large array of nuts is already available and will certainly be a good deal larger by the time this book is published. These days most types are tapered in two directions so that each nut will fit at least two sizes of cracks. These will be bored so that a sling can be fitted without getting in the way of either of the two basic placements. Exceptions are some of the older nuts which are drilled straight through, allowing the nut to be used in only one direction. The lighter nuts of this variety are actually rather useful, since they can be carried on slings without reducing their strength or adding significant weight, thus providing a little extra versatility to the runners carried.

The most common nut shapes are wedges and hexagonal forms, and a range of sizes using these two shapes provides a good basic selection. Cylindrical nuts with knurled surfaces to help them stay in place are not quite so versatile, but they work particularly well in some situations, such as in old piton scars. All these forms are gradually being refined so that versions that weigh less will have adequate strength. Chouinard has developed a variation of the hexagonal nut called a "hexentric," which has shorter sides at the top, rendering the nut slightly more stable in normal positions and also making more effective camming placements possible. Newer hexentrics are also asymmetrical, allowing finer matching of crack sizes. Even better camming is achieved by Bill Forrest's revival of the

T-shaped chock. Various solutions are being tried for the protection of very wide cracks.

Nuts are commonly strung with either webbing or rope slings, as mentioned in the last chapter. Most should be carried on slings long enough to go over the head (with the helmet on). A reasonable number of slings and nuts can be carried around the neck. On more difficult climbs, when large numbers are being carried, some slings can be doubled and clipped to the hardware sling or the waist loop.

Smaller nuts do not have enough strength to protect a leader fall if they are threaded with rope or webbing, so they may be cabled. Cabled nuts can sometimes be placed in spots that are difficult to reach, but they are dislodged even more easily than chocks on short slings. To make insertion at a distance easy, those with double cables should have a few drops of epoxy put in the holes at the top, to keep the cables from slipping. Forrest's single-cable nuts are slightly less prone to being jiggled loose than the stiffer double-cable varieties, and they also fit very well into shallow pockets and cracks. When a sling is attached to a cabled nut the connection should normally be made with a carabiner, since the sharp bend over a cable will reduce the sling strength.

As with runners, the trickiest aspect of nut placement is often keeping the protection in after you have passed. Like slings, nuts are usually good only in some directions, often only in one. A tug on the rope can dislodge a very strong chock, and carelessness in the placing of one anchor can ensure that a fall will pull out every other point of protection below. All protection points must still be viewed as a whole, and the effect of each anchor on all the others has to be considered.

The tactics of keeping nuts where you want them are very similar to those used with runners. A long sling can be added to the nut; several carabiners can be used; heavy steel 'biners may add stability; another sling or nut can be used to direct the forces in a direction that will make a placement stronger rather than weaker.

The technique of aiming forces in different directions can

LEFT

A copperhead placed for protection. A sling needs to be attached to prevent jerks of the rope from dislodging the nut. The girth hitch used here over the nut cable greatly weakens the sling.

RIGHT

Better. Attaching the sling to the cable with a carabiner is much stronger. Passing the doubled sling over the cable would also be stronger than the girth hitch, but too short a sling would make it likely that the nut could be shaken loose.

also be used in more subtle ways. Two or more placements can be made in opposition, so that a sling pulled in one direction reorients the force to pull the two opposing placements against one another. This enables the leader to use formations like horizontal cracks to protect against falls.

It is usually helpful to set the nut by jerking the sling downward (or in the direction of pull). In marginal placements it may also help to tap it with a hammer to seat it more thoroughly. If one resorts to bashing, the nut eventually becomes a badly shaped piton or bashie, and those concerned with the ethics of clean climbing often argue that only hammerless ascents are truly clean. The degree to which people concern themselves with such arguments, one way or another, is a personal matter. The important thing is that if you do use a hammer to set nuts, you should use light taps that do not tear up the rock.

Other placement ideas are included in the chapter on direct aid climbing. Wedges (like pitons) can be very useful in camming placements with steel cables for protection on occasion, but this is discussed in the direct aid chapter because it is inherently more marginal and requires considerable experience to be done safely.

A good nut placement, a Forrest Titon slotted in a horizontal crack. Very hard to dislodge accidentally.

A hexagonal nut slotted shallowly in a vertical crack—a strong placement which would be dislodged very easily if a long sling were not attached before the carabiner was used to clip in the rope. The possible effects of additional placements have to be watched.

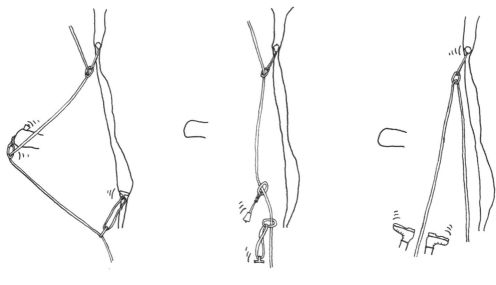

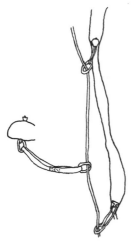

PROTECTION COMBINATIONS. In the upper left, the leader has placed three nuts in such a way as to create rope drag and so that they tend to pull one another out; all are good for a downward pull, but they are pulling each other to the side. If the lower two jiggle each other out (center) and the leader falls, he then (right) has to hope that the top nut holds, since it is now the only protection he has.

The lower drawing shows the correct way to use the same placements. A sling is used on the middle nut to prevent sideways forces from developing.

Two points about nut placements are difficult to overemphasize. First, practice in using chocks is essential to develop a feeling for how well a nut will stay put and the directions that it will be pulled by the forces involved in hauling the rope up or in falling. A standard-length sling is required for nearly all nut jams to prevent the rope from jiggling the nut out, and many placements require far more elaborate precautions. The second point is that the nut jam must always be carefully examined to ascertain what is holding it. If a good chunk of solid rock or aluminum would have to be sheared away to pull the nut out, then it is trustworthy for protection against a fall; but if only a tiny bulge of rock or two little ridges of the nut are holding it, the placement is worthless. With plastic nuts, considerably wider areas are required to resist shearing force and provide a safe placement.

ROPE DRAG

The problem of friction building up against the movement of the rope has already been discussed in several connections, but it is worth stressing here. Each bend in the rope makes pulling it up harder, and when the climber moves over a bulge or around a corner, the drag may be increased a great deal.

Looking up at a roof climbed with aid. Rope drag was reduced by not clipping to the last two placements in the right crack or the first placement in the left crack and by using a sling and extra carabiners to lessen the angles through which the rope was bent. Each time a rope bends through a sharp angle, drag is increased. The cumulative effect is usually noticed when the leader is much higher. In this case, the drag would have become unmanageable as the leader climbed over the edge of the roof and tried to start free climbing.

It is very important to anticipate such situations, because often just at such points the climbing is thinnest, and the backward pull of the rope may pull the leader off. He is then forced at least to haul out enough slack to allow him to get across the move, making for a longer fall in case of a slip.

The best antidote to rope drag is good protection placement. Long slings attached to each protection point are a great help, particularly under a bulge or overhang, before going around a corner, or when the leader is working back and forth between two crack systems. Occasionally, it is necessary to take out some lower anchors to reduce rope drag. A higher anchor may be left in while the leader climbs down to remove some of the earlier placements. If this difficulty is anticipated, it may even be possible to place a nut or sling so that it can be flipped out with the rope once a new anchor is reached.

PROTECTION FOR THE SECOND

On most pitches, the leader simply places protection for his own needs, but he must always keep the second in mind as well. Whenever a pitch involves downclimbing or traversing for any significant distance, the second may be in a far more exposed position than the leader, and thus more in need of protection. On a traverse, for example, a fall can cause a long swing. The leader would normally try to place a good anchor before a hard move to protect himself, but if he is thoughtless he may then go prancing 40 feet along the easy ground that follows without putting in any protection at all. When the second reaches the hard part, he will have just removed the protection placed by the leader and will face a pretty nasty fall if he should slip on the thin move. Clearly, a good leader has to consider his second's safety as well as his own.

PITONS AND BOLTS

Pitons are rapidly, and properly, fading away as standard protection for free climbs, and they are becoming less heavily used in aid climbing as well. The basics of piton placement were discussed in the last chapter in connection with belay anchors, and there is more information in the chapter on direct aid. As for leader protection, there is not a great deal more to be said. Clearly, like slings and nuts, any pitons that are used have to be considered as a part of the whole system of protection. The placement has to be examined just as carefully for a pin as for a nut. The best pitons will be those placed in a position where they are inherently strong, where the force of a fall would tend to push the piton farther in or exert leverage on the crack, rather than pulling directly outward on the piton. When the crack is deep enough, a longer piton will be stronger than a shorter one.

The best and easiest piton placements tend to be in horizontal cracks, while the natural nut placements are more often in vertical cracks. Either can be used in other ways, but the climber usually has to look harder.

The carabiner is normally clipped directly into the eye of the piton, and it is important to make sure that it will not exert leverage outward on the pin in case of a fall; that the gate will not be opened in a fall by being pushed against the rock; and that the rope will feed through the right way for minimum friction when the climber passes the pin. This is a little trickier with pitons than with most nuts, which usually have a flexible sling attached, leaving the carabiner free to rotate. The usual rule is that the gate of the carabiner should open *down and out.* As with other kinds of protection, slings or chains of several carabiners should be used when needed to reduce rope drag. A piton should be tied off with webbing to reduce leverage if the eye is not driven flush with the rock.

Bolts are also discussed elsewhere. It is particularly important when using them for protection to be sure that the hangers do not ride upside down so that a fall could make the hanger into a lever and pull the bolt. Old bolts and old pitons should be viewed with a skeptical eye by later climbers. It is not generally possible to tell just how good they are. They may have been poor to begin with. Weathering may have rotted

Correct orientation of a carabiner clipped into a piton. The gate opens downward.

LEFT
Right way to clip the rope through the carabiner.

RIGHT
Wrong way to clip the rope in. It is essential to visualize exactly how the rope will run after you have passed an anchor and, more subtly, how it will run in case of a fall, both before and after still another anchor is placed.

Reducing rope drag over an edge by attaching a sling to the same piton.

out the rock around, loosening them, or pitons may have become brittle from sitting in a crack under compression for a long time. When nut or sling placements exist, it is usually better to use them. A hammer can be carried to test old fixed pins. They can then be re-driven. Never try to improve a bolt by hammering it; an old bolt will only be loosened. Examination will tell you something, if not much more than the general age of the anchor. No one solution to this problem is possible, but it is important for the climber to remember that old hardware cannot be looked on as permanent—eventually it comes out. Some climbing routes with bolt anchors require the climber to carry hangers and machine nuts or cap screws to fit them. Talk to local climbers to find out what sizes and types are involved.

FALLING

The leader has to develop at least an intuitive idea of the consequences of a fall—of the forces and the dangers involved. These are what he is placing protection against, and each anchor and each climb represents some evaluation of these factors. The forces developed in a fall can be very strong; fortunately modern climbing equipment is also quite strong. This section will describe some of the magnitudes involved, as well as some of the other factors which make falls dangerous.

When a leader falls, he may drop completely free through the air until the rope checks the downward plunge, or he may scrape and bounce against the rock on the way down. He may end up hanging at the end of the rope or hitting a ledge. Obviously a whole complex of factors is involved in determining the sequence of events. In leading a pitch, the climber must continuously evaluate what that sequence would be as accurately as he can.

Modern ropes are designed not only to be very strong, but also to absorb the shock energy produced by a fall. The elongation curve under stress is really more important for a climbing rope than the static breaking strength. A steel cable strong enough to stop a long fall would probably pull the top anchor of the leader's protection and kill the falling climber as well, because all the force of the fall would be transmitted very rapidly through the cable, while a good rope absorbs much of the energy and transmits it over a far longer period. Very strong cables will, in fact, break under the impact of a fall, since they cannot stretch much to absorb shock.

The U.I.A.A. test for ropes uses a 180-pound weight dropping 16 feet on 9 feet of rope. (The rope passes from an anchor, up 1 foot, through a fixed carabiner, and then up 8 feet to the weight, which drops free.) The main test requires that the rope be able to sustain two such falls without exerting a force on the weight (the leader) of more than 2640 pounds. All 11-mm European ropes currently being sold in American climbing stores and American ropes made for climbing can pass this test.

(There are other tests having to do with handling and stretch under small loads.)

This fall is a severe one, because not much extra rope is in the system to help absorb the impact of the fall; but it is certainly not an unrealistic test. To sustain a 16-foot fall on vertical or overhanging rock, the leader would only have to climb about 6 feet above his belay (with an additional 2 feet between his feet and his tie-in). Longer distances than this are not uncommon between protection points, although the force on the climber's body in a longer fall will be about the same, because there is more rope to absorb the extra energy. Thus, forces in the neighborhood of 2500 pounds have to be considered realistic possibilities in leader falls, and each link in the safety chain should be considered in this light.

The climber's body is vulnerable to many kinds of injuries during a fall, but at this point we are concerned simply with the force exerted by the rope in stopping the fall. A severe leader fall can kill or injure a climber tied in with a simple waist loop of rope, because great force is concentrated in a small area of a vulnerable part of the body. The bowline-on-a-coil and other tie-ins like it distribute forces a little better, but most climbers prefer a system which distributes force more evenly and uses less rope. One method is the *swami belt*, consisting of 20–30 feet of 1-inch webbing wrapped around the waist. The force of a fall is thus transferred to the waist over a wide area. But there are still two defects. The waist is not a very suitable part of the body to take the whole force of a fall; and if the leader is left hanging free, his diaphragm will be paralyzed and breathing will stop after a short time hanging on the rope. Unless he can do something quickly to get the weight off his waist, he will die.

The safest alternative tie-in method is a full *harness*, including a pelvic harness with waist and leg loops, and a chest harness. When properly designed, such harnesses should not restrict climbing. Most American climbers have so far found the full harness too cumbersome, and have settled for the pelvic part alone. A good pelvic harness also makes an adequate belay and rappel seat. It reduces the dangers of a leader fall by transferring some of the force to the thighs and by eliminating the possibility of an injured leader suffocating. If part of the full harness is chosen, the chest harness should never be used alone. Besides the danger of slipping out, a little experimentation will convince the climber that hanging free on a chest harness rapidly paralyzes the arms, leaving the climber helpless.

Rope and webbing strength is clearly an important factor, particularly in the case of the climbing rope. The strength of a rope is reduced when it is bent sharply, because the fibers on the outside of the bend are stretched and those on the inside may be cut. This is why a knot in a rope weakens it. Although knots vary, a good rule of thumb is that the strength of the rope is halved by a knot or sharp bend. In addition, it must be remembered that as a rope becomes worn in normal use it loses some strength. Thus, while 9-mm and ⅜-inch ropes might seem to have adequate strength for use as climbing ropes on first inspection, when one allows for the reduction in that strength which can be expected from knots or other bends and from wear, a rope with a new breaking strength of under 4000 pounds does not really have an adequate reserve of safety for leads on high-angle rock. By the same token, any climbing rope should be retired after it shows heavy wear.

Webbing and sling strength is also reduced by knots and by the sharp bends that often occur when they are threaded through nuts. In general, the strength of a sling loop should not be estimated at much over the single-strand strength of the material if the loop is joined with a knot or bent sharply. The 1-inch webbing and ⅜-inch or 9-mm rope runners are thus to be preferred as having plenty of reserve strength. Slings smaller than 9⁄16-inch webbing, 5⁄16-inch laid rope, 7-mm Perlon rope, 5⁄32-inch single cable, or ⅛-inch cable loop should be used only for limited leader protection; that is, one should not assume they would catch a hard fall. Bear in mind that webbing wears more quickly and less obviously than rope, so retire it early.

The leader must remember how easily nylon is cut under

tension. Naturally, not all kinds of cut in a fall can be foreseen, but one should at least be aware of the possibilities. Thus, if a fall from a particular spot might cause the rope to saw across a sharp edge, protection might be put in to avoid the possibility —or a different route might be chosen. It is difficult to describe how frighteningly quickly a nylon rope holding a climber's weight can be cut.

Carabiner strength has been discussed briefly before, but should be mentioned again in light of the forces being discussed here. Many older oval carabiners of good quality tested only to about 2000 pounds. Newer ovals will stand loads ranging from 2500 to 3000 pounds, depending on the manufacturer. A number of climbers prefer the handling of ovals and continue to use them despite the fact that their strength is just about in the range of the stresses that can sometimes be expected in falls, leaving a rather slim margin of safety. Those making this argument can point to the fact that when properly placed and loaded, ovals have a fairly good safety record after a lot of experience with real falls.

Those who prefer the D or modified D-shaped 'biners can point to much higher breaking strength and assert that in climbing equipment the maximum strength possible is barely adequate. Actually, the problem does not need to be taken too seriously. Most climbers who like ovals prefer them mainly for direct aid climbing, because of handling characteristics when one is standing in steps clipped to a carabiner. Since far more 'biners are needed for aid climbing, the extra carabiners used for aid can well be ovals without sacrificing the strength of D's for leader protection on free climbs. The strength of reasonably well-made aluminum alloy D's ranges from a little over 4000 to over 7000 pounds.

Climbers should be wary of second-hand carabiners of older vintage. Aside from checking for damage, one must avoid certain dangerously weak models that have appeared in the past. There have been many poor designs; some of the most notorious are those European models of various shapes which have no catch, but merely a slanting junction at the gate. Most of these are strong enough when loaded lengthwise, but if accidentally loaded across the carabiner will fail at 200 pounds or less. Some early REI and SMC locking 'biners were also incredibly weak. Non-locking models and all those made in the last few years have been excellent, so this criticism should not apply to the new merchandise with these labels.

The *strength of nuts*, providing they are properly placed, is generally limited by the strength of the sling or the rock rather than the nut itself. Plastic chocks should be used with a little more caution but since they are now only made in large sizes, there is no problem except in marginal placements, when metal chocks should be used in preference. Some small chocks are made of stainless steel to provide greater strength, but the advantage will only show if one finds an unusually advantageous slot. Very small chocks are usually dubious as leader protection not only because of the small amount of metal-resisting movement but also because of the small amount of rock that would have to be broken off for the nut to pull free.

The well-designed American chromolly *pitons*—larger than knifeblades—if they are well placed are very strong. Some European chromolly pitons have not been well made, while others are quite good. Soft iron pins should be viewed a little more circumspectly, particularly in vertical placements. In general, soft iron pins should only be trusted for protecting a possible long leader fall when a fairly long piton has been well placed in a horizontal crack, or where protrusions in a vertical crack would absolutely prevent rotation. Remember that chromolly pins are much stronger than soft iron ones. Three-quarters of the soft iron pins placed in horizontal cracks and pulled by Dr. L. J. Griffin came out under less than 2000-pounds force, while nineteen out of twenty chromolly pins held over 2000 pounds. (Reported by John Armitage in *Summit*, June, 1966.) The climber should be particularly wary of soft iron pegs with eyes that stick well out from the blade, allowing much extra leverage to develop.

Pitons with welded rings instead of eyes are not uniformly

reliable because the weld is doubtful. Many such pitons are found fixed in established climbs; they should not be trusted too far.

OTHER SAFETY MEASURES

Falling is never very desirable, even if one is wearing a good harness and all protection is strong and well placed. Aside from the possibility of having the rope cut by the rock, there is always the chance that you will be cut yourself. The likelihood of being badly hurt this way depends on the nature of the climb and the rock, on the length of the fall, and on possible protective measures. Smooth rock, like that found in Yosemite, is a lot less dangerous to fall on than bumpy, abrasive stuff like that in Pinnacles National Monument. A fall on vertical rock is safer than one on a slightly lower-angle face, unless the climber hits a ledge before the fall is stopped. Such comments are only of use to evaluate one's situation accurately in placing protection; once one is airborne, it no longer matters.

A few protective measures are possible. The most important is to wear a helmet. Besides providing some protection from rockfall, *a helmet will greatly reduce the chances of death or serious injury if the climber hits his head in a fall.* The leader will also be in a somewhat better position in many situations if his belayer has a helmet on as well. If a belayer is hit on the head by a rock or if he hits his head while holding a fall, he is quite likely to lose the belay.

If the falling climber pushes himself away from the rock as he comes off, and tries to ward off the rock with his feet, he is less likely to be hurt. Beyond this, he is in the hands of the belayer.

9

RAPPELLING AND OTHER
SPECIAL TECHNIQUES

There are a number of special skills more or less incidental to climbing which every competent mountaineer has to be able to handle well. These include descent using a rope (rappelling or abseiling), climbing a rope using rope slings or mechanical ascenders (prusikking), various forms of self-rescue, tying off a fallen climber, and basic methods of rescuing a fallen companion.

Like all mountaineering skills, these must all be practiced to be of any use. No two climbing situations are the same, and improvisation is often necessary, but the best basis for improvisation is a solid fund of experience. By actually tying off a climber hanging on the rope, the beginner will realize the importance of having the slings he needs readily accessible. Trying a real crevasse rescue will swiftly drive home the difficulties of getting over the lip.

RAPPELLING

One of the most commonly used techniques in mountaineering is the rope descent. It is better known than most climbing maneuvers because it is so photogenic, and it has also become more and more common as routes of increasing technical difficulty are undertaken.

Rappelling is a common means of descent to reverse difficult pitches. The basic principle is simply to use some dependable and easily controlled way of producing friction against the rope and to slide down it. The climbing rope may be doubled through an anchor at the top of the rappel and pulled down

A rappel. The climber's legs are spread to make his position more stable, as he moves past a hole in the rock, just before the rappel becomes overhanging.

afterward; or a longer rappel can be made by using a special rappel line or another rope tied together with the climbing rope.

There are dozens of different methods of producing the friction needed for a rappel. The reader can easily devise his own unlikely combinations, but a few tested methods that have proved generally applicable are presented here.

THE DÜLFERSITZ

This old standard is not much used any more, but it should still be known by all climbers. It is easy to get into, provides enough friction for any situation, and requires no equipment at all beyond the rappel rope. It is particularly useful in general mountaineering.

The main reason for the decline of the Dülfersitz is that the friction is all against the body. This can cause nasty burns if light clothing is being worn, so the method is naturally not very popular for descending from rock climbs made in shorts and T-shirts. On the other hand, in heavy clothes the rappel is easy enough. Safety precautions for all rappels are discussed below, but each type has certain peculiarities. With the Dülfersitz, the rope going over the shoulder can accidentally run against the neck unless a hooded shirt or parka is worn. Putting the shirt collar up and buttoning the shirt all the way to the top generally protects you against this problem.

As with all rappels that are not overhanging, leaning back is important to give the feet traction. With the Dülfersitz, however, it is important not to let the legs get above the body, and particularly not to step high with the leg under which the rope passes, lest it ride under the knee. This possibility can be simply avoided by beginners if they turn sideways so that the leg under which the rope passes is lowermost.

A climber getting into position for a Dülfersitz or body rappel. He stands below the rappel point, where the rope goes through a descending ring on a sling that is looped over a horn. He has passed the doubled rope between his legs and behind one thigh.

The braking hand with the Dülfersitz is the one holding the free end of the rope—the end heading downward. Beginners should practice letting go with the other hand to over-

LEFT

The rope is now passed across the climber's chest, over the opposite shoulder from the leg around which the rope runs, and behind the back. It is important that all parts of the body over which the rope will run be protected by heavy clothing, especially the neck and the braking hand.

RIGHT

Starting the rappel. After the rope passes over the back, it is grasped by the hand on the same side as the leg that the rope runs around. The climber descends with the side of the braking hand slightly downhill, body perpendicular to the rock. The uphill hand holds the rope lightly, and the forefinger of the braking hand is kept between the ropes to avoid twists from interfering with retrieval later on. As the slope becomes steeper, the body becomes more horizontal. Any rappel, including an overhanging one, can be made safely with the Dülfersitz, providing that all parts of the body coming in contact with the rope are adequately padded. To stop, the climber merely moves his braking hand around his body, as in a belay. To anchor himself in mid-air, he can make several turns of the rope around the leg opposite the braking hand. Note that belays on rappels are essential for beginners and prudent for all climbers.

come the natural tendency to clutch with it. This upper hand should normally hold the rope only loosely to prevent upsetting in an accident or to hold the prusik safety open if one is used. (Prusik safeties are discussed below.)

Nylon clothing is quite likely to be damaged somewhat in a body rappel like the Dülfersitz, because of melt-abrasion by the rope.

A CARABINER BRAKE RAPPEL

There are numerous rappels which eliminate all or some of the body wraps that produce the friction in the Dülfersitz, each having its adherents. They all require a sling of some kind from which the body is suspended. The rope goes through a braking system which reduces the force that has to be exerted by the hand to hold the body. Such brakes produce one or several sharp bends in the rope, and the energy of braking goes into heat absorbed by the rope and the braking system. Climbers wearing harnesses can easily attach the braking system to the harness—a safe and effective method with many advantages. If no harness is worn, a diaper sling can be used for rappelling. A diaper that is too loose may cause problems if the climber makes a mistake—one side can ride out to the knee, for example—while one that is too tight gets the rope uncomfortably close to clothing that may then be pulled into the braking system. Climbers using diaper slings should carry one sling that is just the right length for the purpose, although it can also be used for other purposes during the climb.

The simplest braking system is to twist the rope several times through a carabiner. There are many other methods and special devices. The one illustrated and recommended here uses five or six standard carabiners. It is easily controlled, uses no body friction except for that provided by the hand, and is simple to check visually. The two doubled sets of carabiners act as safeguards, so that an accidentally opened gate cannot cause a disaster. Each set is clipped on together, and one of the carabiners is then turned 180 degrees, so that the gates are on

Putting on a diaper sling for a carabiner-brake rappel. A climber normally wears a harness and will simply use it for a seat, but the diaper provides a quick alternative when a harness is not being worn. A long sling is passed doubled around the waist, and a bight from one side is pulled between the legs. This leaves three loops at the front of the climber's waist for attaching the brake system. A comfortable seat is formed, with one loop going around the back of the waist and one under each thigh. Any belay ropes or safeties, not shown here, should be attached independently to the body.

Setting up a carabiner brake. In the system shown here, two oval carabiners are first clipped through the diaper sling (or, better, the climbing harness). One of these is turned over so that the gates are on opposite sides. Another pair of oval carabiners is clipped through the first two, and again one is turned over so that both gates cannot be pushed open from the same side. One or two more carabiners are needed to form the brake. Here the one to be used is being held in the climber's left hand.

LEFT
Getting into the rappel. A bight of the doubled rappel rope is pulled through the outer pair of carabiners so that the rope coming from the anchor comes into the far end of the carabiner chain.

RIGHT
While the bight is held with one hand, the brake carabiner is clipped around the pair of 'biners through which the rope has been pulled.

The braking carabiner is shown here correctly clipped in; the gate is on the opposite side from the bight of rope, of course, so that pressure from the rope cannot open the gate. For increased braking, a second carabiner can be clipped in beside the first.

Starting the rappel. The right hand is the braking hand, and a finger is kept between the ropes to prevent twists. The left hand is used only for balance. It is not even gripping the rope here.

Here the climber has easily stopped in mid-rappel. To hang in position and free the hands, he has only to wrap the rope around one leg a couple of turns.

opposite sides. One 'biner is usually sufficient for the brake, but two will provide extra friction if it is wanted. For special purposes, such as rescue, this same braking system can be doubled, the rope passing through two whole brakes, and can be used by a man standing at the top to lower a load, a climber, a litter, or whatever. A double brake or the use of three carabiners going across in a single brake may be desirable when rappelling on a single strand of rope or a doubled small-diameter rope.

There are several major advantages and disadvantages to carabiner brake rappels generally. The obvious advantage of not depending on body friction has already been mentioned, and if a climbing harness is used, it is impossible to fall out of this type of rappel. Brake rappels are particularly comfortable on long "free" rappels (those going down an overhanging section, where the body hangs away from the rock). It is easy to tie off this type of rappel along the way down, if that is necessary. Momentary loss of control does not lead to disaster quite so readily as with a body rappel, since the rope will still be going through the braking system. Properly tied safety knots at the ends of the rappel rope can be used to make it impossible to run off the end of the rope (without tying the two ends together as is necessary to safeguard a body rappel). These safety methods are discussed below. On the other hand, trivial and easily made mistakes can lead to disaster with any rappel using a brake. The hardware has to be got out and prepared for the rappel, a waste of time for occasional rope-downs on the descent of a big peak. Great care has to be used to avoid getting clothing or very long hair caught in the rappel system, and rope twists and jams occur more often and cause more trouble with brake systems than with body rappels.

SETTING UP THE RAPPEL

The first step in rappelling is naturally to set up the rope. At this point it is worth considering whether downclimbing the pitch might not be simpler. On easy and moderate terrain, climbing down may well be faster than setting up a rappel anchor, tossing the rope down, rappelling off one at a time, and either recoiling the rope or roping up for climbing again. Added to these factors is the fact that downclimbing is usually more rewarding and is an art well worth cultivating.

If a rappel is chosen, one must first find an anchor. A large block of rock, high enough and properly angled so that the rope could not possibly slip over it, with a smooth surface for the rope to run over when it is pulled down, is ideal. Such perfect anchors, located where they are wanted for a rappel, are also rather rare. Of the various desirable features, solidity is the most important. A rappel anchor must be every bit as solid as a belay anchor. A rappel will not put nearly the strain on the anchor that a leader fall would, but the weight of each member of the party *will* come on the anchor. Unlike a belay anchor, it is not a back-up; it is the only thing standing between you and oblivion.

The rappel line is doubled in some way so that it can be retrieved when the whole party is down. This means that it has to run freely around the anchor when pulled from below, even after the weight of each of the members of the party has dangled on it. The pull-down is usually made more difficult by the rope running over a lip after leaving the rappel anchor, so the friction of the lip (and any other bends farther down the rappel) has to be overcome in addition to the resistance of the anchor itself. The practical meaning of this is that the location of the anchor often has to be chosen to facilitate retrieving the rope, and that every possible effort must be made to reduce friction at the anchor. In order to reduce friction when a natural anchor is used, a sling is usually wrapped around it, and the sling is used for the rappel anchor. Rock flakes in particular usually have rough surfaces, and the rope would often be caught in tight cracks or on sharp edges. The use of a sling for the rappel solves these problems. Friction is further reduced if a rappel ring is used. Both the sling and the rope are threaded through the ring, reducing possible friction or binding of the rope by the sling, and also preventing the rope from causing melt-abrade damage to the sling if it is to be used by a second party.

Always use a sling around a living tree, regardless of the ease of pulling the rope. The bark of the tree will be cut and injured when the rope is pulled down if no sling is used.

Several basic principles should be observed in using rappel slings. The first is to avoid old slings that may be in place. Leave them as a back-up if you like, but unless you know who put them there and when, and are sure that a rope has not been pulled through (causing weakening from melt-abrasion), use your own sling. Ultra-violet radiation will damage slings left in place, gradually weakening them even if they look quite

LEFT

A properly placed rappel sling, using a descending ring, with the sling having enough slack to form a fairly acute angle.

RIGHT

The rappel sling shown here is too tight. When a wide angle like this is formed by the lower part of the sling, a very high tension force can be created in the sling by a relatively small downward force. Webbing like this is also relatively inelastic and easily weakened by wear, so this tight sling is risky. The same factor applies to slings used for belay anchors and protection.

new. (This weathering causes the slings to feel brittle and crackly in texture, whereas they feel softer and silkier when new and unweathered; but one should not rely on feel to estimate the strength of the sling.) Any reasonably strong sling material can be used. The tendency is to take whatever is at hand, but there is a good argument for using several loops of lighter material (½-inch webbing or ¼-inch rope) rather than single heavier slings. If several loops are used, they are best tied independently, so that the parting of one would leave the anchor intact. This can be done without cutting the sling into separate lengths by doubling it back and forth and tying the whole sling with a sheet bend or double-sheet bend, either of which will hold all the remaining strands if one breaks.

Another important point to remember in setting the rappel sling is that it must not be too taut—that the angle formed by the two sides of the sling where the rope or the rappel ring pulls on it must be small. If the sling is taut and the angle wide, tremendous tension can be set up in the sling—far higher than the load placed on the rope. This is true of any anchor, of course, but the mistake is more common with rappel anchors, perhaps because the sling is to be left, and the stingy climber wants to waste as little material as possible.

Artificial anchors are frequently used in setting rappels when no suitable natural anchors are available. They are placed in the same way as anchors for belays or protection. As with belay anchors, at least two should normally be used, since unquestionably bombproof artificial placements are rare. Remember that with rappels a failure is generally fatal, so take no chances.

When several anchors are used, the load between them should normally be equalized in one of the usual ways. Separate slings can be tied, both going to a rappel ring. A good method of equalization which does not require too much sling material is shown on page 109.

When a sling is hung from an anchor using thin metal stock or thin wire, the strength of the sling will be increased if the acuteness of the bend is reduced by tucking a loose end of the sling under the load-bearing portion.

Avoid welded rappel rings. Lightweight aluminum rings are available now which do not have welds and which test to several thousand pounds.

Make sure that the rappel rope does not pass over sharp edges against which it might saw, and make sure that it can be pulled down. If the rope runs over a lot of rough ground and then over an edge, it will be very hard to pull down, particularly if there is a knot above the edge. When two ropes are used, the knot must obviously be a good one; but try to tie one as smooth as possible, so that it will be less likely to hang up.

Subject to the rappel reaching bottom and to the difficulty of take-off, set the rappel up so that the knot between the ropes is past as many obstructions as possible. Make sure you know which rope is to be pulled; if the two look the same, tie a knot (or a different knot) in the one to be pulled. When the first man gets down, he should test to see if the rappel can be pulled down. Often, when the ropes are long enough, the last man down can slide the knot past obstructions near the rappel point.

Try to see that the ropes reach bottom. This is not always possible, but if the first man goes off without knowing whether there is a good landing spot before the end of the rappel, he should take special precautions.

Throw the two sides of the rappel line separately, so that they will be less likely to snarl. Coiling each side in small coils —about 3 feet around, rather than the usual 5 or 6 feet—will work better for getting the rope to the bottom. Throw the coils well out from the stance. Taking a hitch of rope around the coil gives a grip for throwing.

MAKING THE RAPPEL

Whether the rappel itself is to be belayed or not, the climber should be belayed while he is getting into the rappel if the spot is precarious at all. Before going off belay or unclipping from the anchor, the rappel position or braking system must be double-checked. *This is a vitally important habit to acquire.* There are too many mistakes one can make, particularly when rappelling has become familiar enough for the climber to be casual about it.

The hardest part of the rappel is usually at the beginning. The rappeller may have to lean back against the anchors at an odd angle for the first few feet until he is down far enough for the line to run parallel to the surface or straight up. He may have to pass an overhang. Leaning well back and walking down usually suffice to get one over the problems, even past an overhang; but if the lip is really sharp or the anchor is very close to it, the take-off may be difficult. There are many schemes for getting past such difficulties, including leaps into space with slack in the rope. Easing over the problem usually works well and puts far less strain on the system. With a very sharp lip or an anchor very close to the edge, try sitting on the edge and sliding off, keeping the braking hand on the outside to protect it, and using the other hand to let yourself down and to ward off the rock.

After the initial fear of rappelling is past, many climbers get rather euphoric about the exercise, sometimes becoming partial to great leaps and bounds, zooming drops followed by rapid braking. Later still, most climbers who have been at the game long enough to have become aware of the large number of accidents, usually fatal, which have been sustained by experienced climbers in rappels come to regard rappels as a necessary evil, to be executed as carefully and conservatively as possible. It is just as well never to become blasé about rappelling, regarding it instead with appropriate suspicion and respect.

BELAYING RAPPELS

Ideally, all rappels should be belayed, and without any question *novices should always be belayed on rappels.* There are simply too many things that can go wrong on a rappel to take chances. By its nature rappelling is normally done in places with extreme exposure, so mistakes are likely to be fatal. It is therefore vital that on all practices for beginners and on early climbs, all rappels be belayed, and adequate ropes must be carried for the purpose. If possible there should be an independent anchor for the belay.

The difficulty normally encountered by experienced climbers is that too many ropes would have to be carried to belay most rappels. If a climb has a long rappel, say 140 feet, then two 150-foot ropes have to be carried just to make the rappel. For the last man down to be belayed would require two more 150-foot ropes, so that the weight begins to become ridiculous even if a special light 300-foot rappel line is taken.

The practice followed by some is to belay all but the final rappeller. An abseil can be made on a single strand by all but the last man, and he uses the other side to belay his companions. This means at least that the anchor has been tested by the time he comes down and that the odds for an accident have been reduced. Presumably, the most experienced climber will be the last person down. Since the last down cannot be belayed, each party has to decide whether the method is worthwhile. In case of pressing time, as with a late descent or a threatening thunderstorm, experienced parties must also weigh the additional safety of the belay against the danger presented by delay. In no case, however, should a climber let such dangers tempt him into using dubious anchors or becoming sloppy about the rappel itself.

SAFETIES

Slings for prusikking (a technique described later in the chapter) should be carried on all rappels, because they provide a means of getting back up the rope in case of problems. A prusik sling can also be used as a safety on any rappel, by attaching it to the rope above the rappelling rig. The safety prusik, when used, should be attached independently to the harness or the body. The prusik knot is held open and sliding down the rope by the upper hand, which is not needed for braking. If something should go wrong with the rappel, body weight will come on the prusik, and it will tighten and prevent a fall. If he is able, the rappeller can then attach another sling in which to stand. A prusik sling for this purpose must be made of the heaviest material that will grip the rope well. A very light prusik sling will be cut through by melt-abrasion before a fall is caught. The safety sling must also be short enough so that if it comes tight, the rappeller can reach up to loosen it.

Prusik safeties should not be considered as a substitute for a belay. They provide the necessary redundancy only for the rappel brake or body wrap, not for the anchor and upper rope.

A prusik safety may be used on a nasty rappel by the last man down after others have been belayed. It should always be used on any rappel where there is danger of rockfall, unless the rappel is belayed, since a rock hitting the rappeller on the hand or head can cause him to lose control. Some climbers prefer not to use the safety on normal rappels, however, because it can become fouled in passing an overhang or other projection, and because they feel that in most circumstances the additional safety gained is not enough to compensate for the problems that can be caused by the prusik's jamming or fouling.

Several other types of safeties will not catch the descending man in the middle of the rappel, but are designed to keep him from going off the end of the rope. Large knots can be tied in each end of the rope, which will jam in a mechanical braking system. For the carabiner brake system shown earlier, I prefer to use a *figure-eight loop* tied in each end. This knot is large enough so that it cannot possibly work through the brake as some smaller knots have occasionally done. The knot will even

A carabiner-brake rappel with a safety prusik kept sliding with the left hand.

jam completely on a single-strand rappel. For body rappels, one has to tie the two ends together to get a safety, although this is not usually desirable because the ends may twist together toward the end of the rappel, causing some problems. When the ends are tied together, a safety sling of heavy material can be tied between the two strands and around the body.

Some kind of safety measure to keep the climber from going off the end of the rope should be used whenever this might be a possibility, particularly if there are complications—darkness, fatigue, or the possibility that there is no ledge below within reach.

ADDITIONAL CAUTIONS ON RAPPELLING

It is hard to overemphasize the need for extreme care in setting up and making rappels. While not technically difficult and generally executed without incident, rappels have claimed the lives of many very competent and experienced climbers. Because of their nature, most rappels are done in very airy spots and, as stated previously, the failure of any point is likely to mean *total* failure. Thus, it is vital to double-check every aspect of the rappel. Anchors and anchor slings in particular should never be taken for granted, nor should the possibility of belaying be rejected out of hand.

Besides the numerous precautions already mentioned in previous sections, some others should be pointed out. Gloves should normally be worn whenever one is rappelling. In addition to providing protection against rope burns, this might be considered a corollary of the general principle that any part of the body which is a point of friction against the rappel rope should be protected, if only because the pain caused by rope burns can make one lose control of the rappel or divert attention to the pain from where it should always be—on the safety of the rappel.

With various brakes it is extremely important to tuck in any clothes that might get caught in the braking system, such as parka hems. Climbers with very long hair should tuck it under the parka or shirt. If the rappel should jam, take the time to get out a sling, set a prusik knot above, and take the weight off the brake so that the jam can be worked out. Do not try to use a knife. A nylon rope under tension needs only the slightest stroke from a knife to be cut.

Beginners should practice stopping and tying off a rappel in mid-air, once they have learned the basics. They should learn to use prusik slings to take tension off the rope and climb back up if necessary.

Hard hats should be left on during rappels. The danger presented by rockfall is obvious, but you can also hit your head on the rock in a minor mishap. The hard hat will keep it minor. There is the possibility of one's companion above dropping a piece of equipment as he gets ready to follow, and if you are hit on the head in an unbelayed rappel you might never have a chance to point out his error later, unless you are wearing your helmet.

Setting up the rappel to run as freely as possible when it is pulled down is an obvious safety precaution if you can visualize being stuck in the middle of a face with a rappel that has been pulled down part of the way. A rappel that has refused to come down at all is bad enough; one has to climb all the way back up the rope to free it, at best a tiring and time-consuming job. If, however, the rope is pulled part way down, and the free end is already hanging high above, the situation is far more unpleasant, since if one started climbing the rope it might suddenly decide to come loose.

Remember to untie any knots in the end of the rope that is to slide through the anchor, double-check the correct end to pull, and be sure that any twists are out of the rope. This should be done by each man as he descends, usually by keeping one finger of the braking hand between the two ropes. The first and the next-to-last man should also have checked to see that the rope will pull freely. The rope should be pulled down as smoothly as possible, since jerks tend to throw the end into possible jams. The rising end and the knot joining the ropes should be watched carefully, so that pulling can be coordinated to try to keep them out of any crannies where they might catch. If the rope does get caught, it may be possible to pull it down by tying loops in it and having all members of the party get into positions where they can exert maximum force.

PRUSIKKING

The technique of climbing back up a rope is as important a part of the climber's repertoire as descending, although it is used much less often. It is the standard form of self-rescue from a host of unpleasant situations, and slings for this purpose are also commonly used to tie off a fallen climber, as well as for various other tasks. Such slings should always be carried in an accessible place. They are not much use in the pack if an emergency occurs. In glacier travel, a prusik sling is normally tied to the rope in advance in case of a fall into a crevasse.

In order to climb back up a rope in the kinds of circumstances that can be expected on mountains, some device is needed to which slings can be attached for the feet, which will grip the rope and hold the weight of the body, but which can be easily moved up the rope. The oldest effective method is the use of prusik knots (named after their inventor). A prusik will easily hold body weight, and when the weight is taken off it can be unjammed without too much difficulty and

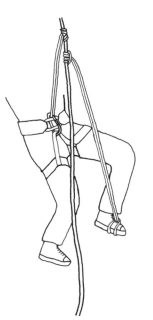

PRUSIKKING. The method shown here is the one most commonly used by climbers. The foot sling (which can have loops tied so that both feet can be used) is tied onto the line below the sling going to the harness, so that the climber can sit and rest in the harness while moving the foot sling up.

moved on up the rope. It is easily tied with one hand, once the climber has practiced it a bit. In case of slipping, extra twists can be taken around the rope. A prusik should still be considered the standard ascender knot, since only a sling is required. The Bachman knot is considerably easier to use than the prusik, particularly when passing an overhang or trying to manipulate the knot with cold or mittened hands. It is also easily tied with one hand, and extra turns will give more grip. For most purposes it is the best of ascender knots.

Many types of prusik slings are used by different climbers. I believe it is important to carry a special set, which is not used for other purposes, because otherwise there is a danger of being caught without. Obviously any available sling can be used, including webbing, although that does not work quite so well as rope. Rope slings for prusikking must be of a smaller diameter than the rope to be climbed. A soft laid rope of the type sold for yachting, or kernmantel that has not been heat-treated, works better in marginal conditions (such as with an icy rope) than the normal hard laid climbing line. Virtually any small-diameter nylon rope can be used, however. The length of the slings will depend on the methods and preferences of the climber. Some prefer to carry short prusiks and to clip other slings (such as aid slings) to them for steps. Otherwise the prusiks can be pre-tied to the correct length for steps, after experimenting with this technique.

If the climber wears a harness, he normally uses two slings —one clipped to the harness as a safety and a seat and the other used as a step for one of his feet. The sling for the seat should be long enough so that the knot will be about 6 inches overhead when one is hanging from it. The length of the foot sling should be adjusted so that when the prusik knot tied in it is raised to be on the rope just under the seat sling prusik knot, the foot in the sling will be raised as high as one can comfortably step. Progress is made by standing up in the foot sling, moving the seat knot as high as possible, sitting down in the harness, and moving the foot knot up, just beneath the seat knot. The most difficult problem is working past overhangs,

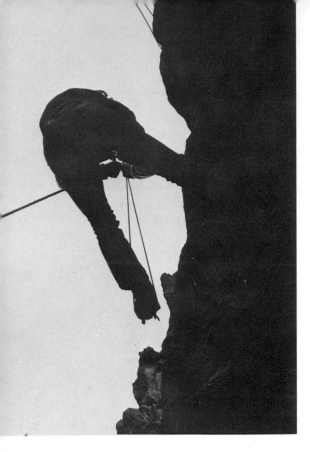

Prusikking.

where the knots are pressed against the rock or into the snow. This is where Bachman knots prove superior. In any case, either the weight must be gotten off the rope by using holds, or the rope must be pulled up off the surface enough to move the knot. With prusik knots, gloves will help in this operation.

If a harness is not worn, three prusiks are needed. The highest forms a safety sling around the chest, and it should be long enough so that if one hangs from it, the knot is about at the height one can conveniently reach. The next length sling is such that when it is tied just below the first, the leg is at the top of a comfortable step. The last sling is for the second foot. When one is standing up in the first foot sling, the second one is tied around the rope just below it and should be long enough so that the second leg steps as high as possible to reach it. The technique is similar to that with two slings, except that both legs are used for lifting, and three slings have to be moved successively.

Several methods can be used for actually tying the slings, none of which seems clearly superior. I use loops for all three and have not found it necessary to tie the loops to the boots, since a little pressure from the toe keeps the foot in. A clove hitch, girth hitch, or overhand keeps the foot in, if something is wanted. The chest safety is perhaps best tied with a fixed loop in each end and a single line between. One loop is used for tying the prusik or Bachman knot and the other is the right size for the chest. This method makes the safety a little harder to slip out of than a plain loop.

A climber using the three-loop method on an unbelayed prusik should take care not to climb out of his slings after passing an overhang, since they constitute his only safety equipment.

Prusik and other ascender knots work even better around a doubled rope.

TYING OFF A FALLEN CLIMBER

This is another of the smaller skills one hopes never to use, but which should be practiced periodically. The exact mechan-

Tying off a fallen climber. The belayer has just held a fall with his (right) braking hand. In cases where the climber is injured, is hanging over a severe overhang, or is unable to help himself for some other reason, the belayer must tie the climber off and free himself from the belay before he can help his companion. In this photograph, the belayer's anchor rope comes around from behind him, around his left side, and is tied into his harness at the front. The belay rope to the fallen climber goes through a carabiner clipped to the harness to prevent it from riding up or down.

ics will depend on the length of the slings available, but the steps shown in the illustrations are typical. Note that if the climber is hanging free on a waist loop or swami alone, it is very important that he get some other support quickly, before his breathing becomes stifled. A climber hanging on a waist

As a first step, the belayer, maintaining hold on the rope with his braking hand, ties the rope off around his body by taking two half-hitches with a bight from the free rope just past his braking hand around the rope going to the fallen climber.

The fallen climber is now tied off with the half-hitches, which are themselves secured with a carabiner. The belayer's hands are now free, and he is getting out a prusik sling with his left hand.

The belayer now ties a prusik onto the rope going to the climber. He has both hands free, though he should be able to tie a prusik with only one. Other ascender knots or mechanical ascenders can be used in place of a prusik, but the need for a ratchet knot in this situation is one of the reasons why a set of prusik slings should be within reach at all times during a climb.

A second prusik is tied to the anchor behind the belayer, the two slings are clipped together, and they are pulled tight. Different anchoring arrangements may require slightly modified set-ups. For example, if the anchor rope goes around the anchor and comes back to the belayer to be attached with a clove hitch, one prusik has to be attached to each line to the anchor, and both must be hooked to the prusik on the belay line.

The belayer can now remove the half-hitches, slowly allow the weight to come on the prusiks, and get out of his belay position. He is then free to do what is necessary. The first thing that must be done is to tie the line going to the climber directly to the anchor, to back up the prusiks. If the climber has to be hauled up, the prusiks will be used as a ratchet on the line. Actual hauling will normally require padding the edges over which the rope passes and setting up a hauling system with some mechanical advantage.

loop will die within about twenty minutes, so if he is injured and unable to help himself, this is all the time his companion has in which to do something. If the fall is into a crevasse and the belay is from an arrest or an ice ax, the belayer clearly has to set up an adequate anchor before he can tie the fallen man off safely.

CREVASSES AND OTHER SELF-RESCUES

The most obvious form of self-rescue when a climber has fallen into a position out of which he cannot climb is to prusik up the rope. It is well worth spending some time practicing this when actually hanging free, particularly if a waist loop or swami belt is used as a tie-in. With either of these methods, the climber will find his breathing rapidly being cut off. If a prusik sling is already attached to the rope, one has merely to pull the other end out of the pocket and step into it, so this practice is standard in glacier travel. If a sling is not attached to the rope, some immediate relief will be felt if one turns upside down, so that the weight falls on the hips rather than the lower chest. If a pack is being carried, this maneuver may be rather tricky. To sit back up again without suffocating, a short sling is pulled over one leg, around the rope in front of the climber, and over the other leg. One can then work up to a sitting position again and be able to function well enough to rig prusik slings. Wearing a harness makes all this unnecessary.

Self-rescue from a crevasse normally requires some help from above, even with an uninjured climber. A companion should first manage to work something under the rope at the lip, to prevent it from cutting in further. The man below should get on all the clothes he can, since one of the main problems tends to be that one rapidly becomes too chilled to function. Tying off the pack if it is at all heavy is also necessary, since it is difficult enough to get oneself out. If the job is not too difficult, the pack can be hung by a carabiner in the loop formed by the climbing rope between the climber and his prusik sling; this will lift it part way as the climber goes up, with a two-to-one mechanical advantage. Otherwise, the climber will either have to tie the pack to a line dropped from above or fix it to the end of the rope and untie himself before prusikking up.

There are several methods for easing the job of the man below. One is to lower the other end of the rope to him and to set up prusiks (or a substitute) from the anchor to each of the ropes. The man below will already be standing in a sling on the end to which he is tied. The other end is tied in a loop, which is then passed through his waist loop or harness and down to form a step for the other foot. The man above then alternately raises each side of the rope and sets the ascender knots. The man below has to do most of the work by stepping up each time, but he is relieved of the need to work the knots, and has a better chance of getting out over the lip.

Really serious difficulties are encountered when the climber who has fallen is too badly injured to raise himself, or when the lip of the crevasse is so large that it cannot be passed.

In the second case, it may be possible to cut or dig through far enough back to get the man out, but so much snow will have fallen on him that he is likely to be suffering badly from the cold by the time he can start to move up. If there are enough climbers, the second rope can be dropped from the far side of the opening; with tension from both sides as he comes up, the lip can be passed more easily. This problem and the one of raising a hurt climber are the main reasons it is so much safer to travel in parties of three or more on snow-covered glaciers. Some systems for hauling which can be adapted to crevasse rescue are indicated in the chapter on big walls. Other systems can easily be devised on the spot if the climber has practiced the basics beforehand, but the chances of one man being able to get a badly hurt companion out of a big crevasse are slim indeed.

CREVASSE RESCUES. There are a number of rescue methods to deal with crevasse falls. In *a*, one climber has fallen, and his two companions on the rope have arrested the fall. Preparation and advance practice will enable the unhurt climber to rescue himself, after his companions anchor him and place an anchored pack under the rope to prevent its cutting further into the lip of the crevasse.

A method of tying in for glacier travel to avoid injury and facilitate self-rescue is shown in *b*. A harness with leg loops is essential to prevent the rope from paralyzing breathing. The one shown is a commercial harness, but a tied one like that illustrated in the knot section is equally good. Two slings, one long and one short, are already attached to the rope either with prusik slings or ascenders. The short sling is attached to the seat harness, and the longer one is attached farther up the rope with a foot sling, which can be kept in the pocket while climbing. A person climbing in the middle of a rope should attach one sling to the rope ahead and one to the rope behind; one can later be changed, depending on which rope catches him. If a heavy pack is being carried, a simple chest harness is essential to prevent the climber from being turned upside-down by the weight of the pack. In the drawing, a sling is formed into a figure-eight, and the arms are slipped through the loops, with the central X behind the back. A carabiner can be clipped into

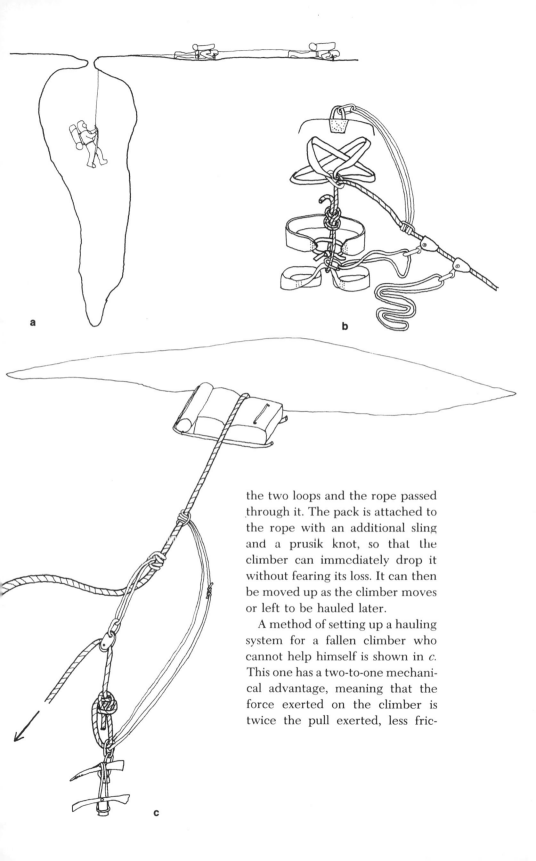

a

b

the two loops and the rope passed through it. The pack is attached to the rope with an additional sling and a prusik knot, so that the climber can immediately drop it without fearing its loss. It can then be moved up as the climber moves or left to be hauled later.

A method of setting up a hauling system for a fallen climber who cannot help himself is shown in *c*. This one has a two-to-one mechanical advantage, meaning that the force exerted on the climber is twice the pull exerted, less fric-

c

tion. A pack has been pushed under the rope to the fallen climber to prevent its biting further into the lip. Though it is not shown for clarity, the pack should be anchored. Two ice axes are being used as an anchor, one backing the other up. Other snow anchors could be used in different conditions. The anchor *must* be absolutely secure.

The upper prusik knot holds the rope between pulls. When the rope is pulled as shown, force is transmitted through the pulley to the lower prusik, which pulls the climber up until the pulley reaches the anchor knot. The upper prusik is then moved to hold the rope, tension is taken from the pulley, and the lower prusik is moved up for another cycle. If only one man can haul, the system should be set up so that the hauling is done with the stronger muscles of the legs, using a foot loop.

HAULING A FALLEN CLIMBER

On rock, there is a somewhat better chance of getting a companion up, even if he is too badly hurt to help himself. Letting him down to the next ledge is usually the logical procedure. If one does have to get him up, either of the hauling methods described in Chapter 16 will work. The easiest to use, providing it is safe, is the technique of hanging on the other end of the haul line with a pulley in between, pulling oneself down about 30 feet to the end of a safety (thereby pulling the injured climber up), and then prusikking back up to the anchor and starting again. If one is hauling from the top and the injured climber is much heavier, a mechanical advantage system like that shown on page 223 can be rigged into the hauling set-up. Any ascender knot can be used to replace the mechanical ascenders, with some loss in speed, and carabiners can be used in place of pulleys, but with considerable extra friction and loss of efficiency.

MECHANICAL ASCENDERS

Several types of mechanical ascenders are available to speed things up when much rope climbing or hauling has to be done, and to simplify rescues. In most climbing they are simply an unnecessary burden and expense, but they can be a great help when needed. The most common types are discussed briefly here.

Jumars are the commonest ascenders used by American climbers, because they are the best suited to big wall climbs. Their use is discussed in Chapters 16 and 18. Several disadvantages and cautions should be mentioned in addition to those discussions. To begin with, the handles of jumars are made by castings and are rather brittle. If they are dropped, they can shatter or develop minute cracks that are very hard to detect. Since they are expensive, and since one's life may hang from them, they should be treated with care.

Under high loads, a jumar can pull the sheath off a kernmantel rope, although the normal form of failure is deformation of the cam. These problems do not need to be considered in normal use of the ascenders, but they should be taken into account before one uses them for other purposes for which they were not designed, such as self-belays in solo climbing or holding heavy loads in rescue work.

If the safety catch does not close properly, the cam of a jumar can come off the rope when loaded from the side. Most of the accidents with jumars have resulted from safety catches not closing on a diagonal rope. Slide the ascender up a little, in line with the rope, to make sure the safety is closed, before you put weight on it. If the jumars are used on a small-diameter rope, note the safety precautions discussed in Chapter 18.

Jumars often cause problems on ropes covered with ice, slush, snow, or mud. The teeth become caked and the cam then slips on the rope. Clearing the rope ahead with your hand will help considerably, but the teeth may also have to be cleaned periodically, and a prusik safety should be used if the ascenders are tending to slip. Clipping through the top eye will improve the grip considerably. When the snow is dry, there is usually not much of a problem, but with wet, slushy snow, the clogging can be severe.

Gibbs ascenders are made in the United States, and they

LEFT

Jumar ascenders. The slings tied to the bottoms distribute any shock over the castings; direct aid slings or special jumarring slings are clipped to these with carabiners. The cams of the jumars grip the rope more strongly as pressure is applied. They grip by friction on the outside of the rope, so that on perlon rope they depend on the strength of the sheath. The triggers below the cams are safeties that prevent the jumars from being accidentally removed from the rope.

RIGHT

A jumar hazard. In clipping a jumar onto a diagonal rope, it is easy to neglect being sure the safety catch is engaged. When it is not, the jumar can be twisted off the rope. Note here that under torque, the cam is holding the safety catch open. The body of the jumar should be run parallel to the rope to engage the catch, and the catch should be carefully checked each time an ascender is attached to the rope.

TOP

A method of improving the grip of a jumar on a muddy or icy line. Attaching a sling to the top makes the rope bend, so that less friction is required from the cam. Worn teeth on the cam reduce grip, as does ice or mud clogging the teeth.

BOTTOM

Gibbs ascenders are simpler, more foolproof, and less expensive than jumars but do not fulfill all the climber's requirements. They are normally attached to the rope using one short foot sling and one longer foot sling together with a knee tie. Climbing a rope is much faster with Gibbs, but they are poor for seconding on big walls. The ascender on the right is attached to the rope; the one on the left is disassembled, as it must be to attach it to the rope or to remove it. The body's weight presses the cam directly onto the rope after it is attached with the quick-release pin.

are superior in many respects to jumars. They are lighter, faster in direct ascents of a rope, stronger, virtually impossible to dislodge accidentally, and better on dirty or icy ropes. Unfortunately, they do not work very well for cleaning an aid pitch, which is the main reason most climbers buy ascenders. For auxiliary uses, the Gibbs are often clearly superior. (If used for self-belay on vertical pitches, Gibbs often catch slowly, because they fall free with the climber. A spring can be added to solve the problem.)

Hiebler ascenders are very simple in design and quite light. They grip the rope mainly by bending it into an S-shaped curve. They are not particularly popular among American climbers, partly because they have no real safeguard against the rope's slipping out under sideways loading.

Clog ascenders use a spring-loaded cam like the jumar, but, like the Gibbs, they are designed so that they must be taken apart to be removed from the rope. (The carabiner must be removed from the bottom, so that the cam can be pulled back.) This is a safety feature, but one that is often a nuisance in practical situations. Some care should be taken if Clogs are used for self-belay or for rescue, since the pins attached to the cams can jam them open if forced against the rock.

IV

Technical Climbing

10

FREE CLIMBING ON ROCK

The most basic elements of rock climbing have been discussed in earlier chapters, as have the techniques for protecting the climber. The meat of the climbing is not in the protection, however; protection is merely a means to an end, the precondition that allows one to come to grips with rock, snow, or ice. Snow and ice climbing are discussed in the next two chapters, and the use of mechanical aids for rock climbing is also the subject of a later chapter. Rock climbing, in one form or another, is the area in which Americans have done their best climbing, pushing the standards of both free climbing and direct aid beyond earlier limits, and developing equipment unsurpassed anywhere in the world.

Free climbing in the United States and Canada means climbing without any use of pitons, bolts, nuts, or slings for making progress up the rock or for resting between belay stances. Obviously, this purist attitude is partly the result of the large amount of rock climbing done in this country in non-alpine settings, where objective dangers and the need for speed are somewhat reduced. This attitude has resulted in pushing the standards of free climbing to extremely high levels.

The how-to-do-it sections of this chapter are fairly brief. One can make a few suggestions about the ways that people might try to develop their skills, particularly in some of the less obvious uses of holds, like jamming. Basically, however, beginners have to teach themselves to climb. Others can describe proper use of equipment, mention safety principles, and encourage novices to push their limits; but climbing itself is done by the body and mind working together in a harmony and mutual understanding that can only be acquired by actual experience. Get out on some local boulders or the side of a building and try to learn what your body can do and what it can't. Then see if you can force yourself to do something harder. Get people to take you out on real climbs and find what you can do on those, building the rhythm, stamina, and understanding needed on long climbs, learning to rest in the middle of a pitch, and practicing the elements of belaying and placing protection, so that you will later be able to lead climbs yourself. You can only learn to be a mountaineer or rock climber by getting out on the peaks and the rocks.

EQUIPMENT

All the standard items of equipment have been discussed before except for specialized rock-climbing shoes. These should not really be considered essential, although they may be of some help. It is quite possible to climb difficult rock in mountaineering boots, and to some degree in good tennis shoes. In fact, every beginner will probably one day have the experience of complaining of not being able to do a boulder problem because of his footwear, and having some resident expert walk up and do the move in question wearing loafers, moccasins, or galoshes.

Rock shoes are a help, though, particularly on hard climbs. If one does a lot of climbing, it is also cheaper to have rock shoes in addition to mountaineering boots. They cost about half as much, and with prices climbing as they are, it is getting rather expensive to wear out boots on local boulders.

There are many kinds of rock shoes; what is worn in a given area at a given time is likely to have more to do with fashion than anything else. This may be important for the novice, however, since if he is convinced that he cannot do something because of his shoes, he will be distracted from the real reasons.

Rock shoes *(varappes, klettershue)* can have lug soles, usually a little thinner than those on boots, or smooth soles; and soles can range from very flexible to rather stiff. Most modern rock shoes have rubber extending part of the way up the sides to improve wear and adhesion in some climbing situations. Split leather tops wear a good deal better than canvas ones. Canvas-topped shoes will last much longer if one has them faced with leather. The life of all rock shoes will be extended if the stitching is smeared with epoxy cement.

It is convenient to consider rock shoes as falling into two basic types: friction shoes, with flexible soles and toes, usually with smooth bottoms; and stiffer soled types, normally having lug bottoms and hard-capped toes. Again the choice has more

Two types of specialized rock climbing shoes. In front are the more flexible PAs, which are especially good on friction and in very narrow jam cracks. To the rear is a pair of Red Spiders, which are stiffer, better for edging and on slimy rock, and do not have to be fitted quite so tightly. There are many versions of each type of shoe, as well as variations and compromises between them. The importance of a particular type of footwear is often overemphasized.

to do with one's personal climbing style than anything else, although since each has some definite advantages, one or the other tends to predominate in a given climbing area. The friction shoes work particularly well on smooth slabs, on scooped sloping holds, and in very narrow or flared jam cracks, into which the uncapped toe can be inserted. The stiffer soles make edging on small, sharp holds considerably easier, and they are far more comfortable, because only a snug size is required, in contrast to the painfully tight grip of a well-fitted friction shoe. Lug soles, on whichever kind of shoe, are far better on wet, sandy, or greasy rock.

Some typical friction shoes are EB's, PA's, and RD's, all named in the European fashion for the famous climbers whose initials they bear. Of the stiff-soled varieties, examples are RR's (for our own Royal Robbins) and Red Spiders.

MODES OF CLIMBING

Both climbing problems and the techniques used for surmounting them can be classified in a variety of ways. Such analysis helps us to talk about what we are doing, but its relevance to the actual process of learning to climb is often obscure. A climb that is a pure example of one type is rare indeed, and so are moves and holds that fit well into our neat categories. As a climber goes up from one hold to another, he is likely to use the same nubbin in half a dozen different positions, moving smoothly from one way of utilizing it to the next, and certainly not thinking about any particular type of hold at a given time. We become more skillful climbers as we learn to coordinate the knowledge of our bodies and minds to work on each individual climbing problem.

Because I think that one really learns to climb by climbing, I don't propose to make the usual detailed analysis of holds here. The description tends to be meaningless until one has used the holds—and pointless afterwards. There are a few kinds of holds and particular techniques that are less obvious than others, especially certain jams. Pointing these out may be

Top-roped slab climbing.

of some help; however, the emphasis they receive does not reflect the fact that they are used a great deal, but rather that they are somewhat obscure because of their limited applicability.

Face climbing and slab climbing are the most common and perhaps the purest kinds of climbing. They come rather naturally, which is not to imply that they are easy. The main trick in both that the beginner tends to disregard is to keep the body upright and away from the rock. Leaning into the rock makes holds hard to see, causes the feet to slip, and allows too much weight to come onto the arms. The less weight a climber puts on the fingers and the more he can climb in balance, the more easily he will be able to surmount the pitch with poise and confidence. The difference between face and slab climbing is that face climbing works up a fairly steep piece of rock using protrusions as holds for the hands and feet. Slab climbing usually refers to a more gentle slope with smaller holds. When climbing a slab, one may use edging on tiny ridges or friction on little pockets with a slightly lower angle than the surrounding rock. In either case, it is important to strain as little as possible. The climber should rest whenever he can, stopping in a position in which the muscles are not straining and resting them while the eyes work out the sequence of holds above.

One should cultivate the ability to move up a sequence of difficult moves and then to come back down again, rest a bit, and go up again. This tactic will enable the climber to find out what lies above without committing himself beyond his ability. The whole art of downclimbing should be pursued as assiduously as the technique of getting up; there are times when one must be able to climb down as a matter of survival.

The arms should be kept as low as possible. Long reaches are undesirable when lower holds will do. Stretching for holds throws the body out of balance, tends to make the feet slip, and is tiring for the arms. Standing for long periods with the hands on holds above the head is even worse, since the resulting poor circulation makes one's arms tire very rapidly.

Using tiny edge holds requires both strength and practice.

Time is necessary to find out the limits of adherence, and more time again is needed to work on the strength and technique to extend those limits. It is usually better, however, to rely on short steps from one small hold to another than to make long and awkward lunges from one large hold to another. Scoops and pockets may give better purchase if the foot is "smeared," the lower side placed on the hold, and the foot twisted into the depressions.

Many holds can be used which point off in odd directions. A flake sticking sideways can be grasped and leaned back on, enabling the climber to reach for a higher hold with the feet or his other hand. Holds pointing straight down can be grasped by the hands, allowing the feet to be held on sloping ledges below. Many very tenuous holds are good for brief intervals between one large bucket and another, but all such rugosities must be used in control, not in desperate leaps.

Get into the habit of testing all your holds. You will find many that look solid but are not. Discover their weakness before you trust your weight to them. Aside from the danger of falling yourself, your climbing companions will probably consider it bad form to drop blocks on their heads, and you will certainly do just this if you blindly clutch at holds without testing them. Twisting, tugging, kicking, and thumping will often produce a warning movement or hollow sound. Some loose holds are strong in one direction, but not in another. You should also cultivate the habit of moving one limb at a time whenever possible, so that when a hold does fail, you will have a better chance of staying on the rock.

Climbing cracks and chimneys tends to be a less natural exercise for most people than face climbing. Progress is often made not by stepping on a projection and pushing the body up, or by grabbing a knob and pulling, but rather by using some sort of cross-pressure between different parts of the body to get enough adherence to the rock. Such tactics—often known as *counterforce* or *opposition holds*—are used often when climbing a cleft in the rock.

Long fissures in the rock frequently provide climbing

Crack climbing on Castle Rock in Boulder Canyon. The climber is using jam holds with both hands and his right toe and a counterforce friction hold with his left foot.

routes. In the smaller ones, ranging from the thickness of the fingers to about 5 feet or so, one can often climb by pushing against both sides at once in opposition, using various methods. Conventional holds are often employed, and the climber frequently moves back and forth from one to the other. Cracks ranging from finger size to about a foot wide, when climbed using counterforce holds, are generally known as *jam cracks*, since various parts of the body are jammed and wedged somehow into the crack. Wider cracks, into which the whole body can enter, are called *chimneys.*

There are many kinds of jams and chimneying techniques. Like most kinds of climbing, they have to be practiced to be learned at all, much less mastered. Some opposition climbing is easy once the climber gets the hang of it, and some is desperately difficult. The most important principle to remember is always to try to use a jam that wedges some rigid part of the body, so that muscle tension is not required to keep it in place. This enables you to rest. The next best kind of jam is one which

Climbing in a dihedral or open book using a variety of types of holds. On the Medicine Bow Diamond.

relies on the muscle contraction making a part of the body larger, so that it stays in a wider part of a crack like a nut placement. This requires some muscular strain, but not too much. The worst kind of opposition hold is one that strains one muscle against another, which is very tiring and cannot be sustained for long. A classic example of this latter type is the lieback.

With a little thought, one can often find rest holds. For instance, in a chimney that is climbed by pushing the feet

Easy crack-chimney climbing near Gem Lake in Rocky Mountain National Park. The climber has jammed his right foot in the smaller inside crack and has his left foot on an outside hold. His left hand is on a cling hold, and his right arm is using pressure on the wall of the chimney.

Easy chimney climbing using small ledge holds for the feet, while the back and arms use pressure holds on the other side.

A pure lieback. The hands use the crack for cling holds, and the feet are pushed against the wall for friction. Many liebacks have small holds for the feet, which only need to be improved by leaning back on the arms. Pure liebacks on vertical rock are rather strenuous.

against one wall and the back against the other, the leg muscles have to do a good deal of pushing during the actual climbing, but they can be rested often by locking the legs straight out, so that the body is jammed without any strong muscle tension.

The illustrations on pages 240–242 show a few typical jamming and chimneying holds.

A finger jam. The climber is using small holds on the face for her feet, gaining purchase on them by leaning her body out against her jammed fingers.

A hand jam. The hand is inserted in a crack, preferably in a locally wide spot, then a fist is made to expand the hand. There are many types of hand jams, obvious enough with experimentation. The most secure ones use a fist or a wide joint like a climbing nut. Less secure ones rely on muscle power to hold the hand expanded.

RATING SYSTEMS

With the growing number of climbers, there are some good reasons to feel that perhaps communication about route descriptions might best be dropped. Climbers in some areas have, in fact, deliberately chosen not to publish guides or route descriptions. If we do want to talk with each other about routes, however, rating systems improve the quality of the information exchanged.

A rating system is essentially designed to convey some feeling for the difficulty of a route by comparing it with others. If two climbers have both spent much time in Yosemite Valley, for example, and one is trying to tell another what sort of climb a route in Boulder, Colorado, is, he might say, "It's about the same level of difficulty as the regular route on Higher Cathedral Spire." Rating systems give a somewhat more general means of comparison between climbs, both within one particular area and between climbing regions.

There are certain natural difficulties that arise with all rating systems. Every climb is different, and problems in various kinds of climbing are hard to compare. Besides trying to equate apples and oranges, rating systems bring with them a multiplicity of little rivalries, ego problems, and disagreements in opinion and philosophy. They are as imperfect as most human systems; but as long as one does not take either the ratings or the arguments too seriously, no great harm is done. One should never rely excessively on route descriptions or ratings, but they can be useful. Some understanding of the common ones is needed if only because they are part of the vocabulary of American mountaineers.

Many rating systems have been proposed and used at different times and in different regions and guidebooks. I will not attempt an exhaustive description of these or try to make any judgments. Some of the more common rating systems in North America are briefly described below. Where others are used, a comparison with one of those described will usually be included in the guidebook.

In the United States, a system was widely accepted for a number of years which tried to rate climbs by categorizing the equipment that was needed. The philosophy involved was commendable: the rating would tell you what you had to have along to make the climb safely, and something about the competence required. That is, if pitons were needed, presumably candidates for the climb should know how to use them and be able to climb on the sort of terrain where they are usually expected. The basic system underwent various permutations but survived in its essence for some time. Class 1 meant trail walking, requiring no special equipment. Class 2 indicated that the footing became tricky enough to require proper boots, as with talus hopping, snow slopes, and such. Hands might be needed for balance on occasion. Class 3 indicated that the hands would be needed quite a bit for clambering about, and that a rope should be carried. Non-technical glacier travel would be included in Class 3, since a rope would be needed because of crevasse danger. Class 4 meant that the rope was needed for belaying because of exposure, so that some equipment for fixing belays had to be carried, but running belays would be used only occasionally. Class 5 meant technical free climbing, with suitable hardware needed for the leader to set up running belays. And Class 6 was climbing using hardware for direct aid, indicating that lots of iron, slings, and such should be carried.

In the 1950's this system began to seem unsatisfactory in a number of areas where it was in common use, because climbers doing technical climbing found that all their routes fell in the Class 5 or Class 6 categories, and there were vast differences in the difficulty of the climbs being done. The decimal system was invented at Tahquitz Rock in southern California, breaking these classes into ten categories each, 5.0 to 5.9 and 6.0 to 6.9, ranging from the easiest to the hardest climbs in each category. This system, with some important modifications, is still perhaps the most widely used rating system in the United States.

The current form is the Yosemite Decimal System. Classes

1 through 4 remain unchanged. Thus, to "third-class" a pitch is to climb it unroped; to do a route "fourth class" is to use a rope and fixed belays, but not running belays for the leader.

Technical free climbing in YDS is rated from 5.0 to the mathematically absurd 5.10 and 5.11, the latter two categories having been necessitated by the rising standards of free climbing since the original "hardest possible" 5.9 climbs were done.

Direct aid climbing is now listed differently, in categories ranging from A1 to A5. These are discussed in more detail in Chapter 13.

Climbs rated by YDS are now given three numbers. The first is a Roman numeral, from I to VI, which is supposed to indicate the overall difficulty, seriousness, and effort required for the climb. The grades were first used to rate climbs in Yosemite, because of the range of sheer size of climbs there. The grade is now used (and sometimes misused) in many parts of the country. It is supposed to tell one the difference between an easy morning's recreation, a tough day's climb, and a very hard and committed multi-day bash. As with free-climbing moves, grades have to be determined by comparison and evaluation. To be meaningful the grade must take into account the time needed, the overall effort and difficulty, and the commitment required (meaning, for example, that retreat may be difficult beyond a certain point).

Grade I's are the work of a few hours or less for a competent team of climbers, and generally involve no more than a couple of rope lengths of technical climbing. Grade II's have several pitches of fifth- or sixth-class rock and would normally consume half a day for a competent party. Grade III's are for seasoned climbers and will require a day of solid climbing; while a Grade IV will occupy the same climbers for a very long day or somewhat more. Grade V's and VI's are the big wall climbs, requiring great competence and effort, the times varying with the route and the expertise and conditioning of the climbers. A Grade V will take good climbers anywhere from one day to three (often more on a new route) in reasonable conditions, while a Grade VI nearly always requires several

FREE CLIMBING DIFFICULT

(Generally indicating the greatest difficulty encountered on the climb or the section of the climb being described.)

Description of type of climbing and difficulty	Trail walking	Easy, unexposed scrambling, with hands occasionally used for balance. Good footwear helpful.	More difficult scrambling, often with considerable exposure. Rope should be carried, especially by beginners and on glaciers	Rope required for safe climbing. Fixed belays may be needed. Running belays may be used occasionally, but competent leaders should need only minimal hardware.
Yosemite Decimal System (YDS)	←———————— Class ————————→			
	1	2	3	4
National Climbing Classification System (NCCS)	F1		F2	F3
British Description	Easy	Moderate	Moderately Difficult	Difficult (D)
UIAA System	I	II		III—
John Gill's Bouldering System	Not applicable —————————			

days of effort by the very strongest climbers. The Nose of El Capitan, the first Grade VI route done in the country, spread over a period of a year and a half, and required a month and a half on the wall.

GENERALLY APPLICABLE TO ROCK CLIMBS

FREE CLIMBING DIFFICULTY

Increasingly difficult climbing, requiring placement of running belays by the leader for safe climbing

	Easy technical climbing	Moderately difficult technical climbing	Difficult technical climbing —can only be led safely by strong climbers	Technical climbing requiring considerable effort and nerve from experts

←——— Class ———→

5.0	5.1	5.2	5.3	5.4	5.5	5.6	5.7	5.8	5.9	5.10	5.11
F4			F5		F6		F7	F8	F9	F10	F11

(D)	Very Difficult (VD)		Severe (S)				Very Severe (VS)		Hard Very Severe (HVS)		Extremely Severe (XS)

III	III+	IV−	IV	IV+	V−	V	V+	VI−	VI	VI ǀ	

									B1	B2	B3

The overall rating gives the grade, the rating of the hardest free move or pitch of the climb, and the rating of the hardest aid move or pitch. Thus, D-7 on the Long's Peak Diamond is *V, 5.6, A2.* If a route is normally done with direct aid

DIRECT AID CLIMBING OF INCREASING DIFFICULTY

Straightforward placement of anchors for direct aid, with placements generally as strong and reliable as protection anchors		Anchors more difficult to place and less reliable, but many are strong and all hold body weight	Aid placements generally hold body weight. Awkward and strenuous to put in. Rotten rock common.	Very strenuous and difficult moves required. Cracks marginal and discontinuous or rock very rotten. Difficult to make placements that will hold body weight.	Long stretches of very marginal aid with protection impossible to obtain over considerable heights. The limits of the possible for expert aid climbers.
Use of pitons, slings, etc. for hand- or foot-holds	Easy direct aid using *étriers*				
A1		A2	A3	A4	A5
A1		A2	A3	A4	A5
A1		A2	A3	A4	
A0	A1	A2	A3	A4	
Not applicable					

but has been climbed completely free, both ratings will usually be given. The East Ridge of the Maiden near Boulder might be rated *II, 5.7, A1,* or *5.10.*

Although many areas have clung to the YDS, attempts

OVERALL LENGTH AND DIFFICULTY

A climb that will consume a couple of hours for a team that can climb confidently at the required level of skill. Not more than 2 or 3 pitches of continuous 5th class.	A route requiring 3 hours to one half day for competent climbers. Generally 2 or 3 pitches of aid or very hard free climbing, or 3 to 5 pitches of moderate 5th class.	A fairly demanding route, taking the better part of a day for competent climbers. Usually more than 5 long pitches of serious 5th class or more than 3 long leads of aid or very difficult free climbing.	A long and serious route, generally requiring a full day or a little more technical climbing for a party that climbs confidently at the level of skill demanded. May require a bivouac even after an early start and without unexpected difficulties.	A very long climb requiring a good deal of commitment. High standard climbing for many pitches, normally requiring more than a day on the technical part of the climb.
I	II	Grade III	IV	V
I	II	Grade III	IV	V
No rating				
No rating				
Not applicable				

have been made to replace it with a less regional, or less illogical, or less something system. In the early 1960s, the National Climbing Classification System was born. It uses the same overall grade and direct aid ratings as the YDS, but substitutes the classifications F1 through F10 for Classes 1–5 and 5.0–5.10.

Many other systems have been proposed and compete for acceptance by climbers. One difficulty with any new system is that to be even remotely comprehensible, a system has to be *used*. The climber knows what a 5.6 climb is only by having done quite a few of them. New systems lack meaning because they have not been used, and for this reason added to natural orneriness, climbers are reluctant to change until the old system becomes wholly unworkable or the new system is better known by being validated somewhere.

The most recent entry into the field is the proposed international system, adopted by the U.I.A.A. and the American Alpine Club. This attempts to standardize ratings internationally so that one will, to a degree, be able to equate rock climbs from Yosemite to the Dolomites and mountaineering routes from Robson to Chamonix. The degree of success that will be achieved in this admirable enterprise remains to be seen. So far, the tone taken by the promoters of the system has apparently not impressed much of the climbing community in America. One reason for the lack of acceptance has been the failure to include an overall grade comparable to the Roman numeral in the YDS system; other improvements are negated by this factor.

Rating systems, by their nature, work far better for rock climbs than for those on ice and snow, where changing conditions vary a climb far too much to allow standard classifications to have much meaning. Rock-climbing ratings, however, generally assume good conditions, and great care should be exercised by climbers moving from areas with generally good weather to those where bad conditions are frequent. A little verglas on the rock or drizzle on the lichen can rapidly turn 5.5 climbing into a nightmarish survival battle.

In very difficult free climbing, several refinements have been developed that should be noted; 5.10 climbs have been subdivided in some climbing areas into a hierarchy of relative difficulty by adding letters, so that they are labeled 5.10a through 5.10d. The 5.11 climb has not yet seen such a division, but we have only to wait a little longer. Bouldering has developed its own corps of experts, who can make scarcely credible moves from overhanging protuberances. It has also earned its own rating system, discussed below.

PUSHING THE LIMITS

The general pattern of rock climbing in America for a number of years now has been that new techniques and virtuosity are developed first on local boulders, and then on the shorter-length climbs in areas close to home where the rock and the weather are good, and where one can just go home if the rain starts. Finally, the same level of climbing is tried on the longer climbs, and eventually it is taken to big, remote mountains.

A cataloguing of the current fashions in "games climbers play" would be pointless and rapidly dated, particularly if the sillier sorts of one-upmanship were argued. Some of the real challenges are worth mentioning, however. Many of the best climbers in the last few years have lost interest in aid climbing and have specialized in pushing very hard free climbs, with much sustained 5.10 climbing, and in climbing routes completely free that formerly required aid. One of the happiest trends of all is the elimination of pitons from the normal arsenal of hardware in most U.S. climbing areas. First "all nuts" or "hammerless" ascents are considered significant achievements by many.

A few current usages may give the flavor of modern American rock climbing in its more difficult (and competitive) manifestations. On short, hard free climbs, climbing a pitch "on sight" is an important distinction, meaning that the climber walked up to the bottom of the pitch and climbed it, rather than finally accomplishing the climb after earlier attempts, perhaps using a top rope or direct aid, until the climb was "wired"—the moves having been learned by heart. The standard of a climb is also sometimes reduced by using previously placed protection, sometimes put in by the same party using direct aid or *en rappel* from above. Fortunately, no one is hurt by this exercise, except the climber who thinks he has reached the standard of the climb by his performance or the local egomaniac whose self-esteem is inversely proportional to the number of people that have gotten up the hardest climbs he has done.

Solo climbing has recently begun to achieve an acceptance in the United States it had not previously enjoyed, at least on climbs of the hardest standard. Normally, one of several self-belay techniques is used. As yet none is really satisfactory. After some consideration, it was decided not to include discussion of self-belay techniques in this book, not because of any feeling that soloing is insane or immoral, but because its inclusion in a book of this kind would be certain to lead to solo attempts by people who are not experienced enough to be able to appreciate the dangers involved. Soloing is one of the ultimate challenges of the sport—something many of the best climbers feel compelled to try at one time or another—but, like Himalayan expeditions or climbing big, loose alpine walls, it is inherently dangerous. Also, in order to taste the strongest distillation of one side of the sport, self-reliance, another is wholly sacrificed—companionship. By the time a climber is ready for soloing on serious rock climbs, he will be aware of current self-belay techniques and will perhaps be able to improve on them.

Free soloing is the rather unfortunate term currently used for solo climbing unroped, not necessarily without direct aid. Clearly, this carries the challenges and dangers of soloing a step farther. The climber is unfettered by the constraints of roped climbing, which are especially boring when soloing. He is also unfettered if he should happen to take a fall. Those considering a free solo should recognize that many of the objective dangers inherent in climbing are far more hazardous to any solo climber, but especially to the unroped one. Even in the safest climbing areas, rockfall occurs, and a small rock hitting the unroped solo climber on steep terrain can knock him loose from his holds. This is only one example of the host of fortuitous incidents that would be of little consequence on a normal climb but could be fatal on an unroped solo. Again, this caution is not intended to condemn solo climbing, merely to point out what the rules of the game are. In climbing, as in life, luck plays its part in every outcome, in addition to skill and determination. The solo climber, besides demanding more skill of himself, is increasing the role of chance, and the unroped soloist carries the process a good bit farther.

One of the pernicious side effects of recent advances in technique has been the loss of fear of big routes by many climbers of moderate experience, who expect to be rescued if they get in trouble. As yet, no good solution to this problem has been found. In areas which are supervised by government agencies, perhaps a partial answer is to remove the responsibility for rescues from their shoulders.

BOULDERING

Tackling hard climbing problems close to the ground has always been a favorite conditioning exercise and campground sport for climbers, but it has recently been developed by some exponents into a specialized branch of climbing. The major American boulder expert, John Gill, has roamed the land from North to South and East to West working out acrobatic routes close to the ground, all requiring tremendous strength and control. Gill's own rating system starts above a normal 5.10 level with the B1 rating (hard 5.10 to 5.11), and goes to B2 (hard 5.11 to 5.12) and B3 (harder than B2). Actually, even boulder moves rated 5.10 are likely to be more difficult than similarly rated ones on a long free climb. This is because a move on a roped climb has to be considered as part of the whole pitch. A 100-foot layback consisting of a whole series of moves, none of which would be harder than 5.8 if alone, is not a 5.8 layback; it is much harder. The difficulty of the pitch results from its sustained nature. Bouldering problems, by definition, are 20 feet or less from the ground, so the moves will be rated on their own merits more strictly than on a longer climb.

Bouldering is often done with a top rope when the ground below is inhospitable, although there is clearly a difference between doing the route with or without a top rope. A person standing at the bottom can "spot" the climber, to reduce the possible seriousness of a slip. As with longer climbs, there is clearly an important distinction between a climb done on sight and one accomplished after long practice.

Many bouldering moves, like some of the hard free climbing that has developed from them, are made dynamically, the climber using some small holds to maintain momentum as he goes past, rather than as discrete holds used in separate moves. Some caution is needed when applying such techniques in exposed spots.

Both boulderers and hard free climbers frequently use chalk, resin, or other substances to dust or coat the hands. Chalk serves to absorb sweat, thus helping to prevent slipping. It also keeps the hands from chafing quite so much and has a mild antiseptic effect on scratches. Bouldering routes are very evident in many places, since the chalk spots can be followed. Taping parts of the hands is also common where much jamming is done on rough textured rock. It is sometimes advisable to remove the hairs before taping, and some people may also benefit from swabbing the skin with tincture of benzoin first to help prevent irritation from repeated tape removal.

11

SNOW CLIMBING

Just as on rock, there is a world of difference between easy snow slogging and work on high-angle routes. Progress to real competence goes more slowly in snow and ice climbing. The tremendous variations in the character of snow and ice, in their stability or lack of it, make long experience a vital factor in the climber's training. There is simply no way to learn even the basic tricks of snow in a short time.

The most important characteristic of the snow and ice is change; the most important rule for the climber is to go slowly. Protection is generally trickier to achieve on technical snow and ice than on rock, and it is often dubious at best. Thus, one's own safety and that of one's companions is often dependent on an accurate assessment of the conditions and the skill and competence of the party. Many other factors add to the seriousness of the climbing. Snow and ice climbing is often done in more severe weather conditions than rock ascents. Accurate appraisal of avalanche hazards is a matter of life and death. Psychological factors may be harder to weigh, because on a steep snow climb the borderline between calm and absolute terror tends to be small—a few degrees of extra steepness may suddenly rob the climber of his confidence 400 or 500 feet up.

All these points are merely cautionary. Snow and ice offer a whole new world of interest and challenge to the rock climber, and no one can consider himself a competent mountaineer until he is a reasonably strong snow climber. Climbing in off seasons in most mountain ranges is impossible without some knowledge of ice and snow. Snow climbs may offer the speediest, the safest, or the most interesting routes to the summit. In many areas one cannot even get to the high rock climbs without some steep snow work.

ROPE WORK ON SNOW

The technique of self-arrest has already been discussed at some length, but its importance cannot be overemphasized. As the mountaineer's experience grows, he will find himself traveling on steeper and more exposed slopes relying on the arrest for protection. Only practice and continual examination of conditions can justify this reliance on self-arrest for safety. When it is needed, the arrest must be executed faultlessly. Experienced climbers who are out of practice may be killed just as surely as the beginner who is out of his depth.

Group arrests have also been mentioned already, and this technique is a standard use of the rope in snow climbing. The climbers are roped together, so when one climber falls, his companions can assist in stopping his fall. But the climbers should always ask themselves if the group arrest can be trusted when individual arrest cannot.

Glacier travel is perhaps the most frequent occasion for depending on group arrest. Providing the snow is in condition for arrest (not too deep and soft), the climbing party can move together, relying on arrest to stop a fall by one person into a crevasse. On steep snow the same technique may be useful when short ice patches have to be crossed where arrest would be doubtful, but where only one member of the party will be on the ice at a time. Again, the technique may be useful in case of rockfall danger, so that if someone is hit by a rock and injured, his companions could stop a fall. (A more prudent course, if feasible, would be to avoid the danger area altogether.)

With all this said, my own faith in group arrest is rather shaken by the many cases of climbers yanking each other out of arrest positions all the way down a slope, as each man begins to stop successfully only to have the impact of a partner on the rope hit him and send him flying. Whenever there is any doubt, belays should be used instead. Group arrest techniques are probably best employed only on easier sections of a climb where individual arrest would be satisfactory, in order to avoid taking off the rope in between places where it is needed, or where there are less experienced members in a party. Whenever the group arrest is relied on, there should not be too much slack between the climbers—not more than a few coils carried by all but the top man, simply to allow for differences in pace to avoid having someone pulled off when his companion slows down. Nor should there be too much rope between the climbers; if only two are roped together, one should be tied off in the middle of the rope, so that they are climbing with just a half length between them. One climber simply coils half the rope, ties into the middle, and carries the coils over his shoulder. Normally, he will stay tied to the end so that the whole rope can be redeployed easily.

BELAYS ON SNOW

As on rock, when the consequences of a slip begin to seem alarming, the climbers start to devise methods to anchor themselves to the mountainside. In many snow-climbing situations this can be done with normal rock anchors. When climbing couloirs, for example, it is often possible to find nut or piton placements in the surrounding rock walls. Such positions are often desirable belay spots anyway, because they are likely to afford better protection from falling rock, avalanches, ice chips chopped by the leader, and the crampon points of a sliding companion. Similarly, rock islands in couloirs and snow slopes may provide good belay positions. Often a sling looped over a rock projection or a couple of nuts dropped into crannies will provide a quick and solid belay. Such positions should not be passed up on ice and snow climbs, even if their use results in short leads, since a great deal of time can be saved without sacrificing security by using them.

If a belay must be made on the snow itself, the most secure

method is a sitting belay anchored by a *snow fluke*. The fluke, also known as a *deadman*, is an aluminum alloy plate buried in the snow in such a way that when force is exerted on the attached cables, the plate will dive further into the snow, absorbing energy and becoming more securely buried as it dives. A well-placed snow fluke is very strong, providing security comparable to good rock belays; but considerable care is needed for its placement. On moderately steep slopes, maximum holding power is achieved by chopping out a stance for a sitting belay and anchoring it with a fluke. A standing hip belay anchored with a good fluke is also quite secure, and is the preferred belay on extremely steep snow. With sitting positions, the climber should insulate his seat by sitting on the pack or something else. Cold and cramped belays are a major problem on many snow climbs, and the belayer must get himself properly dressed before beginning work.

The other common snow belay, usually far inferior to the fluke, is the ice ax belay. This is very quick and extremely useful in many situations, but a good deal of practice is necessary both to use it well and to learn its weaknesses. At their best, ice ax belays depend on dynamic braking, because they are inherently not too strong, and they are often extremely tenuous. With parties of three or more, ice ax belays can often be used to anchor a belayer who is himself in a sitting or standing hip belay.

The climber should not be misled by the relatively low forces that may be developed in early practice belays on relatively easy snow. Such practice should naturally be conducted on terrain where self-arrest will stop a fall in case of belay failure. Much higher impact forces will be encountered, however, on the severe slopes where such belays are really needed, so practice should ultimately be extended to such slopes, with appropriate safeguards. Intermediate protection is often hard to place on snow and ice; long falls may produce impact forces that are as great as those developed in high-angle rock-climbing falls.

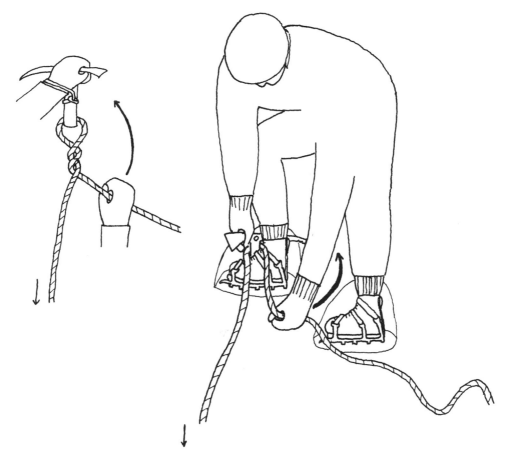

ICE AX BELAYS. At the left is the Saxon Cross belay, popularized in the United States by Larry Penberthy. The climber takes a three-point stance, with the feet in steps or kicked in below, one hand bracing the driven-in ax and the other manipulating the rope, which has at least three half-twists. The small arrow shows the direction of the climber. Braking is done by throwing the brake hand up as shown. In very hard snow, chop a deep groove for the ax before driving it in. In soft snow, stamp it hard first.

On the right is a boot-ax belay; this position is rather unstable on steep snow. To take in or pay out rope, the rope and ax are held as shown. To brake, the belayer moves his hand in the direction indicated by the heavy arrow. Both positions should be practiced thoroughly before they are used.

SNOW FLUKES

The "deadman" principle has been in use for some time. The idea is to bury an object in the snow or ground with a line tied round it, so that movement is resisted by a large area of snow or earth. The method is frequently used when sticks or rocks are buried in soft snow to pitch a tent in winter. Another example is the use of an ice ax for an anchor by chopping a long slot in hard snow, with a perpendicular slot for an anchor line. A metal plate can be carried for use in this way with a steel cable attached as a convenient anchor line.

The anchor plate becomes far more versatile, however, when the plate and line are placed in such a way that the plate is dragged farther into the snow when force comes on the cable, rather than simply pulling against the snow immediately in front of the plate. This allows the plates to be used safely in relatively soft snow, since one is no longer relying, as with a "deadman," simply on the resistance of the snow in front of the plate. Instead, the force is absorbed as the plate dives into the snow.

In order to achieve the proper diving, energy-absorbing effect, the plate must be placed in the snow at the correct angle. If the angle between the plate and the anchor cable is too large, the plate will simply tend to break out the snow in front of it when the force applied exceeds the strength of the snow. If the angle is too small, the plate may simply slice out of the snow rather than diving.

Setting the plate in the snow at the proper angle will ensure diving, but the best flukes have two cables attached so that the angle between the carabiner eye and the plate is maintained correctly. This is a real improvement in design, since the plate will tend to maintain the angle as it dives, even though the consistency of the snow may vary somewhat.

Another improvement is the one which gives the fluke its name, a refinement originated by Larry Penberty of Mountain Safety Research. The two sides are bent back at an angle. This provides side-to-side stability, because if one side strikes more stable snow and is pushed back, the other side will then present more area, and thus more resistance to the snow, so that the fluke will right itself as it travels through the snow. This principle works amazingly well. I have tested it with a number of people dragging the fluke in soft snow and radically changing the direction of pull. The fluke automatically righted itself and continued to dive.

There are several other design features important for belay plates in snow. Size is important. Smaller sizes are useful in harder snow, where large plates take much too long to place and will act as static anchors rather than diving. Larger plates are required in softer snow. Reinforcing bars along the top are helpful in preventing damage when the plates are hammered in, but they tend to reduce diving, so their value is questionable. Cables are definitely preferable to tied rope or webbing slings, because the cables tend to cut easily into the snow, which is vital if the plate is to dive properly. There should be a hole in the upper edge of the plate for installing a retrieving cord.

PLACING SNOW FLUKES

Proper placement of snow anchors is far more important than specific design. The best fluke made will pop out with a slight tug if the groove for the cable is not cut deep enough. The climber must first pick a site for placement. The snow must obviously be somewhat consolidated, even with a large plate; it can be soft, but light powder will not hold any strain. Equally important is the uniformity of the snow. If there is a soft layer on the surface and a much harder layer below, the anchor must be placed in the harder layer. Otherwise, when the plate begins to dive, it will glance off the hard snow below, and the belay may be lost completely.

Snow should be probed with an ice ax to be sure that there is not a much harder layer just below the surface. Loose, unconsolidated snow should be cleared. It is also a good idea to chop or stamp a small platform to place the fluke. With soft

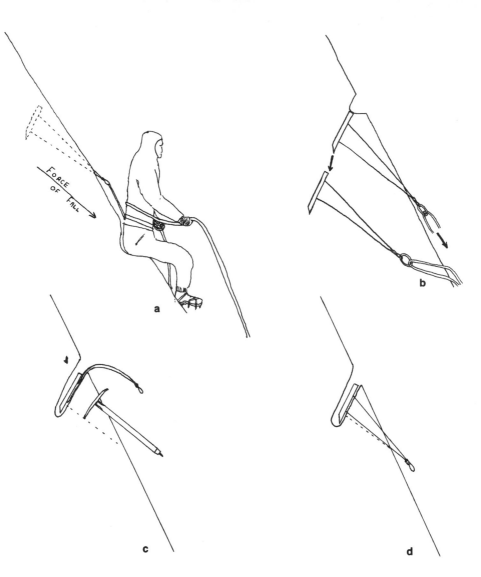

USING SNOW FLUKES FOR BELAYS. A belay using a snow fluke is shown in *a*. The action of the fluke in holding a fall is shown in *b;* the fluke dives deeper into the snow, absorbing energy as it goes. In soft snow (which is still strong enough to give good resistance), the fluke is stamped in, and the cables are pulled through the snow to the proper angle. Placement in harder snow is shown in *c* and *d:* a trench is first cut with the ice ax to hold the fluke, at an angle of about 60° to the slope. A slot must then be cut for the cables, as shown, otherwise the snow lip would simply act as a pulley, and a pull on the cables would pop the fluke out. Proper placement is shown in *d*.

snow the plate can then be stamped or pounded in, but with harder snow a slot will have to be cut with the pick of the ice ax. In either case the fluke should go into the snow at an angle about 30–45 degrees from the perpendicular, as shown in the diagram. A single cable plate should be placed at 40–45 degrees, while a plate with the angle fixed can be placed at 30–40 degrees. A slot must also be cut for the cable, at right angles to the plate. If the cable is allowed to ride up at all, the snow will act as a pulley, so that a force at the cable eye will yank the plate out instead of pulling it deeper into the snow. *The cable slot must be cut deep enough.* It is usually best for the belayer to be at least 4 to 6 feet below the fluke to prevent any upward pull; so if the plate has short cables, a sling should be added to lengthen the anchor line. The two critical factors in placing the belay plate are the angle in the snow and a sufficiently deep cable slot. Flukes can be arranged so that one backs up another, or in load-sharing systems to provide more security or more resistance in softer snow. In such arrangements they should be spaced some distance apart to prevent a failure of the same section of snow from affecting both plates.

Snow flukes are far superior in most cases to other types of snow belays and anchors. They have provided a great deal more security than was ever before available on snow climbs. In snow climbing, however, there is no substitute for experience and judgment. Snow that is too soft will not hold a fall no matter what kind of anchor is used, and an avalanche will carry belayer, anchor, and climber all to perdition.

ICE AX BELAYS

Most common among the various other types of snow belays is the ice ax belay. The fact that it is quick to place and does not require extra hardware gives it a great advantage. Unfortunately, in many conditions it provides dubious security at best. The ice ax belay depends solely on the strength of the shaft and the snow in front of it, so reasonably well-consolidated snow has to be reached for it to provide any security at all. Wooden-shafted axes are not trustworthy for this purpose, particularly if they have been in use for several seasons. Even new axes whose shafts have been tested to some minimum may break at the tangs. Laminated wood shafts are considerably more trustworthy than other wooden ones, since their strength is fairly uniform and the possibility of really weak shafts (when new) is eliminated. For ice ax belays, however, metal shafts are preferable.

Short axes may also cause a problem in trying to provide ice ax belays in any but the hardest snow, since the reduced length of the shaft clearly reduces the amount of snow resisting a pull. Whatever the length of the ax, the shaft must be imbedded as deeply as possible. The ideal condition is one in which the ax can be driven in to the hilt, but only with great effort. The snow cover is frequently not cooperative enough to provide such conditions, and is likely to be so soft as to provide little resistance or so hard it can barely be penetrated. A hammer can be used to drive the ax into the snow, but unfortunately most axes are not designed to resist such pounding.

In the standard ice ax belay, the ice ax is thrust as deeply as possible into a stamped platform and is braced with one foot and held down with one hand in such a way that arrest can be started if the belay fails. The other foot is braced below in the most stable position possible. The rope runs over the toe of the boot, around the shaft of the ax, and back over the instep of the boot, where it is controlled by the other hand. In case of a fall, extra friction can be obtained by wrapping the rope back around the boot. This belay is a dynamic one, however, if the fall is at all serious. The rope must be allowed to slide enough so that the belay is not pulled out.

A great deal of practice is required to use the boot-ax belay effectively. The rope has to be handled with one hand so that the other can stay on the ax head. Only a lot of practice in different snow conditions will give reasonable assurance that the fall can be stopped as quickly as possible, but without applying too much friction and losing the belay.

Obviously, gloves or mittens have to be worn if the belay is to be effective. If a metal-shafted ax is used, the pick should run across the fall line, so that the widest cross section of the shaft resists the pull. This gives approximately 25 per cent more strength from the snow's resistance to the ax. On the other hand, if a wooden-shafted ax is being used, the pick should point uphill to reduce the chance of shaft breakage.

Several other points should be noted in using the boot-ax belay. If there is a much harder layer of snow below the surface, belaying on the surface layer will tend to produce great leverage on the shaft, which may break or bend at the stronger layer. A stronger belay can be achieved by cutting down to the older snow before setting up the belay. Clearly, the belayer must face the path a falling climber would take. If the leader climbs above his belayer and crosses over him, the belay no longer exists until the belayer reverses his position. For this reason the climber must be equally adept at the boot-ax belay on either side. This belay will also become practically useless if the climber above should place intermediate protection.

If the snow is too hard to allow the shaft to be driven in well, a hole can be chopped, the shaft driven in, and snow then compacted around the shaft by stamping with the boots. Try to chop the hole so that the shaft will be well braced by unchopped snow and ice.

Another good ax belay uses the Saxon cross friction hitch around the shaft of the ax. The rope is given three half twists and the ax shaft passes through the bight and is driven into the snow. The belayer can then stand in a stable position below in kicked or chopped steps, bracing the ax head with one hand and handling the rope with the other. Braking is done by pushing the holding hand up so that the twists are pushed tight.

Of the two ax belays mentioned, the Saxon cross is generally preferable, because of the more stable and comfortable position of the belayer. However, in relatively soft snow it is possible to achieve more strength with the boot-ax belay.

OTHER SNOW BELAYS

Besides the common belays mentioned, various other possibilities are useful on rare occasions. Long snow pickets made of aluminum and having a tubular or T-shaped cross section are generally inferior to deadmen and snow flukes, but they are occasionally useful. The same strictures concerning the firmness of the snow and the dangers of leverage with weak upper layers apply to pickets as to ice axes. Unless the snow is hard enough to give a good deal of resistance to penetration, pickets should not be trusted. When hammering them into hard snow, many light taps of the hammer are better than harder, less frequent blows. The pressure from the blows melts the picket in. Finally, the sling or carabiner attaching the rope to the picket should be flush with the surface to reduce leverage; tying off with a sling is better than using a carabiner hole above the surface.

The deadman principle can sometimes be used to advantage, especially in very soft snow, by burying some object, particularly if a shovel is being carried for digging snow caves and the like. For example, a large rock on the surface which is not frozen in well enough for an anchor may be dug into the snow, tied off with a sling, and buried under tramped-down snow to provide a bombproof anchor. This method is sometimes quite useful at a moat on the side of a gully or snowfield, where a rock, ax, or pack can be gotten into the space between rock and snow, with the sling passing through a quickly cut slot in the snow.

Another possibility which is occasionally useful is the snow bollard, created by cutting or stamping a trench around a central pillar or mushroom of snow. The size required will vary with the consistency of the snow, but except in very hard old snow, it must be quite large—generally impractically so. With hard snow, however, a useful bollard can sometimes be chopped with an ax.

One type of crampon. This one is a fixed size with a hinge in the middle to allow the boot to flex, and it has neoprene-nylon straps for a binding. The front-points are for climbing on steep ice or hard snow. Other types are discussed in the text.

CRAMPONS

On snow which is too hard for step-kicking, progress is made by cutting steps, by wearing crampons, or both. A crampon is a metal framework with spikes protruding from the bottom which are strapped onto the feet to give good purchase on hard snow and ice. Considerable development is now taking place in crampon design because of the advancing standards in technical ice climbing, so new types are likely to appear each year.

Most modern crampons are made with either 10 or 12 points each. The 10-point models usually have all the spikes running vertically, although some have the front two points slanted slightly forward. These crampons are intended for use on moderately steep slopes with the feet stamped flat against the slope and all points in contact. With French crampon technique, which requires a great deal of practice and flexible ankles, such crampons can be used on extremely steep climbs;

but in America they are generally used only on moderate climbs. If this is the kind of climbing which is intended, 10-point crampons are probably the best type, since they are somewhat less tricky and dangerous to use than 12-point models.

The 12-point crampons look like the 10-point ones, except that they each have two additional horns protruding nearly horizontally from the front. These "front-points" can be used on very steep hard snow and ice to kick one's way up the slope. The 12-point models are nearly indispensable to those climbers planning routes steep enough to require them, but the additional hazards involved should persuade climbers who do not need the horns to avoid them.

Until recently, crampons have been hinged in the middle to allow the sole of the boot to bend. For most snow climbing and most boots this feature is necessary, but modern technique on technical ice and snow has resulted in the development of the rigid crampon, which forms a platform under the boot. A rigid design greatly eases the strain on the calf which is felt in front-pointing on steep snow and ice, and it also improves the penetration of the front-points. However, rigid crampons make normal cramponing on moderate snow less convenient, and they also require the use of very stiff-soled boots. Using rigid crampons with flexible-soled boots usually results eventually in the crampons breaking. For general mountaineering with normal climbing boots, hinged crampons should be chosen.

Perhaps the most important feature to be considered in choosing crampons is proper fit. The crampons should fit the boots perfectly. If the boots slop around on ill-fitting crampons, serious accidents can result. A really good fit will keep the crampon on the boot when the foot is picked up, simply from the friction of the side posts against the boot sole.

One of the problems with standard crampons is that a pair which fits one set of climbing boots may not fit another set of the same size, because the shape of soles is different. Also, if overboots are worn in cold weather, the crampons may not fit over them. One solution to these problems has been the development of adjustable crampons. The degree of adjustability varies a good deal with the manufacturer, so the same care in fitting is necessary with adjustables as with any other crampon, checking the fit with all combinations. The adjusting mechanism has to be very solid; it is advisable to check the reputation of any particular brand to see how well it has been holding up under use. The adjusting feature, despite its advantages, does add extra points of possible failure. For front-pointing, all joints should be as tight as possible to damp vibration, which reduces point penetration.

The straps are as important as the crampons themselves. They must be sturdy and foolproof. A broken strap in the middle of a climb is too unpleasant a possibility to be risked. Neoprene-coated nylon straps have the advantages of being strong and durable, not stretching when wet, and not freezing up. Crampon straps should be pulled tight enough to hold the crampon on firmly without restricting circulation in the feet, an ideal sometimes hard to meet. The hardware on the straps should be as easy as possible to work with cold, mittened fingers without sacrificing security.

CRAMPONING

Crampons provide the basic means of climbing on hard snow and ice, and their use is a basic mountaineering technique. Even where they are not essential to a climb, crampons can eliminate hours of step-cutting on hard snow, allowing far more rapid progress. And even when steps have been cut, crampons give better footing, so their use is generally preferred, except when snow and ice sections are simply short interruptions of a rock climb.

Just as with step-kicking, when cramponing on snow it is important to keep the weight of the body directly over the feet. Leaning into the slope will tend to break out the crampon points. The crampons, however, should be slapped flat against the slope, requiring the ankles to bend at the same angle as the slope. This takes strong, flexible ankles and a good deal of practice, but there is no substitute in snow and ice climbing. On moderate slopes one can walk straight up or traverse up diagonally. Generally, the climber alternates to put the strain on different joints and muscles. Some thought and care should be given to the danger presented by a falling climber to his companions below when choosing a line. Crampons are very dangerous indeed.

As the climbing gets steeper, the feet can be splayed out to either side for direct ascent, or one can face sideways. The sidehill position comes quite naturally when actually climbing, although it may not seem so at first glance. One simply stands across the slope, raises the lower (outside) leg above and slightly forward of the inside, plants the crampon, and moves up. When the ankles tire, the climber switches sides.

Remember that the keys to smooth climbing with crampons are an upright position and crampons flat on the slope, with the ankles flexed appropriately. If the points are in on one side only, a slip will eventually result. Much practice on moderate slopes or short, steeper pitches should be undertaken before attempting a long climb on steep hard snow. Snow and ice can become very scary a few hundred feet up, even if additional difficulties are not encountered.

Particular care is needed when one first begins using crampons to avoid catching a point in one's clothing or gouging the opposite leg. Snagging a pant leg can result in a nasty fall even if the leg is not laid open. For the beginner it is difficult to overemphasize this point. Walking is instinctive, and a person may have the habit of bringing one foot very close to the opposite leg in certain maneuvers without ever noticing it, since without a crampon nothing will catch. When the irons are first strapped on, the novelty will promote caution, but a few hours later as things feel more natural it is very easy to catch a gaiter or pant leg.

Descent on crampons is considerably easier than ascent, except on extreme climbs. A step-kicking descent on hard snow while facing the slope is difficult, because the human anatomy is ill-suited to the maneuvers required. With cram-pons, however, facing out allows easy flexing of the ankles, pointing the toes downhill. Again, the crampons should be stamped in flat on the slope so that all points bite, and the body should be upright. The main difficulty is psychological. The exposure is all too apparent when one is facing out, and the temptation is to lean back into the slope—just the wrong thing to do. The climber must train himself to stay in balance, heel-ing down when that is possible, and when the snow gets too hard, planting his crampons and ax carefully and walking down in an upright position.

HANDLING THE AX

Proper use of the ax is part of crampon technique as slopes get hard and steep. The climber must, as always, be prepared for self-arrest, but the ax is also used to provide a hold, either for balance or actually to support the climber's weight. If the climbing position allows, the ax should be held in a way that facilitates arrest. When other positions are used, only sufficient practice will enable the climber to shift the ax for arrest as needed. Obviously, when arrest is doubtful, ropes and belays should be used; but even when belayed, the falling climber should attempt to arrest.

12

ICE CLIMBING

Serious ice climbing in America is currently undergoing a revolution comparable to the one which occurred in rock climbing with the development of hard alloy pitons in Yosemite by John Salathé. The interest in technical ice climbing has grown tremendously in the past few years, and standards are beginning to be pushed. Some of the techniques which are currently being popularized are new, but most have been around for quite a while. Because this growth in popularity has only recently begun, equipment and technique are far less standardized than in rock climbing, and route possibilities have barely begun to be explored.

THE MEDIUM

Ice is as varied in composition as the snow from which it often develops. The distinction between snow and ice is frequently not at all clear. Ice may originate in the weathering, packing, and metamorphosis of the snow cover. The two also merge in other ways; snow can cover a layer of ice, or be covered by one. The separation of snow and ice climbing is mostly one of convenience, and fine points are unimportant for our purposes.

The two major ways that ice in the mountains is formed are by the metamorphosis of the snow cover, and by the direct freezing of water. It is again not particularly worthwhile to make too fine a distinction since the two means of formation

272

The slow, safe way up ice—cutting a line of large steps in a diagonal line up the slope.

are often mixed, but the general difference is apparent enough to the climber.

Most ice which is formed directly from snow retains a granular character and tends to be fairly uniform. Glacier ice of this type is similar to the *névé* (compacted snow in transition to ice) from which it is formed. Névé and granular, whitish ice generally make for easy step-cutting and cramponing. When ice of this kind gets older or is subjected to more compression, as with older glacier ice or gully ice, it becomes more similar to water ice, except that it retains its uniformity.

Water ice is normally much harder than névé unless it is full of air pockets or softened by warm weather. Since it tends to be tougher than compacted névé, water ice is usually more difficult for either cramponing or chopping steps, but it often provides more reliable protection when ice screws or pitons are placed in it. Water ice can be very tricky, however. It often forms in a series of sheets, which may be poorly bonded to one another and can peel off in great pieces at the slightest provocation. Water ice in waterfalls may also contain a lot of air pockets combined with sheet ice.

Ice formed in some gullies and sections of glaciers by compaction where there is a lot of falling debris is frequently extremely hard, and may be mixed with grit and fragmented rock, forming a surface not unlike concrete. Such "black ice" makes for tough climbing and it usually occurs in areas of high objective hazard as well.

CLIMBING TECHNIQUES

The most time-honored of ice-climbing techniques is cutting steps with the ice ax. Many classic ascents here and in Europe were made in this fashion, and the abilities of some of the hard men of the past to cut steps steadily by the thousands is legendary. Cutting steps has tended to go out of fashion somewhat in recent years, for several reasons, some good and some bad. Without question it is the slowest and most energy-consuming way one can use to get up a slope. Given a proficient wielder of the ice ax, however, it is not nearly as time-consuming as one would expect—a strong chopper can cut and move almost at normal step-kicking pace. Such feats require practice and conditioning, and the lack of these ingredients is one of the bad reasons for the decline in chopping steps. The knack, even if it is rarely used, is one well worth acquiring. There are occasions where steps *must* be made, and they are not likely to be good learning situations. There are also numerous times when the ability to chop steps quickly and efficiently is useful, even if not absolutely essential.

The most elegant and efficient way to climb ice is by using the so-called *French technique*. Basically, this is the technique of keeping the crampons flat on the surface of the ice, planting all the points, and flexing the ankles so that the body remains in balance. The ice ax is used in various positions for safety and to maintain the balance, but the legs do the work. The ankles have to be very flexible and strong, and the climber's sense of equilibrium honed to a fine point; but this technique is faster and less tiring when it can be used because it depends on skill and rhythm rather than strength. The method has been developed to its highest level by the French—partly because it is ideally suited to the névé conditions often found in France. It has been around in North America for a long time, but has recently been repopularized by Yvon Chouinard.

The final basic ice-climbing method is generally known as *clawing* or *front-pointing*. Crampons are used which have sets of points protruding in front of the toes of the boots. The front-points are kicked into the ice, and the climber stands on them, using them like small toeholds. Handholds are provided by other implements jabbed into the ice; the climber is able to move up very rapidly, making small but adequate holds as he goes without having to chop steps. Front-pointing is easier to learn than French technique, because it requires neither the flexible ankles nor the niceties of balance of the latter. However, it is considerably more strenuous and quite slow if used for descending.

The fast, committed way up ice—front-pointing using an ice ax and an ice hammer.

PROTECTION

Protecting a pitch on technical ice requires even more judgment and understanding of the climbing surface than on rock. The strength, hardness, temperature, uniformity, and depth of the ice layer all have a bearing, as do the air temperature and sunshine. On good ice, the climber has the advantage that he can place appropriate protection anywhere, not having to rely on cracks or pockets. Mostly, though, placing protection on ice is more difficult and its quality more dubious.

When possible, protection should still be placed in rock. In gully climbs it is often possible to place conventional protection along the walls or to drop a sling over an imbedded boulder. Such solutions are obvious enough when they are possible and need no further elaboration.

Perhaps the most difficult ice to protect is névé. Small flukes or "deadboys" should be used whenever possible; driving in a picket is also sometimes possible. Even when the ice is quite hard one can nearly always cut a slot for a fluke, but this is so time-consuming that the procedure often has to be reserved for belays. In ice it is vital that the slot for the cables is cut deep enough and that the angle of the main slot is correct, because the anchor will probably not dive in ice, and it will pop out if not placed correctly. If the ice is hard enough, long ice screws and pitons (around 12 inches) will be fairly reliable. Placement methods are discussed below, but it is particularly important in granular ice to chop away any unreliable surface layers, otherwise tremendous leverage will be placed on the lower, reliable part of the screw or piton.

In either very cold or warm weather the ice on the surface is likely to be unreliable for protection. In extreme cold, the surface is likely to be chilled and much more brittle and easily shattered than the layers below; in warm weather, it becomes soft. Whenever possible in such conditions, the surface layer should be chopped away with the ax and the protection placed in the more solid or less easily shattered lower layer. If the ice is not thick enough this may not be possible, and anything placed in the poor surface ice should be looked on with appropriate skepticism. Layered ice causes similar problems when bonding between layers is not strong. Sometimes it is possible to chop down to better ice below.

Whenever protection is placed on warm days, or particularly when warm sunshine is beating down on the climb, even if temperatures are below freezing, the climber must remember that a screw or piton can conduct heat very well, sometimes melting the ice around it enough to make it very insecure. This difficulty should be particularly watched for with pitons that have to freeze in solidly to develop any strength. Chopping the surface ice away, placing the protection in the hole, and then covering the exposed metal with ice chips will prevent this type of melt-out.

Melt-out will also be caused by pressure on the piton or screw, particularly if the ice is only at freezing temperature. Thus, belays which put tension on the anchors should be used with care, especially if the ice is wet.

SCREWS

Screws have several major advantages as anchors in ice. Since they don't rely completely on hammering to get them into the ice, they are often easier to place without shattering it. The threads will resist a direct outward pull, and they also tend to bite into the ice at the back of the hole (where the ice is usually strongest) when leverage is exerted on the eye of the screw, thus resisting the force tending to pull the screw out. Screws can sometimes be placed with one hand. Finally, they can normally be removed by screwing them out, whereas pitons nearly always have to be chopped out.

The standard ice anchor has become the *tubular screw*, which is available in lengths varying from 6 to 12 inches. These are strong and can be placed in most types of ice, ranging from quite soft to very hard. They are more reliable than solid screws, because for a given weight, they have a larger cross section and thus are less likely to shear through the ice under the stress of a fall. A slot in the threads is an improvement in design which helps the ice core inside the tube to clear.

One of the biggest problems with the tubes is that in cold weather the ice core in the center freezes in place, and the screw cannot be used again until it is cleared. A tool made of coathanger wire should be carried to help clear the tube; but in really cold weather the screws have to be warmed with one's hands or inside clothing before the ice core can be dislodged.

Several design improvements could be carried out on tubular screws, and there are rumors that a properly made screw may soon be on the market. Clever climbers can make some modifications themselves. The front of the tube should be beveled so that all the displaced ice clears to the inside in order to reduce the screw's tendency to split brittle ice. The teeth and the opening near them should also be designed so that displaced ice clears to the inside of the tube. Greg Lowe has suggested coating the inside of the tubes with Teflon so that the ice will clear more easily. Chouinard is reportedly working

Placing a tubular ice screw. After chopping away any poor surface ice, a starting hole is made, and the screw is turned into the ice slowly enough to prevent shattering. The screw is put in at a slightly descending angle. Considerable practice is needed to place screws effectively and to learn their limitations.

on a screw in which the tube will be narrower at the cutting end, with a bevel toward the rear, so that it will clear easily. A similar method is used with the screws made by Mountain Safety Research.

Tubular screws currently available on the U.S. market are all made by Salewa, although several U.S. manufacturers will probably have models fairly soon. The Salewa screws are quite reliable, with no reports of breakage except under high loads. They do vary somewhat in hardness, and therefore more than they should in holding power; but they are uniformly fairly strong, even with an outward pull. Because of variations in the quality of ice, the climber must always be wary of placing too much trust in any ice screw, but a well-placed tubular screw in good ice will hold over 2000 pounds.

Placing tubulars is relatively simple in soft ice, when the angle is not too steep. A small hole is made with the pick of an ax or hammer after any rotten ice on the surface has been chopped away. The screw is turned as much as possible by hand, then leverage is used to twist it in with the pick of an alpine hammer or an ax. When the ice is soft enough and the climber secure, the ax can sometimes even be used like a carpenter's brace to turn the screw in rapidly. When the ice is harder, however, a lot of leverage is required, and tapping with the hammer may be required to help melt the screw in without shattering the ice. Turning slowly will also help to prevent brittle ice from splitting—the colder the ice, the more slowly the screw has to be turned. In very hard ice it is sometimes difficult to get the forward teeth of the screw to cut at all, and a good deal of hammering may be required along with turning to get it in.

The only other type of anchor currently available that is in the same range of strength as the tubular is the *lag screw*. Lengths of 6 or 8 inches are very strong, and lags as short as 3 inches provide some useful holding power. The biggest problem in getting lags now is to find some with closed eyes which have the uniform quality desirable in climbing equipment. The hardware store variety usually have eyes that are merely bent closed. These have to be tied off, and their quality must

As the screw is placed, a center core of displaced ice normally is forced out. The part of the core remaining in the tube usually freezes in and must be removed before the screw can be used again.

be regarded with suspicion unless a large number from the same lot are purchased and some of them tested. European versions made for climbing are hard to get these days, and they also vary a good deal in quality. Those with welded rings should be regarded with particular suspicion. Despite the problems with lag bolts, the properly made ones are very strong in good ice, even stronger than tubulars. They are also quite cheap. They require a good deal of screwing because of the pitch of the threads, but since they are solid, there is no freeze-up problem.

Tubular and lag screws should be considered the standard types of protection on hard ice. Other devices are significantly weaker and must be used with discretion. Hopefully, improved equipment will appear in the next few years which will offer strong protection that is easier to place; but for the moment, protective methods on ice have to take equipment weaknesses into account.

Another type of screw that is very useful has a narrower cross section than the tubulars and lag screws, and thus tends to shear out of the ice more easily. Less force is required to place them, however, so they can sometimes be put in with one hand, a very useful attribute when the climber is front-pointing on steep ice. Since they are solid, they also avoid the problem of core freeze-up, and can be placed even in very hard ice.

The original screw of this type was the *Marwa*, nicknamed the "coathanger" because of its rather disturbing construction. A similar one was made by Stubai. These screws have rather low holding power at best because of their small cross section and soft metal. They also have a well-deserved reputation for faulty workmanship. They should never be regarded as really solid anchors, but they can be occasionally useful for direct aid, for placement on steep ground to allow enough security so that both hands can be used to put in a tubular, or to protect a couple of hard moves over a bulge, with more reliable protection placed above. Only 7- and 5-inch Marwas should ever be used for these latter two purposes. The little 3-inch ones are strictly for direct aid.

The *Charlet-Moser* is a more reliable screw of this type. It is stronger and less subject to breakage than the Marwa, but it must still be regarded as much less secure than a tubular or a good lag screw. Also, although the workmanship is better than on Marwas, there have been incidents of Charlets breaking because of weakness in the metal, probably due to improper hardening. The breaks generally occur at the threads, and the climber may not be aware of the breakage. Other screws of this type that are available in Europe have had similar problems.

These warnings should persuade the climber to be cautious about depending heavily on any one screw of this type to protect a possible hard fall. The incidents of breakage would be more than enough reason to advise against using them at all if there were anything else available that would do the job.

Under current conditions, however, climbers are stuck with what is on the market.

PITONS, WART HOGS, AND SUPER-SCREWS

In some situations, there is a distinct advantage in being able to drive in protection on ice. Both hands may have to be used, as they usually do when placing a screw, but the situation is generally awkward for a shorter time. Often, a hole can be made in which the piton can be inserted with one hand, so that it can then be driven in while the other hand is holding a clawing tool or a chopped grip. After a piton has been driven a short way it also becomes an adequate hold that can be used for balance while the piton is being driven home.

Ice pitons have been made in a number of shapes over the years, ranging from blades similar to a horizontal rock piton to channels and tubes. They are usually rather heavy and have less holding power than screws, and they are largely obsolete, though some climbers carry a few, finding them useful in certain situations. Be particularly wary of those with welded rings, which are of questionable reliability. If a piton with a welded ring is used, it should be tied off around the shaft.

Several problems arise with standard ice piton designs— that is why screws were developed. Pitons generally have to be chopped out if they are well placed and have frozen into the ice. This is very time- and energy-consuming. Screws, on the other hand, can usually be twisted out. Unless they are very well frozen in, pitons may give very little resistance to an outward pull, so that they may accidentally be pulled out as a climber falls past them; this is particularly true in soft water ice. Finally, pitons tend to split out hard brittle ice, which means they are difficult or impossible to place securely when climbing on water ice in very cold weather. This is true of screws also, but generally the ice must become much colder before screws become hard to place effectively.

Several newer piton designs have solved some of these

problems. Two designs are made to be driven in and screwed out. The *wart hog* is made with bulges forming a rough spiral so that the piton can sometimes be screwed out, although it may freeze solid and require chopping. The bulges also improve holding power. The *Nester super-screw* has a fine screw thread and can nearly always be screwed out. Early models were somewhat prone to breakage in the threads because of hardening problems and sharp notches, but the later ones seem to be about as reliable as the wart hogs. The holding power of the two is approximately the same for both perpendicular and outward pulls; the Nester is somewhat lighter. Super-screws have much better holding ability with an outward pull if they are screwed in the last few inches. For maximum strength, the carabiner or sling should go around the shaft rather than just through the loop.

Even with good placements, neither the Nesters nor the wart hogs are as strong as tubular screws, so, like Charlet-Moser screws, they should be used with discretion. Neither piton will work in extremely hard water ice, since the ice will tend to split out if it is too brittle. As the ice becomes harder, the pitons can be placed with rapid, lighter taps. The usual rule of clearing off brittle or rotten surface ice will help; but in very cold ice, the climber will have to return to tubular screws.

Two further types of pitons were developed several years ago by Henry Kendall and others. They are very useful in some situations and are worth mentioning even though they are not commercially available at the moment. One is the *beak*, which is essentially of the cliff-hanger form (a Lowe Alpine Systems modification is called the *grippling hook*). The illustration shows a beak I made from chromolly steel. Since the blade has a sharper curvature than the radius formed by the arm, the hook will tend to stay in without being dependent on freezing into the ice. This characteristic is particularly useful for soft ice, where melting under tension tends to make many pitons gradually upend and fall out; for thin ice; and on steep sections where easy placement is essential. They work in ice only a few inches thick, unlike any other ice protection. Beaks can also be placed, after some practice, in very hard ice, since a hole can be chopped with an ax or hammer pick, and the piton tapped in without fracturing the ice. The holding power of models with beaks of over 3 inches is very good in water ice. Removal is easy with an upward tap of the hammer. When placed for protection the beak should have a sling attached to prevent rope drag from dislodging it, as with many nut placements.

The second type of piton is known as a *thin.* It is straight, but with deep teeth on the shaft on the lower side near the eye and the upper side near the tip, so that a downward pull tends to set it more soundly, even with considerable melting. These are good only for direct aid or for protection on short falls. Three-inch lengths are good only for aid, and 4- to 6-inch lengths can be used for protecting short sections of a climb. They are very quick to set in many kinds of ice. Kendall's design used an eye above the shaft to prevent the piton from camming itself out if it has turned part way out. The Lowes developed a modification they call a *snarg,* using a curved blade which would lock into the ice and be stronger against a straight pull. Unfortunately, the snargs are also somewhat harder to set and remove.

Both these pitons are extremely useful if one is climbing ice over 80 degrees, when speed of placement becomes critical

A home-made beak, for protection in ice. It is normally placed with a sling girth-hitched around the blade and the sling passing down through the lower hole in the arm. A carabiner is clipped to the sling. The beak is discussed in the text, along with other types of ice protection.

because of the strain of maintaining a stance while one is trying to get in a tubular screw. A good deal of experience and practice are required to use beaks, thins, and snargs effectively for protection. When properly placed, they are often very effective; at other times they should only be trusted for temporary security or aid while a tubular screw is put in.

CLIMBING ICE: FRENCH TECHNIQUE

French technique is by far the fastest and most effortless method of climbing ice and hard snow, when it can be applied. In principle, it is also very simple, since it consists essentially of balance climbing with crampons. The body remains upright over the feet, and in balance. It may be leaned slightly onto the ax when one foot is being moved, and the ax is used for a hold in the same circumstances; but the ax and hands are used mainly for balance, with the legs doing most of the work. There is no shortcut to learning French technique. Security and confidence on steep, hard ice will come only after a great deal of practice. The ankles have to become strong and flexible, balance must be acute, and use of the ax has to be sure.

The first rule for proper cramponing (other than front-pointing) is to plant the crampon flat on the slope and leave it there until the next step is taken. Edging with the side of the foot, as one does on rock, works very poorly on ice. All the vertical points should bite in, except when one is using a small step or platform where only the front part of the boot will fit. Even then, the points on both sides of the foot should be planted firmly on the ice—if the points on only one side are in, they will often break out as the climber moves. To make all the points bite, the ankle has to flex.

Planting the crampon is quite easy on hard snow or soft ice, particularly at low angles. In these cases, the points are easily driven in simply by the weight of the body. In fact, this technique works best on the névé and granular ice for which it was designed, where crampons bite relatively easily. On harder ice, technique must become more precise—the crampons have to be planted, driven straight against the ice. They should then be left where they are as the body moves. Edging the crampon as the weight shifts will tend to break the points out, particularly on very hard ice. The harder the ice and the steeper the slope, the better one's technique must be to climb in balance. A climber with really good form will be able to climb far steeper ice without resorting to front-pointing or step-cutting.

Much can be said about the angle of the feet to the slope while climbing this or that angle of ice. Actually, all this comes rather naturally with practice, providing one strives to climb in balance and flex the ankles. The particular position will vary constantly as little depressions are used to advantage and as the climber moves to find the best route and to change position to avoid muscle strain. Clearly, also, the more adept the ice climber becomes, the higher angle he will be able to maintain in any given position.

Generally, when the angle of a slope is low, one can walk straight up it. As the angle or hardness of the ice increases, the feet will have to be splayed out to both sides (*en canard*—like a duck). When the ice gets steeper, or when a relief in position is wanted, the climber begins to traverse diagonally upward, with the feet pointed across the slope. On still steeper ice the same position is maintained, except that the feet point somewhat downward to relieve the degree that the ankles have to be bent sideways. Some writers claim that the climber can, on even steeper slopes, face outward and back up; in my experience, this is an absurd position except on the descent. It is nearly impossible to climb in and to get out of so that one can again face toward the slope.

For foot positions and the ice ax positions which will be discussed below, it is almost meaningless to give particular angles of ice. Technique varies with the kind of ice as well as with the slope (as already mentioned). Walking up 50-degree névé in balance is one thing; doing the same on 50-degree boilerplate is quite another. The angle of a slope is generally very hard to judge unless it is measured with an inclinometer.

Climbing ice in balance (French technique). Here, the climber's weight is on his right (inside) foot with the ax used for balance, pick in the slope, and the left foot being moved up. The crampons must be planted flat against the slope, with the ankles more flexed the steeper the slope is. Climbing in balance is best suited for hard snow and soft ice.

Most people guess that a slope is much steeper than it really is, so descriptions are unreliable. Finally, when a slope is cupped or stepped, the angle of a step may be far different from that of the ice as a whole.

Several ice ax positions are commonly used to assist in cramponing steep slopes. On easy angles the ax is simply used like a walking stick. Normally, the pick should point to the back of the hand, so that it can be readily gotten into arrest position. As the slope becomes steeper, when the climber traverses the ax is normally held across the chest, with the outside hand gripping the pick as for an arrest, and the inside hand holding the shaft near the spike. With the spike jammed into the slope, the ax can be used for balance and for some upward leverage. This cross-chest position is extremely useful over a wide range of slope angles. One may just touch the spike occasionally for balance on easy climbing, or use it as the third point of support in difficult sections.

Often it is helpful to drive the pick of the ax into the ice. Properly planted, a good pick is very strong this way, as long as it is not moved around too much. With the pick sunk in, the shaft or sling becomes a good hold under tension, the pick can be held in one hand and the shaft in the other, or the pick can be held with one hand alone, either like a dagger or below the shoulder in a mantle-type hold. Often a climber will sink the ax head and use the ax in all these ways in succession. The head can also be sunk by the hand holding it, though this requires more effort and is used more for front-pointing than in French technique.

The ax can also be rested directly on the ice—pick into the surface and spike end resting on it for stability—with the hand pushing on the handle. This method can be used ascending or descending, mainly for balance.

Again, practice with these methods will make them seem

The left crampon has been planted, and the right is moving up. Then the ax will be moved.

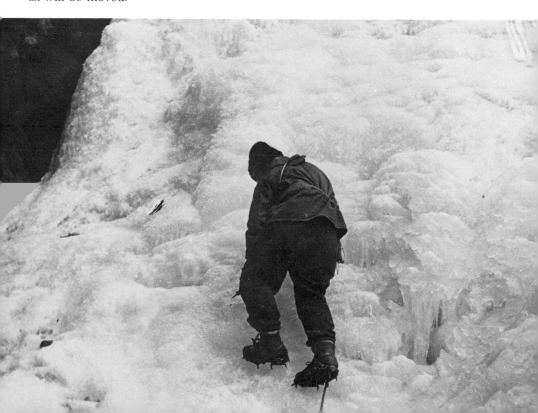

far more natural than any amount of explanation. In French technique the ax is used to provide security while one foot is moved. When both feet are planted, the weight of the body should be squarely over them while the ax is moved. Unless the climber is securely in balance, a minor chipping out of a piece of ice is likely to precipitate a fall.

STEP-CUTTING

Because it is time-consuming and tiresome, step-cutting is always avoided when possible; and because of the improvements in technique and equipment in the past few years, it is used far less than it once was. Still, there are many occasions when the climber must resort to this method, and proficiency is very desirable.

Technique in cutting steps will depend on the angle and consistency of the ice and the type of ax used. Steps are easier to cut in névé and granular ice, more difficult in water ice—particularly when it is very hard. Traditionally, the pick of the ax is used for step-cutting, but the climber will have to experiment with his own ax, since many axes chosen for their anchoring and clawing characteristics have picks that are poor for step-cutting. The adze is often best for cutting certain kinds of steps, because it can be directed more precisely.

Normal steps are cut diagonally up the slope and should be large enough to accept the whole foot. Even though crampons may be worn for additional security when climbing in steps, it is usually better to practice cutting them wearing just boots. This way, it is easier to tell when steps are cut correctly —high enough so that the leg is not forced out, with the bottom of the step angled slightly downward on the inside so the foot doesn't tend to slip out. Steps are cut larger at the end of a line, when the climber wants to change direction. The steeper the slope, the farther ahead the steps will have to be cut. In hard snow or granular ice, a few strokes should suffice once one has had enough practice. Two or three vertical strokes are made with the pick, then one or two horizontal ones to break out the step, and finally a sweep with the adze to smooth the step. In water ice, things are more difficult, particularly if the ice is brittle and tends to flake out.

One method of saving steps when climbing up diagonally is to combine crampon technique with step-cutting, chopping steps only for the uphill leg. The steps should be of adequate size. The outside foot is planted flat on the slope, pointing somewhat downward, as usual when cramponing on steep ice or snow. The position is surprisingly stable even on quite steep terrain. The move up to the next step is made with the aid of the anchored pick of the ax.

Steps may also be cut straight up a slope and used like a ladder for both hands and feet. The width of such steps is minimal of course, but they may have to be cut quite deep, depending on the angle of the slope. Such steps are generally cut with the adze, though in hard ice particularly a couple of strokes with the pick first may speed the process. When proper clawing tools are not available, these steps are the standard method of bypassing short sections of vertical or overhanging ice. For this purpose and any other where a good handhold is needed, the steps must be cupped downward to provide a secure grip for the mittened hand.

Any type of step can be abbreviated—small ledges or little cups may be chopped quickly and used to give crampons a somewhat better bite. Such techniques have to be used with caution, however. One of the advantages of steps is that until they are melted out or filled in with snow (either of which sometimes occurs very quickly), they provide a good route of retreat. Downclimbing generally is more difficult than coming up, particularly if the climbers are unnerved, and tiny steps that may be adequate for upward progress are likely to be useless on the return. Since it is far easier to cut steps going uphill, that is the time to make the steps for your descent.

FRONT-POINTING

The technique of front-pointing on extremely steep ice, developed largely in the eastern Alps and in Scotland, is rapidly revolutionizing ice climbing on severe routes in America

Front-pointing in a gully, using an ice ax in one hand and the other hand for balance.

and Canada as well as in Europe. Equipment for technical ice is now being developed which makes possible a new standard of high-angle ice climbing.

Actually, the revolution in ice climbing is largely dependent on changes in attitude and equipment. Equipment is discussed later in the chapter, but it must be recognized that it is fundamental. Good clawing tools make front-pointing on 60 degree-ice feel far more secure, but on vertical ice of any height they are essential if chopping buckets or direct aid are to be avoided.

The technique of front-pointing is not difficult to learn in its basic form. The front points of the crampons are kicked into the ice and left without jiggling them around. With some styles a slightly downward motion in the kick sets the points better. Learning when the points are set securely in various kinds of ice is a matter of experience. One can simply use the ice ax for a handhold in the standard anchor position, one hand on the head and the other on the shaft.

More commonly, the climber uses one tool in each hand, so that three-point support can be maintained at all times. Only one foot or one hand is off the ice at any given time,

The feet during front-pointing. The points must be kicked in and then held steady. Moving the feet around may break the points out. On vertical ice, holding the upper body against the ice is critical.

allowing far more secure climbing and also permitting the climbing of ice at angles where the climber is overbalanced without his having to resort to chopping holds. In the early development of front-pointing technique, the ax was commonly used in one hand and an ice screw or piton in the other. This method can still be quite useful for short pitches on an alpine climb, but as more front-pointing was done on steeper ice, specialized tools were gradually developed. Ice daggers were tried first to replace the piton. Such devices were made essentially obsolete by the development of modern clawing tools.

EQUIPMENT FOR ICE CLIMBING

One of the biggest problems in discussing ice-climbing equipment is that there is far too much dogmatism based on limited experience. In Europe advocates of French technique and front-pointing often get into this difficulty, which results mainly from the fact that the two schools were developed from different climbing conditions. Obviously they overlap, but each has special advantages. Even greater difficulty arises when one is trying to design *the* ideal ice ax or *the* perfect ice hammer. One can change technique in the middle of a pitch but one can hardly carry three or four axes to meet different conditions. Added to this inherent problem is the natural inclination displayed by the designer and manufacturer of a particular piece of gear for his own stuff. Finally, there are natural differences in technique and personal preference among climbers. Just as there are differences in preference for various styles of rock-climbing shoes depending on technique and types of rock, so there are disagreements over the proper length for the handle of an ice ax and various other matters. These controversies are exacerbated by the fact that modern ice climbing is far less developed than rock climbing, and thus more experimental.

There is generally more agreement on the subject of crampons than anything else, so we will dispose of them first. All modern crampons designed for technical ice have twelve points each. The length of the points varies somewhat. Shorter points are advantageous on hard water ice, since crampons do not penetrate deeply and additional length merely makes the climber feel as though he were walking on stilts. Longer points are ideal for snow and granular ice, and for conditions where a layer of rotten snow overlies ice and short points don't go through to bite the ice properly. For most American conditions a compromise length has proven suitable.

Front points should be slanted down from the horizontal around 30 degrees. Points that stick straight out would require tremendous tension in the calf to keep them in the ice. The points should also be held rigid by a front bar in the crampon to reduce vibration that shatters ice when they are kicked in. Rigid crampons with no hinge action in the middle help to reduce this vibration also, as well as providing a platform for the foot which is less tiring to stand on. However, as mentioned earlier, rigid crampons are less suitable for general climbing and require an extremely rigid boot to prevent breakage. Breaking a crampon on technical ice is a serious matter. Hinged crampons are more tiring for front-pointing, but better in the other respects. One compromise that has been tried with moderate success is to hinge the crampon around the arch of the foot rather than the ball; this allows some flexing and is less prone to breakage than a rigid crampon, but it gives better support on steep ice than a crampon hinged farther forward.

The advantages and disadvantages of adjustibility have already been mentioned in the preceding chapter. Most climbers and companies have opted for at least partially adjustable crampons. For our purposes it should be sufficient to say that on technical ice a good fit between the boot and crampon is essential.

ICE AX DESIGN

If the beginner recognizes that many contradictory demands are made on the ax, controversies over design will take on a truer perspective. A pick that is ideal for a handhold while front-pointing is not likely to be as good as possible for step-cutting. A handle long enough for efficient cutting on moderate slopes, going up or downhill, will be longer than convenient in many other situations. Examples are innumerable, but the point is simply that there is no ideal ice ax. Each climber will have to weigh the characteristics he wants, his climbing style, and the kind of climbing he does against available axes and possible modifications.

In terms of length, about the only point on which there is general agreement is that the handle should not be much longer than the distance from the palm to the floor. This length is very convenient for general snow work and for ice ax belays, and it is still preferred by many mountaineers. It can be inconvenient, however, on steep technical ice and snow, and such a long ax can be cumbersome on rock pitches of mixed climbs. Thus, many technical climbers prefer a shorter ax. Lengths between 25 and 30 inches, depending on the climber's height and style, are still usable for most standard purposes including French technique, but tend to get in the way less than full-length axes. Some climbers prefer still shorter axes, sometimes down to 12 inches, for front-pointing and cutting steps on steep ice walls. Some metal-shafted axes are now made with extensions to allow short technical axes to be lengthened for normal snow climbing and French technique. The weaknesses of wooden shafts, particularly in ice ax belays, have already been discussed.

Probably the most important feature for the technical climber is the droop of the pick. In the anchor position in French technique, and especially for use in clawing while front-pointing, it is the droop of the ax that makes it stay in the ice. An ax with insufficient droop has to be held in by the climber (with leverage by the hand or by pulling the spike end of the handle out), or it is kept in simply by the grip of the teeth. This is rather absurd, since the idea is for the ax to hold you in position rather than vice versa. The droop becomes particularly critical when the ice gets really steep and really hard.

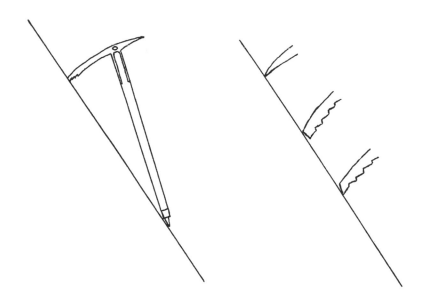

DROOP OF AXES. At the left is an ax as it might be held for a hold on hard ice, with only the tip penetrating. The curvature of the pick is greater than that of a circle that would be formed with the ax handle as a radius, so the pick tends to stay in. At the right are three types of pick. The pointed one will bite because it is pointed. The center one will skate unless it is driven hard enough for the lower edge to catch. The lower one will bite immediately.

The principle of correct droop is illustrated above. There are two interdependent factors—the downward curve of the pick itself and the length of the handle of the ax (or hammer). In most circumstances, the spike end of the shaft will serve as a point of rotation, and it will often be resting directly on the ice. If the radius of curvature of the pick is greater than the length of the handle, the pick will tend to rotate out of the ice; if the radius of curvature of the pick is less than the length of the handle, it will tend to rotate in. Even though other factors (teeth, holding the handle out, etc.) may keep the improperly curved ax in, the climber will have a far more stable hold if the ax has sufficient droop.

One of the points which is often ignored by manufacturers of modern axes intended for technical climbing is the importance of the length of the handle. At the time of writing, only Grivel was selling an ax which had a more extreme curvature for each shorter length. This is extremely important, particularly on water ice. If the curvature is just right for a 70-centimeter ax, it is not just right for a 55-centimeter one. One point about modern axes is clear: the radius of curvature of the pick near the point should never be greater than the length of the handle.

There are several other points about droop that are somewhat less clear. An extreme droop (radius much shorter than handle) has several advantages: properly placed, it will tend to bite more as weight is put on it and may feel very secure; one can even pull out on the pick while moving up on vertical or slightly overhanging ice. On the other hand, the more extreme the curvature, the more the pick will tend to stick in névé and softer ice, making removal difficult. It will be poor for chopping steps, unless the cutting blade is wide; and if the droop is really extreme, ice may tend to break out under the tool.

What all this means is that climbers in different areas with different kinds of ice are likely to find that different degrees of droop work best. An ax with essentially perfect droop for the soft ice found in the Sierra Nevada will tend to pop out of the hard winter ice of the Rockies a little too easily. On the other hand, a point that hangs into that hard ice well enough really to inspire confidence is likely to be far too hard to extract when sunk into granular hard snow.

Ice hammers of one kind or another are carried by most high-angle ice climbers as additional clawing tools and for the placement of pitons and screws. Not infrequently, the climber may carry three implements—most frequently two hammers and an ax, but the variations are numerous. Two hammers may be used for clawing on extremely steep stretches, and the ax reserved for use on lower angles, for example. One very useful technique when two hammers are carried is to hammer one in with the other for a temporary self-belay or for direct aid while protection is being placed. A sling is usually attached to the hammer for the purpose. Some axes have hammering anvils that allow them to be used this same way.

A number of kinds of hammers are available, but all of

them have a pick generally like that of an ice ax on one side of the head, with a hammer head replacing the adze on the other side of the head. If there is a shaft and a spike like those on an ax, the tool is usually called a *North Wall hammer.* Others, like Chouinard's *Alpine hammer,* have a short handle like a piton hammer, with no spike. The droop on a hammer is even more critical than on an ax, particularly if the handle is very short, because small bulges in the ice effectively change the point of rotation significantly.

Only recently have tools begun to appear which are suitable for modern ice climbing on hard water ice. Many climbers in areas with this type of ice have found it necessary to modify existing equipment—by changing the pick shape, by having picks drooped farther and then rehardened, by adding or deepening notches. Such modifications sometimes weaken the tools and pose the danger of breakage in critical situations. Unfortunately, it is not only home-modified implements that have shown an inclination to break at awkward times. Much of the commercially manufactured gear has such poor-quality control, particularly in hardening, that breakage has been common.

A few other features are worth mentioning in ice ax and hammer design. The spike, if any, should be quite hard, so that it can be kept sharp when needed for French technique on hard ice. Many spikes are much too soft and need to be filed almost constantly. A narrow angle of cleavage (the sharpness of the pick viewed from above) will go into hard ice much more easily and with less shattering than a wider angle, but obviously the pick must not be so thin that it is weak. As I said in the chapter on arrests, my own experimentation has led me to agree with Penberthy that in difficult arrests on hard snow and ice, the lower edge of the point of the pick should hit the ice first, or the point will tend to skate. This is of no importance if the ax will only be used on ice of such high angle that arrests will never be relied on; but approaches generally steepen gradually, so this is rarely the case. For this reason, I feel that chisel picks should always be filed so that the lower edge will hit first. Many climbers vehemently dispute this argument.

Teeth are very helpful in an ax or hammer which will be used for clawing or in the anchor position. To be effective teeth must be deep, extend almost to the tip, and come back some distance. There are great variations in adze design. The most important features seem to be that the adze does not droop very much and that it is sharp. An adze with a broad, chisel-like cutting bevel works poorly on hard ice. A carabiner hole is frequently useful for various purposes, but it should not be used for belaying. In the undesirable case of the pick driven in for a belay, it should at least be tied off as close to the ice as possible to reduce leverage.

Slings, wrist loops, and the like on axes are the subject of considerable disagreement, simply because no one has succeeded in finding a very satisfactory solution. Most climbers find the prospect of losing an ax in the middle of a serious climb too horrifying to risk leaving the ax completely unattached to the body. The old maxim that one must always "hang onto the ax" is fine as far as it goes, but the main principle which has made modern extreme climbing feasible is to build back-up safety devices wherever possible. Further, when screws and other protection are being placed, one frequently must let go of the ax briefly. It can be slipped between the pack and the back, passed through a carabiner on the hardware loop, clipped with a carabiner through the head (if there is a carabiner hole), or, in the case of a short ax, put in a hammer holster. Regardless of the method, in my opinion it is still best to have either a sling attached to the ax head or a wrist loop which slides on the shaft as far as a stop screw. Clearly, these do not have to be used all the time, but much of the time they should be.

A sling going to the head (through the carabiner hole or in a girth hitch) should be of a length which allows the hand and wrist to be locked in at the end, as with a ski pole strap, a few inches above the spike. Then when the ax is used for a reaching hold going over a bulge, one does not have to depend completely on the grip of the hand. If the sling is twisted around the shaft, it will serve as a good brace for the wrist when cutting steps one-handed. I find it convenient to sew or tie another loop in the sling about 6 inches up from the first to give a brace farther up the shaft. Obviously, the sling can be clipped to a carabiner when desired to attach it to the body. The wrist loop is standard on many longer axes. It is short and convenient for many purposes. If the spike of the ax is jabbed in or held against the snow or ice in the cross-chest position for balance, the ax has to be reversed across the body when the climber turns to traverse in the opposite direction. The wrist loop stays on the same arm, merely being slid to the other end of the shaft when the ax is shifted. At other times, however, a sling is more convenient. When the ax is being used for a cane in places where losing the ax would be dangerous—on glaciers, for example—the sling can be clipped into a hardware loop and still be moved back and forth from one hand to the other without the nuisance of switching the wrist loop. Some prefer to leave the ax unencumbered with wrist loop or sling and to attach a sling to the head or prusik to the shaft. I would rather put up with the sling when I don't want it than run the risk of losing an ax in a bad spot.

Helmets are even more important for safety on ice than on rock. Besides possible injuries that might be prevented during a fall, the helmet protects the head of the belayer from chunks of ice chopped off by the leader. Finally, there has been at least one belayer killed with crampons when the leader fell from directly above.

13

DIRECT AID CLIMBING

Direct aid climbing means using something other than the pressure of hands and boots on the rock to make progress. In American climbing, any use of protective hardware for holds or for resting points in the middle of a pitch is generally considered to be direct aid. This is of some importance for those who want to repeat a route in its original style, and it makes a good deal of difference to the rating of a pitch. The use of a nut for a handhold or stepping onto the head of a pin may make a move much easier, but the climber will be deluding himself if he decides he can climb 5.9 because he has hauled himself up a route rated as a 5.9 free climb by using a chain of fixed pins as holds.

Although there has been a strong movement in many climbing areas recently to push free routes that were formerly done on direct aid, there are still many established routes in most regions that require aid, whether for the entire climb or for a few moves. Aid has become a standard part of the repertoire of American climbers, and proficiency in direct aid climbing is required for many of the classic routes in the country.

While any use of shoulder stands, rope tension, or protection as holds is considered to be direct aid from the viewpoint of style, aid climbing generally uses more sophisticated methods for making progress up pitches where free climbing is not feasible. There are many variations in these methods, which depend on the technique of the climber, the sorts of routes he does, and so on. The methods described here are effective, but they can hardly be considered definitive. Each climber will

Direct aid climbing using only nuts. Here the climber is moving out of the sling in which his left foot is standing to make a free move.

find his own tactics in direct aid climbing, and will make modifications that suit him. I have not tried to describe all the variations and tricks that might be included, but rather to give a general approach on which the climber can build his own repertoire.

ETHICS

The ethics of aid climbing have been the subject of various hot debates ever since it was invented. Most of the arguments have been tempests in a teapot, and the only ethical questions that will be considered here are those having to do with degradation of the rock. It ought to be each climber's business how he wants to do a route, providing he does not spoil the climb for others. Thus, if a party aids an entire climb that was originally done free, their style is certainly poor; but this is of little interest except to the climbers themselves, providing they do not litter the route with bolts and piton scars that were not there before.

Even more than with free climbing, the main ethical and aesthetic problem confronted in aid climbing is the destruction of routes by people for their own ego gratification. The question often comes down to one of equipment. Nuts, runners, camming, and similar techniques leave essentially no mark on the rock, and therefore, to my mind, pose no general ethical problem. On the other hand, when a bolt is placed, it permanently defaces the rock. If pitons are driven and removed on a popular route, they may completely destroy a crack system in a relatively short time.

The techniques of aid climbing without using pitons have only begun to get a lot of attention fairly recently, but they have come a long way in that time. Several of the big, hard

Misuse of bolts. The two lower ones have been chopped, and another has been placed above. The rock is increasingly disfigured as the childish competition between choppers and placers continues.

walls in the country have been done without using pitons and some without hammers. Pins have not become obsolete for use in aid climbing, but they should now be considered a last resort, particularly in popular climbing areas, just as bolts generally have been thought of for years. There have been major exceptions, but as a rule the idea of bolting up blank walls has met with distaste, if only because if this tactic is used one can ultimately engineer one's way up any reasonably sound rock that is not plagued with objective dangers. With skill, verve, routefinding, and uncertainty eliminated, climbing would become a poor thing. Thus, bolt ladders have generally been used reluctantly to link up natural lines, and they have usually been placed with restraint dictated by the feelings of the local climbing community at the time. Some fine souls refused to place them at all, but even among users, it has generally been felt that bolts were only justified when the best climbers and techniques could not surmount a blank section any other way. So it has nearly always been considered improper to place new bolts on an established route, except to replace a bad original or sometimes to add a second bolt on a belay stance or rappel anchor. If similar attitudes are applied to the use of pitons, the problems of route degradation will be minimized.

AID SLINGS

Direct aid pitches are usually climbed using short ladders variously known as *étriers, aid slings,* or *aiders.* In the United States these are normally made of 1-inch flat webbing, and they can be either tied or sewn. Commercially sewn ones are available if one doesn't mind the price; they are a little lighter and less bulky and are normally reinforced at points of heavy wear and stiffened so that they are easy to use, but they cannot be adjusted for individual reach and climbing style.

The number of steps, length, and size of webbing used to make *étriers* are not critical; advantages will vary with the individual and the climbing. Because webbing wears quickly, 1 inch is preferred for safety and strength, but for slings carried to do brief sections of aid on long routes that go mostly free, lighter and less bulky material may be better. The distance from one step in a sling up to the next should not be an unmanageably long reach or movement will be strained and awkward. The whole sling should be long enough so that when the

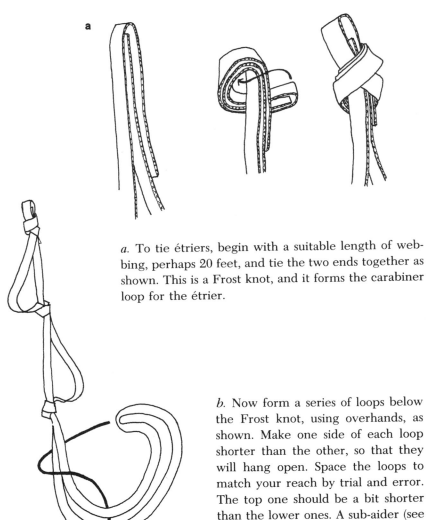

a. To tie étriers, begin with a suitable length of webbing, perhaps 20 feet, and tie the two ends together as shown. This is a Frost knot, and it forms the carabiner loop for the étrier.

b. Now form a series of loops below the Frost knot, using overhands, as shown. Make one side of each loop shorter than the other, so that they will hang open. Space the loops to match your reach by trial and error. The top one should be a bit shorter than the lower ones. A sub-aider (see text) can be tied in through the carabiner loop, with or without a Frost knot.

climber stands in the top step of one and reaches at full length to place the next, the lowest step in the second is within easy reach. Obviously, many factors combine to make one length of step and number of steps convenient for a particular climber. The slings shown in illustration *b*, opposite, will work well enough for most climbers; modifications can be made after a few climbs if they are needed.

Four-step slings are perhaps the most commonly used, but five steps are preferred by many. Robbins's idea of attaching an extra short, lighter *étrier* to the top of each of the two main ones is very helpful, particularly on overhanging pitches. Only the top two or three steps are duplicated with the *sub-aiders*. I now generally use two four-step slings with sub-aiders and carry one extra three-step sling for occasional use. Tall people would be more likely to use five step slings with sub-aiders and a four-step extra.

BASIC DIRECT AID

The standard procedure for leading an aid pitch is for the leader to stand as high as possible in his slings and put in a nut, sling, piton, or whatever. He then tests his placement, attaches a carabiner to it, and clips an aid sling on with another snap link. He steps into the upper sling, generally bouncing slightly to test the placement further before relinquishing his hold on the lower sling. He retrieves the lower *étrier* and moves up on the new one. When his waist is at the level of the placement, he clips his rope through the carabiner that is attached to the placement, moves as high as possible, and repeats the process.

Climbing on aid is actually rather complicated at first, and smoothness requires a lot of practice. Since progress is slow at best, confident and efficient movement is essential. There are also a number of qualifications and fine points that must become part of the working knowledge of the climber. Even the second must be reasonably well aware of the problems faced by the leader and of the mechanics of aid climbing, because the second has a considerably more complicated job than he does on a free pitch.

LEFT

Basic direct aid sequence. Here the climber is standing in a sling, sitting back on his right foot, which is in a higher step in a sub-aider (or a second direct aid sling). The rope goes through a carabiner attached to the anchor on which he is standing. He is placing a nut in the crack above.

RIGHT

A carabiner has been clipped into the nut, and the climber is clipping an *étrier* to it with another carabiner. (An *étrier* should not normally be clipped directly into a nut or piton with only one carabiner.)

Rope drag is even more of a problem on direct aid pitches than on free ones, and the leader must exercise a great deal of care to minimize it. Clipping the climbing rope directly into the placement may not always be advantageous; it is often necessary to use runners or extra carabiners to reduce rope drag. Sometimes it is worthwhile to reduce rope drag by not clipping the climbing rope through some aid placements. One may reach back and detach the rope from an earlier placement after clipping it through above, particularly if the upper one is bombproof and the lower one dubious. Obviously, the leader should be circumspect about reducing rope drag at the expense of protection.

The method described assumes that the gate of the carabiner used to clip into the nut or piton will open under body weight. Since the climber is already standing with his weight on the 'biner when he clips in, this is essential. Some carabiners, especially older ones, will not open when weight is placed on them. If the gate will not open, or if the snap link will be pulled hard against the wall by his weight, the climber will

LEFT
The climber tests the new nut before shifting his weight to it by bouncing on the *étrier* that has just been attached to it.

RIGHT
Having moved onto the higher nut and *étrier* and climbed up so that his waist is level with the placement, he clips the climbing rope through the carabiner that is attached to the nut. In some cases additional slings or 'biners would be used to reduce rope drag. The climber is now ready to reach as high as possible and make another placement.

either have to use an extra carabiner to clip in or clip the rope through the 'biner before moving up onto it. The disadvantage of clipping in first is that the leader has to pull out enough slack in the rope to reach up to the next protection point and then back down again, so that if the placement pulls out when he steps onto it, he will fall an extra 3 or 4 feet before the belay even begins, putting that much extra strain on the lower anchor. In practice, the climber will have to learn to use his experience and good sense. Sometimes it is more convenient to pull out the slack and clip in before moving up, and if the lower placement is really solid, this may cause no particular problem. When one is standing on a very shaky anchor, it may be best to pull out the slack needed to clip in above in order to avoid straining against rope drag on a poor step. As a rule, however, it is best to clip in when one reaches the level of the anchor.

Tension with the climbing rope is a time-honored form of direct aid, and it is still sometimes useful. Basically, it tends to be an awkward and inefficient device, and when the leader is on steep or overhanging sections, so that he needs to lean back against his anchor to make the next placement, it is generally better for him to provide his own means of support. The standard rest position in aid climbing is to sit back on one foot while standing on the other extended one. This position may seem unlikely, but with a little practice it becomes second nature. When the climber is standing higher in his slings, he may require tension at his waist harness to free or to rest his arms. A sling attached directly to the harness or swami can be easily clipped into the anchor to provide this tension. Convenient refinements that may or may not be worthwhile are a sling with a line of knotted or sewn pockets (a *daisy chain*) so that length can be adjusted at will, and a hook (*fifi hook*) instead of a carabiner for easier removal.

PLACING NUTS FOR DIRECT AID

Nuts are somewhat trickier to use for direct aid than for free climbing, but the advantages are great. Because there are so many more anchors used on an aid climb, faster placements and faster cleaning will yield substantial savings in time. Aid climbing is often rather strenuous, and the use of nuts rather than pins reduces the effort that has to be expended considerably.

Two main problems immediately face the climber when he starts to use nuts for aid. The first is that his range of choice is more limited than when protection is being placed on a free climb. He cannot say to himself, "Gee, this is getting hairy and that last sling was about fifteen feet back." Since his progress depends on hardware, placements will only be between 1 and 5 feet apart. The consequences are that many of the nut placements in aid climbing will be more marginal, and that a far greater selection will have to be carried, since more will be placed and one can rarely reject a possible slot because the proper nut is not available.

The second problem immediately apparent when using nuts on aid is that the usual solution for eliminating directional difficulties is not available—one can't just hang a long sling on the nut and forget it. A great deal of care has to be exercised in placing the nut to anticipate the changing direction of pull throughout the time the climber will be using that nut, and the pull itself must then be adjusted accordingly. If the section is slightly overhanging and the nut is good only for a pull straight down, another placement will have to be made before the climber gets high in the slings, for high up he will have to put a lot of outward pull on the anchor. More nuts than pitons generally have to be placed to climb a given pitch.

The ideal design of the nuts will be somewhat different for aid climbing. Wire slings that are only occasionally useful in free climbing give a welcome extension of reach to the aid climber. Nuts that are threaded correctly for free climbing with rather long slings cannot be used for aid, without some modification, since the clip-in point is farther from the nut than the climber can reach. When nuts are to be used for aid, the slings either have to be tied off close to the nut or an extra sling or pocket should be attached to clip in aid slings. I often add a lightweight, very short sling to each nut for this purpose.

Copperheads and wedge nuts are available with short wire slings for aid. Short slings of light webbing or rope (or in extreme situations, parachute cord) can also be looped over the top of the nut, although leverage generally makes this undesirable. Extra short slings or high stops knotted or sewn in are to be preferred. In any of these cases, when the nuts are also to be relied on for protection after the climber has passed, the normal length sling should be used for threading the climbing rope, and standard procedure should be observed to prevent its being dislodged.

With nuts and other aid techniques, all placements do not have to be strong enough for protection. A number of the smaller nuts are, in fact, designed mainly for aid and could not

LEFT
A nut rigged for aid by having an additional short sling tied in. The long sling is used for protection on both free and aid climbing, while the short sling allows the climber to clip his *étrier* close to the nut for maximum reach.

RIGHT
Moving off aid to free climbing is often tricky.

possibly hold a fall of any length. The aid climber is free to use all manner of marginal jams, taking special care that a small shift of his weight does not dislodge the nut. Once familiarity has begun to breed contempt, however, it is important to remember that it is occasionally necessary to have a really strong anchor, so that the house of cards is never allowed to become too high.

There are various ways of stacking nuts which can be quite useful, particularly in wide cracks. The general principle of such jams is illustrated below. Some combinations produce such good wedging action under tension that the placements will work even in parallel-sided cracks. When well placed, some stacking arrangements will provide good protection, but extreme care should be exercised in trusting these arrangements to hold leader falls, since they are easily dislodged by a jiggling rope.

Lowe's cam nut is excellent for direct aid and can be very useful over the range it covers; but it should be used with care for protection since it is easily shaken loose in many placements. Prototypes using double cams have solved this problem. Unfortunately, they are not yet available on the market at the time of writing.

Stacking nuts. A downward pull on the left chock tends to expand the whole arrangement and jam it tighter.

CAMMING

The system of using steel cable to jam with pitons or other wedges was suggested in a *Summit Magazine* article by Greg Lowe, and it has proven to be extremely useful for direct aid. The illustrations show camming with pitons, but a range of lighter and cheaper aluminum wedges will work as well. The

LEFT
A camming placement. Here the cable of a wired nut is used with an angle piton. The piton is wedged in by hand over the cable, and the cable is then jerked to set the wedging action. Pulling on the cable pushes the piton more securely against the rock. The cord secures the piton against loss in case the cam pulls out.

RIGHT
Cable cams are often stronger in an upside down placement like this than the piton would be if it were hammered in, and the rock is left unscarred.

piton is pushed in by hand over a swaged loop of steel cable. Jerking out on the cable serves to wedge both into the crack, and stress on the cable simply wedges them more strongly, up to the limit of strength of the rock or the cutting of the cable. As with nut and piton placements a good deal of practice is required to use the technique effectively, but it works well in many situations where nothing else is very good—in overhanging cracks, for example. The possibility of cutting the cable should always be considered in examining placements that may have to hold a fall, and one should try to use larger sizes of cable (³⁄₁₆ of an inch and up) in these situations. When smaller sizes are used for protection, it is often possible to stack one or more cables behind the first to provide a back-up in case of cutting action on the first. Tying the piton or wedge to the cable with webbing or cord prevents loss.

SLINGS

Slings can be used for protection in aid climbing just as with free climbing, but as a rule sling placements over nubbins can rarely be used for aid. Generally speaking, if nubbins are large enough to accept slings, the section will go free. Occasionally, of course, a sling can be pitched over a chickenhead that is out of reach and then used for aid, but this is the exception rather than the rule.

Large numbers of short slings of ½- or ⁹⁄₁₆-inch webbing are very useful in aid climbing for a number of purposes, ranging from tying off anchors to use above the top step of the *étrier* to gain an extra few inches (a *hero loop*).

CLIFF HANGERS AND LOGAN HOOKS

In extreme direct aid it is sometimes possible to hang an aid sling from a hook over the edge of a flake, ledge, or other small protuberance. The three shapes currently available are all useful in some circumstances. The newer Chouinard cliff hangers have the superior base design of the Logan hooks

made by Ed Leeper. A loop of webbing should be used on the bottom of the hook and a carabiner clipped to this. Care should be taken not to put any more rotational stress than absolutely necessary on the hook when moving on it. Precautions are also necessary to avoid losing the hook and everything attached to it in case of a fall or when moving off the hook to the next placement.

NAILING

Until quite recently, direct aid in North America was practically synonymous with nailing pitons; and even though more and more climbers are avoiding this style of climbing when possible, there are times when nothing else is suitable. The basic principles of piton placement have already been discussed, and nailing in direct aid is not a great deal different from placing pitons for protection, except that on hard direct aid routes much more tenuous placements may be used.

Because of the number of pitons placed on direct aid that is nailed from bottom to top, cleaning can be very laborious and time-consuming. This problem should be far less applicable today, since even when pitons are used, nuts or camming can be employed on much of the route, thus minimizing both the possible damage to the rock and cleaning. But on occasions when long stretches of nailing are done, climbers often try to make a point of not "overdriving" their pins. Bashing away at chromolly pitons in good rock often makes them very difficult to remove, and on aid climbing this should be avoided when possible. However, concentrating too much on shunning over-driven pins is likely to result eventually in a very spectacular fall, the leader pulling one peg after another and thus proving that none are overdriven. It is not always possible to tell how good a piton is, even when one has driven thousands, so when there is any doubt at all, the piton should be hammered in until it is solid.

Unfortunately, one is not always in a position to decide whether or not to overdrive a pin. In difficult nailing, it is hard enough to get one to stick at all. Clearly, any pitons that can be driven only part way must be tied off. The more tenuous the nailing becomes, the more important it is to reduce leverage as much as possible. Sometimes when there are hollows inside a crack one can wedge a webbing or wire sling into one of the spaces and then drive the piton to eliminate any leverage effect.

Pitons can be stacked, just as nuts can, either with other pins or with nuts. This method is particularly useful in shallow cracks. It is sometimes possible to wedge a nut in against one side of a crack and to drive a pin between the nut and the other side. More frequently, pitons will be stacked with each other.

A tied-off Leeper.

Stacked bongs in a very strong placement. Ideally, it is best to have the open sides facing the rock, as with the right hand piton here.

Stacked Lost Arrows.

A tied-off angle. Here simply looping the sling over the pin worked well.

A copperhead nailed into a crack with an angle for a strong placement that otherwise would have required a bashie.

An angle and a long dong (the longest Lost Arrow) stacked and tied-off.

They can be laid lengthwise together, back-to-back or with the eyes together, depending on the types of pitons. Angles can be stacked fitted together, but they tend to be hard to remove, and this method is hard on the pitons. Angles of all sizes are best stacked by crossing, as shown in the illustration on the next page. Many combinations will work. For example, Leepers stack beautifully with angles. The climber will have to experiment with different combinations to get a feeling for those that will work. Don't forget to tie everything together with a sling, so that you won't lose pins if they pull out accidentally.

KNIFEBLADES, RURPS, AND CRACK TACKS

Just as there are nuts which are too small to be seriously trusted for protection, so there are a number of pitons made primarily for aid climbing. *Knifeblades* are relatively thin horizontal pitons, and they are in the borderline area. Properly placed, they can be quite strong, but one would not cheerfully take a long leader fall on one. Most currently available knifeblades in America are made by Chouinard; the long one, solidly driven, is strong enough to protect a fall, but the short one should be used strictly for direct aid.

Rurps (realized ultimate reality pitons), invented by Chouinard, and *crack tacks* are tiny pitons designed to be hammered into seams in the rock and cracks that have just begun to form. They work essentially by chopping their way into the slightly rotten edges of the seam. When they are hammered in correctly they will often support body weight. These represented a major breakthrough when they were invented because they allowed the climbing of nearly blank sections of climbs that would previously have required bolting.

When placing a rurp or tack, it is important that they are hammered straight in. Glancing blows will crumble the edges of the rock, and every grain may be needed. It is also helpful to hold the pin between the fingers in such a way as to damp vibration as it is being hammered in. Obviously, leverage has to be minimized with these pins. Normally, a loop of webbing

ABOVE
Angles incorrectly stacked. Doing this ruins the pins and makes them hard to remove.

LEFT
Angles correctly stacked.

is tied through the bottom hole for vertical placements, and a knot is jammed in the center hole when the orientation is horizontal. Sometimes simply looping a sling over the blade works best. A good deal of practice is required before rurps and crack tacks can be used safely. Rurps work better in hard rock; while the thicker, more chisel-shaped crack tacks hold better in some types of softer rock and fit into many corners.

BASHIES, MASHIES, AND TRASHIES

These are pieces of soft metal, generally aluminum of various sizes, which are smashed with a hammer until they conform to some pocket in the rock. They do permit passage of some sections without bolting, but they are only occasionally justified. They are often difficult to remove without almost chopping them out of the rock (or falling on them). If bashies are used at all, they should generally be threaded with wire slings, since if they are left in place and threaded with nylon, the sling will soon rot out leaving the bashie not only unsightly but unusable (a "trashie").

Nuts are sometimes used in a similar manner, although they rarely require a great deal of beating to make them stick in the obscure hole that inspired the attempt. *Copperheads,* which are malleable and have a single cable swaged in, are particularly suitable for this type of placement. If one is trying to climb a route clean, smashing a nut in like a piton clearly is inappropriate.

BOLTS

Since placing a bolt permanently defaces the rock, it is a far more serious matter even than putting in pins. Pitons only scar the rock slightly when they are placed and removed properly, unless a route is heavily climbed, in which case repeated driving and removal of pins can be more destructive than use of bolts. Thus, a climbing community as a whole may decide that in a particular area pitons should be avoided if at all possible, or that pitons or bolts should be permanently placed. For the individual climber, however, the decision to place a bolt should not be taken lightly.

Obviously, many factors are involved. No one is likely to become particularly excited about the use of a bolt ladder on a wall in the Alaska Brooks Range, because a first ascent party in a remote area has to make its own choices—the route may never be seen by another human being. Safety conditions are very different in severe conditions three weeks' walk from the nearest settlement than they are on local cliffs near home. A few of the points that should be taken into account are whether the climb is a first ascent, the nature of the rock and the other possible protection or aid placements, the difficulty involved, the popularity of the area, and local ethics. It is generally considered improper to place any bolts on a route that has already been climbed without them. The only usual exceptions are the replacement of a bad bolt; securing a bad belay stance, where one bolt may have been trusted on the original climb, but where later parties cannot have the same faith in it; and in situations where the original ascent party felt that a bolt should be placed but did not put one in.

The difficulty of the climb, and the use of other possible placements, should also be considered. On a short rock climb, it is hardly appropriate to place bolts simply because one does not have the right nut or piton along to make a move. It would show far more taste to return to the climb later and complete it without bolting. By the same token, on short rock climbs most climbers would not put up a bolt ladder on a pitch which would obviously go free on another day. There are always matters of style and ethics involved, which depend on the climbers and the area.

Local standards are perhaps the most important consideration. Whether one is a regular climber at a particular spot or a visitor, it is only common courtesy to respect the standards that have been developed by the people who put up the routes. This is not to say that everyone has to become regimented, but simply to recognize that many can enjoy the rocks with a little mutual consideration. It means that you should not use bolts to climb an established free route. If you aren't good enough to climb it in the original style, save it for a time when you can. Pick a route that is within your abilities. By the same token, if local climbers have been saving an obvious route for the man who can do it free, do likewise. Before you put up a new route with a bolt ladder, either talk to local climbers or climb a number of routes in the area to get a feeling for the local standards, both traditional and current. Then, if your route is compatible with those standards, do it.

All this does not mean that climbers of modest abilities ought not to be able to climb an established aid route just because someone has done it free. Chopping out bolts placed by the original ascent party to "raise the standard of the route" is often as stupid and reprehensible as putting in bolts to lower the standard of an established route. However, first ascents in popular areas should be done at the level that is considered appropriate by the local climbing community.

In general, bolting has been thought justified for protection or direct aid on sections which could not be surmounted in other ways. The standards have naturally tended (with major exceptions) to go higher as other tools became available to replace bolts. Thus climbers doing an aid climb in Yosemite, for example, should expect to find fewer bolts on an equivalent climb done in the late sixties than on one put up in the mid-fifties. In areas where the quality of the rock is poor and crack systems infrequent, bolting is naturally far more common.

The mechanics of placing bolts are simple enough if the rock is good, although it may be quite strenuous work. Simplicity is one of the things that makes bolting so unaesthetic. Thus, bolts are more likely to be considered justifiable when only a few are needed on an otherwise intricately pieced-out route. On rotten rock, placing bolts may demand incredible delicacy and courage. Smaller or shorter bolts may be used for direct aid, with better ones occasionally placed for safety; but whatever size one is using, each bolt should be placed properly both for your own safety and for that of future parties. The wisdom of placing bolts too short to be safe as protection may be questioned because they may mislead later parties. If faster placement is needed, it would be better to place bolts of a smaller diameter, since a later climber can see that a bolt is only $\frac{3}{16}$ of an inch thick, while there is no way he can tell one is only 1 inch long.

Specific types of bolts will not be discussed here in detail. Some mention was made in Chapter 7 of types of bolts and their placement, but I believe that anyone intending to place bolts should inquire locally, both about bolt ethics and the best types for the specific kind of rock.

Hangers should be left on bolts once they are placed. The cost of hangers is not so high that they need to be removed after use. Because of the large numbers of possible combinations, removing hangers encourages the placement of other unnecessary bolts by climbers following the route who have different equipment from the first ascent party. If you have left bolts without hangers, be sure to include the needed information in the route description.

When climbing an older route which may have bolts on it —particularly if it is infrequently repeated—a party should be sure to carry a selection of hangers and nuts (to thread onto stud-type bolts) to avoid unpleasant situations. The ¼- and ⅜-inch bolts with standard threads are most frequently encountered. Phillips (self-drive) bolts require Allen-head cap screws and hangers. In a few climbing areas nail-head bolts are left and climbers are expected to carry keyhole hangers to make use of them.

If you are climbing a route which requires belay stances to be anchored with bolts, particularly with hanging belays, be sure to place at least two good bolts for the belay. Because they are generally very strong and because weaknesses may not be visible, there is a dangerous temptation to rely on single-bolt anchors. *Resist it.* A number of very competent and experienced climbers have died as a result of this error.

BAT HOOKS, RIVETS, DOWELS

On some recent climbs of big walls which required bolting over great distances because of their rather unnatural lines, a number of shortcuts have been tried to avoid the time- and energy-consuming task of placing all the hundreds of bolts needed. One such technique has been to drill shallow bolt holes, and to use ground-down cliff hangers to make upward progress using the holes. *Bat hooking* in this fashion, a tactic invented by Warren Harding, is certainly more attractive in some ways than bolting; but it has a major disadvantage, which is that the edges of the holes erode and weather rapidly, leaving the hole unusable. This technique would be best avoided on routes that seem sufficiently attractive to warrant repetition, since new drilling will be required in a relatively short period.

Rivets are very short bolts, used in the conventional manner except for the amount of trust with which they may be regarded. *Dowels* function similarly; they are short sections of aluminum rod which are driven into short bolt holes and tied off with webbing.

A climber follows and cleans a roof.

ROOFS

A *roof* is a severe overhang, and passing a roof is one of the more common direct aid problems. It is always strenuous, because of the need to lean far over while performing most tasks. The actual placements may be relatively easy and quite secure, or they may be extremely difficult, depending on the cracks available. Rope drag is often a great worry, because the rope may make several right-angle bends. Unless the climber is careful, the rope drag is likely to reach the unmanageable stage just at the difficult point of emerging over the roof. Both leader and second should also be careful about the possibility of falling on a roof, since extricating oneself from the resulting position can be awkward.

EXPANDING FLAKES

Many flakes which may have to be used by the climber, either for free-climbing holds or direct aid, can be pulled or wedged farther way from the rock. "Expanding" refers to the crack behind the flake. Clearly, some such flakes may be too weak to be used at all, but others are relatively sound. It is best to use nuts for protection, if at all possible, and when direct aid is needed, camming and nuts both work well. Long pitons with a gradual taper are best when pins have to be used, since the extreme wedging forces produced by pitons will tend to expand the crack. The major problem with expanding flakes occurs when a climber has to use pitons behind one for direct aid, since one pin will be driven a few feet from the last, and driving the new peg may expand the crack and cause the one he is standing on to drop out. Besides proceeding gingerly, it is a good idea to clip into the pin you are driving with a sling, in hopes that it may hold you if the one on which you are standing pops.

PENDULUMS

A *pendulum* is used to move from one crack system or series of weaknesses to another when the space between is too devoid of holds to be traversed with normal methods. In principle the technique is simple enough; in practice its difficulty varies a great deal. The climbing before and after the pendulum may either go free or require direct aid.

To do the pendulum, the leader climbs up to the pendulum point and places the anchor, which should normally be as strong as a belay anchor, unless the pendulum is very short— in other words, at least two good placements should be made for the pendulum point. Normally, all the equipment at the pendulum point must be left, including a carabiner (or a descending ring, if the climber stops and goes through the laborious task of threading the rope through). The leader either climbs down or is lowered by the belayer. He then gaily trips across the pendulum, which may require swinging back, running, and all manner of lunging and desperate grabbing. Once over, he simply climbs to the new stance and belays his partner.

There are many ways to follow a pendulum, depending on its difficulty and the equipment carried. The most important point is to be absolutely clear how things are going to be managed before the leader starts. The obvious method—not always the easiest—is for the second to climb back up to the pendulum, cleaning all the protection up to the pendulum anchor, and descend or be let down as the leader was. The second then crosses just as the leader did. On reaching the first anchor at the other side of the pendulum, he can tie into a bight in the climbing rope, untie from the end, and pull the rope from the pendulum anchor.

Frequently, it will be faster and simpler if the leader cleans the pitch up to the pendulum as he is let down, so that the second does not have to reclimb it. If a second rope is available, the leader can trail it and pass it through the first anchor on the other side, so that the second can use it to pull himself across. If the second rope is the hauling line, the second can follow the hauling bag across, making the pendulum simple for him and keeping the bag from taking a wild swing. Both hauling methods and seconding with jumars are discussed in a later chapter.

CLEANING

Cleaning an aid pitch differs from seconding a free pitch mainly in that there are more things to remove. On the other hand, except on horror pitches, one usually has a reasonable place to stand and puzzle out a nut placement or bang away at a pin. Normally, a climber can unclip the rope from a particular point before stepping on it, although occasionally this is undesirable because of the swing that might occur if a nut or pin popped. Having unclipped the rope, the second can move onto the placement and clean the one he just left. All this varies with the pitch, and sometimes it may even be easiest to climb up 10 or 12 feet, clip the *étriers* end to end, and climb down to clean a series of placements. One should take care of equipment that is clipped to an anchor from which the rope has been removed, lest it be lost if something pulls out.

Cleaning nuts that have been used for aid is often more difficult than taking out protection points, because aid nuts have born body weight. A hook of stiff wire and a long, thin piton will often help, as will any number of homemade gadgets designed for reaching into cracks to joggle the nut.

On long aid routes with a lot of nailing, both time and wear on cracks can be saved by using a piton hammer with a carabiner hole, attaching an old carabiner to each end of a foot-long piece of chain, and using this arrangement to pull the pins, driving them out.

RATING SYSTEMS

Just about all the rating systems now in use in North America rate aid sections of a climb separately from the free climbing, with numbers running from Al, the easiest, to A5. The meanings naturally vary somewhat with the climbing area, but a general definition follows. As with the ratings for free climbing, using the system is the only way to develop any precise feeling for each category.

A1—The easiest aid climbing classification, including use of a sling over a nubbin for a bit of help, a shoulder stand, straightforward nailing in a good crack, easy nut placement, or a normal bolt ladder.

A2 Placements are trickier or strenuous, but they are reasonably secure and require no really difficult moves.

A3—Placing aid becomes quite difficult or awkward. Rock may be loose, and problems like bottoming cracks, expanding flakes, difficult overhangs and pendulums, and doubtful protection are encountered. Placements may include insecure nuts, tied-off knifeblades, crack tacks, and so on.

A4—Very difficult aid, with many placements or rock of a very dubious nature, so that even with expert use of hardware, support is doubtful. Skyhooks, rurps, and tied-off piton tips are frequent.

A5—Either placements that will hold body weight are almost impossible, or a long sequence of A4 placements is necessary with no protection in between, so that any failure guarantees a long fall, even for an expert.

14

MIXED CLIMBS

Mixed climbing is the term often used to describe mountaineering routes that may involve a wide variety of rock, snow, and ice climbing in alpine terrain. Much of the climbing in Europe is of this type, as are the classic routes in some ranges of the United States and Canada. While there are no highly specialized techniques involved in mixed climbing, it seems worth some special consideration, partly because many U.S. climbing areas offer only pure rock climbs or spring snow climbs.

What is different about mixed climbing is the versatility of technique and equipment that is needed. Rock-climbing shoes, great loads of hardware, and similar specialized gear are generally not appropriate. Equipment should be as lightweight and versatile as possible. In general the technique of mixed climbing is to go light and fast.

Many mixed routes are much longer than those to which most rock climbers are accustomed, so a smooth, confident technique and good physical conditioning are very important. The climbers should be comfortable on snow, ice, and rock of the level that will be encountered on the route. For beginners in alpine technique it is important to remember that 5.6 rock climbing on wet rock with mountaineering boots and a pack is quite different than on sunny rock with a little day bag and *Klettershue*. When one is beginning at mixed climbing, it is well to be conservative in estimating one's abilities.

Mixed climbs are likely to alternate back and forth between snow and rock. When steps can be kicked in the snow this presents no real problem, other than getting used to kicking the snow off the boots as one steps onto the rock, and allowing for wet soles. When the snow is really hard, however, the climber is faced with the choice of wearing crampons over rock, cutting steps on the snow, or having to don and remove crampons frequently. Normally one ends up doing all three at one time or another. Rock climbing on crampons is an art in itself, and often cannot be avoided when one is going up steep, icy sections with no place that one can put on and remove the climbing irons. When there are long stretches of rock with short ice patches or gully crossings, chopping steps tends to be simpler than bothering with crampons. A couple of new kinds of crampon bindings using quick-release cables have been developed in Europe which greatly simplify the task of putting on crampons or removing them, and these have real advantages on mixed climbs. Safety straps should be used with them to prevent accidental loss.

Ice ax management can be a problem in mixed climbing, particularly when one is just getting used to it, since the ax is needed whenever the climber encounters snow or ice but is an encumbrance on rock. On occasional moves it may be allowed to dangle from the wrist strap or chest loop. The ax can also be got out of the way for a short time by slipping it into a hammer holster or a carabiner on the hardware loop, and very short axes are often carried this way all the time. Generally, however, the simplest way to get rid of the ax is to slip it between your rucksack and your back, passing the spike between the two straps of the pack at the top and on down to one side, above the spot where one of the straps is attached to the bottom of the pack. The head of the ax thus rests on the top of the pack straps. The ax is secure, easy to get at with one hand, and easy to put back the same way. Accidental loss is very unlikely, unless one forgets to retrieve the ax before removing the pack.

Objective dangers are often far greater on mixed climbs than on pure rock or snow ascents, although this will not always be the case. Since mixed climbs are generally on large

Easy mixed climbing. The climbers have stowed their axes between ruck-sack straps and backs as they moved off the snow onto rock.

peaks, the attendant weather hazards and the possibility of avalanches and rockfall must always be taken into account. Areas of severe rockfall can be identified by the accumulation of debris at the bottom and by scars on both rock and snow. A snowfield peppered by channels and imbedded stones is a sure sign of danger. In the high peaks, frost at night may stop the stonefall, and a climb may be justified if one can start early enough and climb fast enough to be out of the danger zone before the sun hits the slopes above. Naturally, in places and seasons with regular lightning storms, one should be in a safe place by the time they normally come up.

There are almost certain to be many loose blocks and sections of bad rock, because of the weathering effects of snow and ice. Great care is needed to avoid dislodging pieces of the mountain onto one's companion or other climbers. Wearing a hard hat and exercising prudence in choosing belay spots will also widen the margin of safety.

The climber must make a careful choice of tools and protective hardware that are to be carried, balancing the need to travel fast and light against that of having the equipment necessary for safe climbing in a place where an accident might be very serious indeed. The more difficult the route, the more difficult the choices will be, and the more careful the climbers should be to choose a route well within their abilities. Slings and nuts will usually be adequate for protecting rock pitches, except in chimneys or gullies where one expects to find all the cracks iced up. In such cases, it may be necessary to carry pitons and hammers. Angles and Leepers (Z-section pins), within the ranges they cover, are more effective than regular horizontals in iced-up cracks, because they tend to displace the ice and to concentrate pressure in smaller areas, so that the ice that is left will be more likely to melt out. An Alpine hammer may be of more use than a regular piton hammer, particularly for the leader, since the pick can be used to clear cracks and for the ice climbing that is likely to be encountered wherever there are iced cracks. Some climbers may prefer a north wall hammer to substitute for the ice ax, piton hammer, or both, depending on the nature of the climb.

Routefinding problems tend to predominate on mixed climbs; routes will change from week to week and hour to hour. The preferences of the climbers themselves will vary with their own skills, the condition of different parts of the route, and the equipment they have on the climb or at a given moment. Verglas tends to make snow or ice alternatives more desirable, while sun that rots the ice and snow may dry out the rock and make it attractive. Climbers who have crampons on at a particular point in a climb may pick an altogether different way up from those who have their climbing irons strapped to their packs. These factors and others will also make route descriptions gleaned from guidebooks or other climbers much harder to follow; you may use the same general line as those

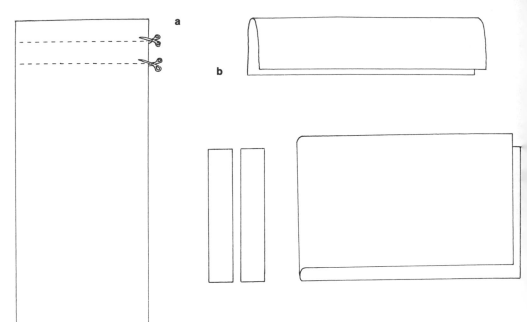

a

b

MAKING A BIVOUAC SACK. The sack shown is designed for two people and is made from commonly available lightweight coated nylon 45 inches wide. The length should be figured so it is a little longer than your height; get material three times your height plus 2 feet. You will also need thread, grommets and a tool for setting them, 2 feet of 1-inch webbing, three cord clamps, and about 20 feet of light-duty nylon cord. A sewing machine helps.

Cut the material as shown in *a*, removing two 8-inch strips from one end to make tunnels for face openings and cutting one-third of the remainder off. The resulting pieces are shown in *b*. The smaller of the two big pieces is folded in half along its length as shown above, and the larger one is folded in half along its width as shown below.

Cut the webbing into two pieces, each 1 foot long. Form each into a loop, as shown in *c*, making a 2-inch overlap, and sewing back and forth along its length for 24 passes with no. 24 polyester thread, 10 stitches to the inch. The loops will then be nearly the full strength of the webbing and can be used for tying in. Those who do not need tie-ins in the sack can use lighter webbing and fewer stitches.

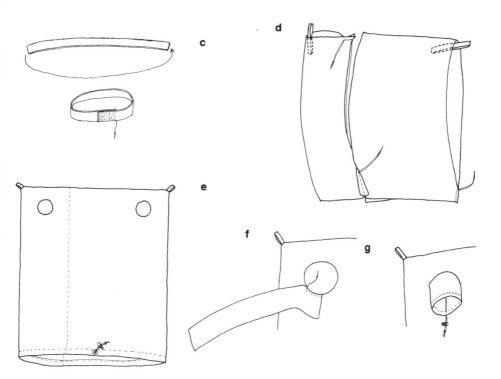

Sew the body of the bag together as shown in *d*. First sew together one end of the shorter folded piece, inserting one of the webbing loops in the corner. Then sew one of the long sides of the longer folded piece, again inserting a webbing loop in the corner. (When placing the loops, remember that the finished bag will be turned inside-out.) Finally sew the two together to form a large envelope, the loops on one end, and the other end open.

Turn the bag inside out, install a grommet in the center of one side, 1½ inches up from the open end. Make a 1-inch hem along the whole open end; the grommet will be in the hem. Put a safety pin on the end of the cord and work it through the grommet, around the hem, and out the grommet again. Put a cord clamp on the cord, knot it, and cut off the excess. The finished hem is shown in *e;* the drawcord allows the bottom of the sack to be pulled tight.

Cut two holes in the upper corners of the bivouac sack on the same side as the cord clamp. The holes should be 9 inches in diameter, and the edges should be 5 inches from the top of the bag and 7 inches from the sides. Sew one of the 8-inch strips to each hole to form a tunnel, stitching the long edge of each strip along the outside of a hole, as shown in *f.* When the strip has been sewn all around the circumference, cut off the excess, sew the ends of the strip together, and install a grommet, hem, drawstring, and cord clamp, as in the bottom of the sack. A finished tunnel is shown in *g.*

who came before, and yet climb a completely different route. One must rely on one's own routefinding skills rather than trying to adhere blindly to the descriptions of others.

On all big routes, whether mixed or not, one will sometimes have to bivouac. The important factors are advance preparation and settling into a good spot when the time comes. Warm clothes and protection from the elements should always be carried, together with enough water and food, on any climb in the mountains—particularly on long routes. Shell clothing, extra sweaters, jacket or insulated parka, and spare socks and mittens should be standard. Some sort of bivouac sack is also really helpful, particularly on big mixed routes. Two- and three-man bivy sacks are available commercially, and plans for making one are shown on pages 334 and 335. A bivouac sack should be made of waterproof material (light enough so that one does not leave it at home), should have ties or grommets so that it can be suspended, and should have flaps or tunnels at the top corners which can be closed against the elements or opened for ventilation, visibility, or safety tie-ins. It has major advantages over individual waterproof protection in that it is more efficient, pools body warmth, and greatly improves team morale.

A small lightweight stove makes bivouacs more comfortable and may be essential for melting ice and snow. Food is important to maintain warmth and energy, but adequate liquid intake is even more vital, whether the weather is warm or cold. Dehydration has insidious effects, sapping strength and common sense, and lowering the resistance of the body to other enemies like cold.

Whether a bivouac was planned or not, it makes sense to stop early enough to pick a good spot and prepare it adequately. One will climb far better in the morning if the night has been relatively comfortable than after a really miserable ordeal. Besides the equipment already mentioned, a small foam pad to sit on helps a great deal and weighs very little. Boots should be loosened or removed. Those who tend to get cold feet may wish to carry down booties.

15

WINTER MOUNTAINEERING

Climbing in winter has always represented one of the great challenges in mountaineering. Whether for seasoned climbers in search of a more difficult arena in which to test their technique or for new generations of tigers looking for frontiers, the mountains in winter are familiar ground with a far more serious aspect. The basic climbing techniques, of course, are the same in winter as in summer, but the climber new to the winter months should avoid overconfidence. The mountains in winter are very different indeed, more changeable than ever, and presenting rather strange permutations of their normal conditions and difficulties, problems which can easily be fatal to the unwary. On the other hand, winter mountaineering is often the way to find the mountains at their best —grander, lonelier, and generally more challenging.

THE MOUNTAINS IN THE WINTER

The first trick of winter mountaineering is to learn to anticipate changed conditions. Weather patterns are likely to be far different from those in summer, not just colder. Each range has a special set of winter idiosyncrasies, which may be quite the opposite of its summer ones. In the Sierra Nevada of California, for example, which is known for its generally fine summer weather, winter storms are frequent and often violent. The Front Range of the Colorado Rockies has much less snow but is particularly susceptible to extreme winds in the winter. The list could go on and on, but it is important to note that the winter climber must understand the nature of the weather in the particular mountains where he is planning to climb. It will influence a host of decisions: whether to take clothing suitable for wet cold, the likelihood of avalanches, the amount of ice to be anticipated on the route, and so forth.

Everything in cold weather tends to take far longer, and there is less daylight available. Drinking and cooking water must often be melted; deep snow will greatly prolong both approaches and camping chores; bulky clothing makes movement awkward and slow. Realistic time estimates are difficult to make because the condition of the snow will affect nearly every phase of a climb. It is vitally important, however, to carry enough food, clothing, and fuel to get one through the trip, including the time needed to wait out possible storms. Running short of supplies during a storm where one has skied several days or a week to get in may not only abort the anticipated climb, it may result in the deaths of some of the party.

Winter storms in the mountains are of a different order from those of summer. It is often quite impossible to keep going through a serious winter storm. The mountaineer must take shelter or court death. In such circumstances, bivouac equipment and emergency rations obviously need to be heavier and more carefully planned than for a summer climb. Relatively light clothing may suffice when one is moving, but adequate protection from the elements is essential at night and for the belayer on a technical climb. Food can be consumed in incredible quantities when one is working hard in a cold environment.

The winter mountaineer needs to be aware of the special nature of climbing in the winter, and also of the vast changes which often occur on different sorts of routes. Such changes will vary a good deal both from one range to another and from day to day and year to year in a particular chain of mountains. Occasionally, routes will go better in good winter conditions than in summer. A dangerously loose gully may fill in with snow, becoming a straightforward climb when the snow is good. Many climbs which are a nightmare of rockfall in the temperate seasons may be more technically difficult but less dangerous to good climbers in the winter, because the stones are well frozen in cold weather. Most commonly, however, climbing on any route is both harder and more hazardous in winter.

The climber may be surprised in his first winter season to find that difficulties can be reversed by the seasons. Sections of a climb which verge on the trivial in the summer may turn into the touchiest pitches in winter, while the most serious leads of the summer may change little. For example, D-7 is the easiest summer route on the Diamond, the great vertical wall on the east face of Long's Peak in Colorado. It is probably not the easiest route in winter; but, more important, the most dangerous section of the climb is the exit ledge at the top, which in summer is an easy walk-off. Direct aid in the cracks below is not a great deal different from the summer, except for the bulkiness of clothing and the need for hauling more gear. This reversal of difficulties is not at all uncommon. Poorly protected third- and fourth-class climbing is often far more serious in the winter than difficult fifth-class leads in between. Other fifth-class pitches that are normally difficult in summer may turn nearly impossible in the winter if ice fills up the holds and cracks. With careful consideration, the climber can anticipate some of the changes. The interest remains, however, for he will always find surprises, even if he climbs the same route each winter.

WINTER APPROACHES

Approaches in winter generally require skis or snowshoes to keep the climber and his pack from disappearing into the snow cover. There is not space here to argue their relative merits in detail, and the interested reader is referred to my *Complete Snow Camper's Guide* for discussion of this and other aspects of winter travel and camping. Basically, snowshoes are preferred for those without previous ski-touring experience, and they are also more appropriate in areas with

Heading in for a winter climb, one climber on skis and the other on snowshoes.

heavy brush or rocky terrain which is not adequately covered by winter snows. Skiers are generally not willing to concede many other advantages to snowshoers, and since I am a skier my prejudice is plain. On winter traverses, however, even the skier may choose to carry a light pair of snowshoes on the back of his pack to ease the descent and the trek back to camp. The new short, wide skis are quite practical as well, but they are rather expensive for their specialized purpose.

   With either skis or snowshoes, more surface area provides more flotation in the snow. When one has to carry winter camping equipment, food, fuel and climbing gear, packs in the winter are heavy, so careful consideration should be given to ensure that the skis or snowshoes chosen are adequate. Sturdiness is important, particularly for long wilderness approaches. Equipment should be tough and well tested, and adequate repair kits must be taken for contingencies—spare ski tip, binding repair items, and the like, depending on the equipment used.

There has been a strong tendency in the past few years toward lighter ski-touring gear for mountaineering approaches. This may range from moderate-weight touring skis with special bindings accommodating mountain boots to the use of light skis and touring boots, with the climbing footgear carried in the pack. This method is particularly suitable in areas where not much wilderness skiing is done on high-angle slopes, so that steel edges and heavy skis are not essential. The light weight of touring skis can make progress faster and more enjoyable, particularly as light skis of greater strength are developed. One should be careful, however, of using excessively fragile equipment in deep wilderness or where there will be a lot of trail breaking through heavy crust.

The time required in a winter approach varies incredibly with the snow conditions. With good snow and light touring skis, an approach may be much faster than in summer, particularly when nasty brush can be avoided by skiing over it. On the other hand, with deep, heavy snow, a party can be slowed to a crawl on the same approach. Factors like these give a winter trip much of its intrinsic interest and challenge.

WINTER CAMPS

The greatest problem encountered by the mountaineer living in winter conditions is pumping enough water into his body to avoid dehydration. Besides its negative effects on overall performance, dehydration of the body makes the climber far more susceptible to hypothermia (dangerous chilling of the body) and traumatic shock in case of storm, fatigue, or injury. It is vital to remember to drink during the day, and especially to replenish the body's liquid supply at camp. When possible, the availability of water in liquid form should be a prime consideration in choosing a campsite. Water may sometimes be obtained by chopping into a stream or by filling bottles with runoff during the day. Generally, however, snow and ice will have to be melted for water, requiring both an efficient stove and plenty of fuel. Fuel requirements in winter are usually about three times those in summer. The length of time required to melt snow makes the use of a stove with a pressurizing pump desirable. Kerosene or white gasoline-naphtha stoves are generally more efficient, and users of butane stoves may find that the tanks have to be heated to vaporize the fuel. Plan on plenty of time to melt snow.

Choosing a stove for use in the winter is a real problem. New designs come on the market every year, but at least at this time there are none that are really satisfactory. The bottled gas types are sometimes convenient, but they do not have the capacity or the efficiency to serve well as anything except emergency soup warmers. The traditional small, self-pressurizing white gas stoves (which also burn naphtha canned fuel) work well enough in the summer once one has learned their idiosyncrasies, but they are painfully slow when one is melting snow and fighting heat loss in a cold environment. The best designed of the conventional small stoves is the Mini Enders, which does have a pump and is well thought out in many other respects, but is still too slow at heating and has a rather small tank capacity. The best stoves for winter use in terms of heat output, tank capacity, and convenience of operation are the big pump stoves like the Optimus 111B; however, they are far too heavy. (The 111B weighs 3½ pounds without fuel.) The best stove in terms of heat output, weight, and fuel capacity is the M.S.R. stove, which has a number of clever innovations like the use of a normal fuel can as a removable tank, thus eliminating tank weight and providing a safety feature at the same time. Regulation is poor, so that simmering has to be accomplished with the help of an asbestos pad, which means excessive fuel use for some summer cooking. Nonetheless, in the winter, when melting capacity is of prime importance and simmering is a bad idea because it produces extra condensation, this stove is unsurpassed. Whatever model is used, carry a small piece of closed-cell foam cut to fit underneath to reduce heat loss and to prevent the stove from melting its way down into the snow.

    Shelters for winter camping are adequately discussed elsewhere. Briefly, the best tents for the purpose have frostliners, snow flaps, floors with cook holes, and entrances at both ends. Igloos and snow holes are warmer shelters which are completely protected from wind, but their construction requires some practice that should be acquired in advance, not when darkness is only a short time away. A shovel should be carried for building snow shelters (one with sturdy construction, not held together with a couple of flimsy aluminum rivets). Some snow flukes can be fastened to an ice ax for shoveling. A really sturdy shovel is a farmer's grain scoop. A snow saw should also be carried for cutting blocks if igloos are planned. The merits of the two types of shelter depend mostly on conditions and experience. Igloos are most suitable for large, roomy shelters,

A winter camp. The entrance to a snow cave is visible below and to the far right of the two igloos.

particularly when a stay of several days is planned. A snow cave in the side of a drift is usually faster and better for a quick evening bivouac. In mountains like those on the West Coast, where the snow tends to be wet and heavy, there is nearly always suitable igloo snow; but in regions of cold, dry snow, igloos are far less practical, since it is far more difficult to get good blocks and to get them to freeze into place.

Building snow shelters should be practiced by every winter mountaineer. Snow is an excellent insulator, and a snow cave can be a lifesaver in many circumstances. Even at lunch breaks on cold, windy days, a small snow cave can often be dug in ten minutes that will mean recuperation instead of a bone-chilling ordeal. Each region and season has its own idiosyncrasies, but here are a few tips when building shelters:

—To get consolidated snow when everything is loose, jump around the area on skis or snowshoes for a while, then let it alone for fifteen or twenty minutes.

—There are nearly always drifts in the mountains, which are already consolidated and are deep enough to provide the depth for a cave or plenty of blocks for an igloo.

—For an igloo, take the first blocks from what will be the floor; put in a basement before building above. Then the dome will not have to be so wide or high. Don't step on an area from which blocks are going to be taken, or they will be cracked in advance. Lower layers of snow will usually be better than top ones. Cut blocks as large as possible and bevel them so they are supported by the lower block and the one beside. In moderate temperatures, keep using large blocks. In cold weather and powdery snow, small blocks work better on the top rows; each one is held for a minute until it freezes in place. With good snow, holding the blocks is unnecessary; shaping properly allows them to be held by the preceding block and the row below.

—With igloos and snow caves both, an entrance below the floor level will allow the sleeping space to trap warmer air. A ventilation hole in the roof will provide temperature control and a draft that is essential during cooking. A larger hole gives more draft.

—Digging tools should be kept inside the shelter. You may have to dig out in the morning.

—When digging a snow cave into the side of a drift, don't pick the lee side of a place where heavy accumulation is likely, as on the side of a ridge that runs perpendicular to the direction of the prevailing wind. In an ill-chosen spot like this, 20 or 30 feet can be added to the drift overnight in a bad storm, so that digging out becomes a survival epic. Most drifts result from eddies caused by smaller features in the terrain and are safe from this hazard.

—When possible, dig the entrance to an igloo or cave across the prevailing wind so that it will be less subject to either drifting or wind blowing in. Partly closing the entrance with packs or blocks of snow will often help.

—Carry a ground cloth or use a sleeping bag cover. Those using tents in summer often forget ground cloths. Sleeping bag covers are an aid to warmth and help keep the bag dry in either a tent or a snow shelter.

—Pack down insulated gear in plastic bags or stuff it into sacks whenever it is not being worn. Humidity in a snow shelter (and often in tents in winter) is around 100 per cent and when bags or parkas start to cool off, moisture condenses in them.

—Be sure to maintain proper ventilation when cooking. A vent should be left all night, but there is rarely a problem with oxygen except when a flame is going. A stove uses tremendous amounts compared with a person, and there is also some danger from carbon monoxide when cooking.

—In places where snow is wet, raingear and waterproof mitts should be used during building.

—Don't lose your way if you go out to answer a call of nature in the middle of the night. A snow cave or igloo is such a good sound insulator one can be completely unaware of a 100-mph wind outside—or a companion calling out. Snow shelters blend into the landscape well, particularly in the dark.

There are many other tricks to winter camping, of which only a few will be mentioned here. Because of the time often required to get going and the limited amount of light, an alarm clock or watch is generally needed, even by those who do not use them in summer. Both unfrozen water and heat are often a real problem, so the water bottle may be best carried wrapped up in the sleeping bag to keep it warm, or at least to prevent it from freezing. Another alternative is to carry a bottle inside some of your clothing. All gear left outside in a winter camp must be packed up and put in a spot that is easily found. Even a light dusting of snow will cover over small equipment sitting around at random, and equipment placed in a drift area can be buried irretrievably. Wet gear is always a problem in winter, so every opportunity should be taken to dry everything, even at the risk of losing travel time. Wool is an old standby in winter, because of its relatively good performance in wet conditions. In places where wet, cold weather is common, strong consideration should be given to synthetic insulation in some items like sleeping bags, rather than down, which collapses when wet.

CLIMBING GEAR

Equipment for winter climbing will naturally vary with the nature of the climb, but some generalizations can be made. The balance between adequate gear for a climb and excessive weight is even more difficult to strike than in summer, because so much more must be carried simply to survive and to manage the approach. Winter camping gear alone will weigh more than a carefully planned pack for technical mountaineering in fair seasons. Every choice made must be considered more carefully, because the consequences of a mistake in winter are likely to be far more serious. The same factors govern party size. Going on a big climb with a party of two in winter is considerably more risky than in summer, and because community equipment will be heavier, small parties are also less free to move quickly than in summer.

Personal gear must, of course, be quite a bit heavier than in mild seasons, but how much heavier depends a good deal on climate and the nature of the climbing. In regions where wet conditions are possible even in winter, plenty of wool clothing should always be carried, and this is a good bit heavier than down gear. For general mountaineering, when everyone can keep moving most of the time, less heavy clothing has to be carried, on the assumption that sleeping bags will be used once a long stop is made. When difficult climbing is likely, however, whether it would be difficult in mild seasons or not, the belayer may be stuck in one cramped position for hours, and he will need a lot of insulation to keep from freezing on the spot. Layers and readily opened means of ventilation are particularly appropriate in winter, because one frequently needs only light clothing when moving fast, but as soon as one stops, a great deal of insulation is required.

The extremities present particular problems in winter. Good hats are essential, of course, so that the head gets a plentiful blood supply (and hence a heat supply) all the time. This means that proper insulation of the head, face, and neck are vital if one is chilly, and it also means that when work starts to heat the body too much, baring the head is a good way to get rid of the extra heat in a hurry. Some kind of wool cap with an extension that makes a neck covering or complete face mask is a basic piece of winter gear. Down parkas should obviously have hoods, since the uncovered head can easily waste half the heat produced by the body.

An adequate combination of mittens and gloves is clearly essential, including spares in case a mitten is somehow dropped. (A keeper cord for the outer mitts running through the arms of the parka is helpful.) Mittens are, of course, much warmer, but finger dexterity is often needed. Many good combinations are possible, but my own preference for most conditions is a very light pair of gloves of thin fabric, serving mainly to allow one to touch metal objects without having the skin of the fingers freeze to them. Heavy wool mittens go over these and lightweight fabric overmitts go over everything. Naturally, not all these are worn all the time, and the only spares that need be carried are wool mittens.

Feet are the greatest problem. They can't be stuck in pockets or under armpits to warm them up, and during belays they are often buried in cold snow for long periods without much possibility of moving. For the average winter traveler, frostbite is rarely a problem if the body as a whole is kept warm; but the climber has the added problems of heavy stiff boots and immobility in cramped positions to contend with. When climbing is fairly continuous, many mountaineers will find that regular climbing boots are adequate even for winter conditions, as long as they are not too tight when adequate socks are worn. Obviously, good gaiters should be used to keep snow out of the boots, and extra socks should be carried. In colder weather, or on technical climbs with long belays, it will be necessary to wear double boots, overboots, or both. Well-made double boots allow technical climbing to a fairly high standard, but they have become hideously expensive. Over-boots, particularly insulated ones, are excellent on climbs where crampons are worn continuously, but since they have smooth soles, they are impossible to use on steep terrain without crampons. Fortunately, a good solution has been developed recently by Pete Carman in the form of super-gaiters, which cover and insulate the calf and the whole upper part of the boot, but which leave the sole clear for climbing. Several models are on the market, and more will doubtless follow. Super-gaiters greatly extend the temperature range of any footwear, but it is difficult to get them to fit on some types of boots.

One other possible solution for cold weather climbing is the old army double-vapor-barrier rubber boot, which has an excellent record of preventing frostbite on climbs like McKinley. It is suitable and recommended for non-technical snow climbs, but it is not rigid enough to do technical climbing. The double-vapor-barrier boot is also called a Korean or Mickey Mouse boot.

The technical gear which is carried will, of course, depend on the climb. In principle it will not be too much different from the summer gear, but in practice, the winter mountaineer generally is forced to extend himself more than the summer climber, relying less on equipment for safety and more on his own skill and judgment. The winter mountaineer is already faced with the need to carry a lot of weight in equipment and food before he even starts to load technical gear into the pack. He also has frequently to contend with major approach problems before he even gets on the climb. As a rule, he is likely to find that many more pitches are technically difficult in the winter, while the days are far shorter. The consequence is that many winter mountaineers cut the technical gear they carry to the bone, relying on speed rather than equipment for safety. This is not a decision to be made lightly, but it emphasizes the more dangerous nature of winter climbing. The alternative to paring technical gear may be the use of expedition tactics, relaying loads into the base of a climb and up the first part of it for long periods before an attempt is actually made.

Ice gear and snow flukes will be carried according to the nature of a particular route. Rock hardware may vary somewhat from a summer selection, besides being more Spartan. Slings are used at least as much in the winter as the summer. Although small rock horns may be covered with ice and snow, blocks that would not be trustworthy in summer are often frozen in reliably, and screws may have to be tied off in thin ice. The possibilities for the use of nuts varies a lot, but where cracks are heavily iced, the winter climber will have to rely more on pitons. Even where nuts can be placed, a hammer will often have to be used to clear ice from cracks and to knock the chocks into safe positions. Angles and Leepers (Z-section) are usually better pins in winter than horizontals, because they clear ice in cracks much better.

CLIMBING IN WINTER

Technique in winter is that of the general mountaineer, who is often likely to feel he is scrabbling rather than climbing. There are unlikely to be any pure slabs of dry rock on which one can engage in friction technique. If the slab is found, stiff boots, heavy clothing, and crampons will inhibit one's style anyway. The climber is forced either to rock climb in crampons or to cut steps in ice pitches. Knees are likely to come into play, along with any other part of the body that can be used to get an ounce of adhesion. Ledges and holds tend to be covered with a layer of ice and a pile of powder snow.

The mountaineer's first winter climbs are best restricted to routes that would be easy walk-ups or scree grinds in other seasons. Even second- or third-class summer routes are often exciting and challenging enough in the winter, and they are good places to gain experience in dealing with the problems of the season. Rushing onto a big route in the winter is likely to end in a debacle.

Anyone interested in winter climbing should study the problem of avalanches thoroughly and cultivate extreme respect for the dangers they present. Avalanches in other seasons are serious enough, but they tend to be relatively easy to predict, provided the climber puts a little effort into their understanding. In winter the problems are greatly magnified. More avalanches come down and in more varied circumstances. (The reader is referred to the bibliography for books on the subject.) The climber should talk as much as possible to people who know the patterns and conditions in a particular region. It is also important to know the history of the snow cover in a given year so as to understand overall patterns in a range. Talk to Forest Service and Park Service specialists or to avalanche control people at local ski areas. They will know if there is a layer of ice that formed early in the season and has been bringing down an unusual number of avalanches or if major instability has developed in the snow cover. Digging pits yourself and probing with ski poles can tell you a good deal once you have learned to recognize unstable conditions.

Remember that avalanches are most likely to develop after very heavy snows, or driving wind, or both. They are most likely to develop in size on slopes of between 30 and 45 degrees. Small avalanches will develop on much steeper slopes, however, and they can easily knock climbers off. Avalanches are most likely to occur on lee slopes, where wind-driven snow is dropped. In some regions, avalanche danger rapidly tapers off after a storm has passed, although sudden warming trends will sometimes bring more down; the colder the temperatures, the longer the danger will persist after snow has fallen. In other regions, particularly where high-country temperatures are cold and there is a lot of wind, slab avalanche conditions can persist indefinitely, particularly where depth hoar, an ice layer, or smooth ground makes a good sliding surface underneath. Where the possibility of a slab exists, the only reasonably safe solution is to stay off possible avalanche slopes.

It is important to become proficient in general mixed climbing technique to make winter ascents. Strong, smooth movement is essential, since the climber has to get up the mountain as quickly as possible. Even on multi-day ascents, the climbers are always racing against bad weather. There are a multitude of operations which take longer in the winter, so there is never any extra time to waste. Starts should be made as early as possible, and easy ground is usually climbed in the dark with headlamps.

Winter climbing requires really good physical conditioning. Far more effort and expenditure of energy is required than in summer, and many climbers who are perfectly capable of creditable performances at other times of the year find themselves exhausted before they even finish the approach on a winter climb. The safety factor here is critical. Overextending oneself in the mountains in winter can be deadly. The margin for error is simply not that wide.

Rope-handling techniques may vary slightly from summer practice. A great deal of extra care is required to avoid damage to the rope. Ice axes and hammers are being swung around, and it is all too easy to chop the rope unless one is constantly careful, particularly in a party of more than two when a middleman is climbing with ropes leading and trailing him. Crampons are an even more likely source of damage, whether one is stumbling around on a ledge with numb feet or front-pointing on ice. When belaying in the normal fashion, one should remember that icy gloves on a snowy rope don't give much friction, and a turn around the wrist and forearm of the holding hand is often necessary to ensure adequate control. Belaying devices like the Sticht plate, M.S.R. link, or Lowe ring are particularly useful in winter, both to allow secure belaying with cold, mittened hands and to give the belayer a little extra freedom to eat and adjust his clothing while working.

Short pitches are often helpful in winter, particularly if good belaying spots are available. They allow progress to be made with less hardware, and keep the belayer from becoming quite so chilled. Running belays while both climbers are moving are also sometimes useful to speed progress on terrain where the climbers feel confident. Clearly, this is a calculated risk, and the method should not be used where there seems to be a real possibility of unarrested fall. Such running belays must be bombproof, and normally the rope should be shortened. The most common belay of this type is perhaps the threading of the rope back and forth between gendarmes (pinnacles) on a ridge.

THE CHALLENGE

Winter holds out special difficulties and rewards to the climber, and the person who accepts them will not be disappointed or bored, whatever other reactions he may feel. Winter in the mountains is hard and stark and unforgiving, but for beauty, challenge, and solitude, it is a time which cannot be matched. The climber a few days in from the trailhead is not likely to have to worry about crowds, at least once the first barrier to snowmobiles has been passed. The winter mountaineer is also not in much danger of reaching a point where the success of a climb is certain enough that the challenge is lost. The mountains in winter are too difficult, too demanding, and too uncompromising ever to become stale.

16

BIG WALLS

The great vertical and near-vertical faces naturally present some of the best possible challenges to the climber. They have a way of capturing the imagination of the serious climber as nothing else can. Whether or not one chooses to climb them, the great faces and walls represent the ultimate challenges of the sport.

In one sense it is absurd to talk about special techniques for climbing walls, because they simply present maximum demands on all the skills the climber can muster, and they are as varied as the sport itself. The greatest wall in Europe, the North Face of the Eiger, involves 8000 feet of classical mixed climbing, fraught with serious objective dangers. The Wickersham Wall on Mount McKinley is a huge face that is climbed by standard expeditionary techniques. The North Face of Mount Robson in the Canadian Rockies, which might well be called a wall, is a difficult snow and ice climb. In the greatest ranges of the world, there are monstrous walls requiring both expeditionary techniques and the highest level of technical climbing.

In the United States, "wall climbing" generally refers to the ascent of extremely steep rock faces, often taking at least several days for a strong party. Some special techniques were developed to allow such climbs to be made without the use of siege tactics, and a few of them will be discussed in this chapter. Some methods which were developed on big walls are frequently used on short, hard climbs—seconding with jumars, for example. The techniques described in this chapter are

America's best known big wall and the rock climber's mecca—El Capitan in
Yosemite Valley.

grouped together as advanced methods generally applicable to the great rock climbs of America and Canada. No attempt has been made comprehensively to review all the tactics used on such climbs. Wall climbers are innovative, as they must be. A trick that may work perfectly on the Diamond on Long's Peak will fail miserably on Glacier Point Apron in Yosemite.

This is not a "how-to" chapter on big walls. The challenges are too demanding for any such approach. The first test is that of coldly balancing one's ability against the difficulties that must be faced and one's desire to do a climb. The big climbs have lost some of their power of intimidation in the last few years, but they have also begun to take their toll. On a big wall a party is—or should be—wholly dependent on its own resources. It is best to be sure in advance that those resources, both personal and technical, are up to the challenge.

ANCHORING

Special attention should be paid to anchors on any climbing so steep that the climbers and their equipment are sus-

A climber anchored and set up for hauling with an all-nut anchor. Since both climbers and equipment will be hanging from the anchor in this type of situation, it is vital that the anchor be bombproof and that the load be distributed. At least *three* solid independent anchors are necessary. Here, the top anchor is used to suspend the haul line, the middle anchor supports the weight of the leader, and the lowest anchor supports the climbing rope going to the second, who jumars up, cleaning the pitch while the leader hauls. The lowest anchor consists of two nuts, one directed against an upward pull for a possible leader fall after leads have been switched. Naturally, all the anchors are tied together.

pended from them. This is particularly important on walls, because a tolerance is built up to exposure and constant reliance on artificial anchors may cause the climber to become complacent.

For hanging belays in particular, two good bolts or three good pitons or nuts should be standard. Such total reliance has to be placed on the anchors that one cannot afford even very small risks of failure. Normally, one anchor is used to tie in the climbing rope leading to the second. An additional anchor is used for hauling, and the leader hangs from a third , which is tied to both the first two as a back-up. All three are thus connected, so that even if two failed, everything would be held by the third.

TACTICS

Many strategies have been used in the ascent of big walls. Quite a few ascents have been made by besieging the climbs —setting up camp at the bottom, and running fixed lines up as successive pitches were climbed. Months could thus be spent in the assault, rappelling off in bad weather or to return to a job during the week. Such methods are now generally considered to be a form of overkill. Although climbers frequently climb a few pitches on arrival at the wall and rappel down to spend the first night at the base, full-scale sieges are now rarely used.

Groups of three and four climbers are not uncommon on big walls. With a foursome, one team of two will normally be in the lead, while the other pair cleans the pitches and hauls equipment. With three, the chores will be similarly divided for maximum speed. Such teams have the advantage of spreading the labor and thus being subject to less of a strain than teams of two. The extra manpower also makes for safer climbing, since there is a built-in reserve of strength in case of accident.

Most commonly, however, big wall climbs are now done by teams of two, particularly when previously established climbs are repeated. A three-man team will be slightly faster, but current methods make progress by a rope of two quite rapid. Usually both climbers use mechanical ascenders; jumar ascenders are preferred because they are better suited for cleaning. The normal methods used are described below.

HAULING

Hauling is certainly not restricted to wall climbing; practically every climber occasionally uses a line to haul up the packs. On big walls, however, hauling becomes a major logistical problem, both because of the amount of gear which has to be taken and the fact that it is often quite impossible to climb with a big pack. There are many hauling schemes. The method described here is one of the variations normally used by two-man teams equipped with jumar ascenders. After the leader puts up the pitch, towing one end of the separate hauling line, and anchors everything properly, he gets set up to pull up the extra gear. The second releases the hauling bag below and cleans the pitch by jumarring up the climbing rope, belaying himself, while the leader hauls the gear. This technique saves a lot of time and energy, and it is quite safe on most pitches, providing both climbers are careful.

The hauling bag should be tough, smooth, and as rounded on the outside as possible; packing so that sharp corners are not pushing out is important if one wishes to keep it intact throughout the climb. Everything from rucksacks to dufflebags has been used, but frameless sacks designed for the purpose work best. A good haul sack should have straps which make it possible to carry it as a rucksack without too much discomfort or loss of balance. Carrying straps and hardware should be removable so that the outside of the sack will have a smooth profile. Hauling straps should be very strong, go all the way around the bag, and be arranged so that the pack hangs straight down when suspended from the hauling line.

The standard Yosemite hauling system is simple and straightforward. The hauling line is tied off on reaching the stance. A pulley is put on the hauling rope and clipped to one of the anchors. One jumar is clipped (pointing downward) onto the rope on the same side of the pulley as the bag; its sling is anchored above and the other end of the jumar is weighted, generally with the hardware sling. The other jumar is attached to the haul line on the opposite side of the pulley in the conventional way, with an *étrier* attached. The leader can then raise the haul bag by standing in the aid sling, while the upside-down jumar acts as a ratchet and prevents the bag from slipping back.

Another hauling system is faster for very heavy loads and requires less effort but has more pitfalls for the unwary. The leader attaches himself to the anchor with a 20- or 30-foot safety and attaches both jumars with *étriers* or slings fixed to the haul line on the other side of the pulley from the bag. Holding the hauling line on both sides of the pulley for control, he unties from the anchor (except for the long safety line) and slides down the rock to the end of the safety, letting his body weight lift the haul sack, and jumarring back up to the anchor after each pull.

Hauling. The leader hangs from his anchor. The haul line and sack are suspended from a pulley on the top anchor. An upside down jumar hung from the same anchor acts as a ratchet on the haul line; it is weighted by the hardware sling. The other jumar is also attached to the haul line, but on the other side of the pulley. The climber can step in the *étrier* attached to the second jumar and use his body weight to raise the bag.

SECONDING WITH JUMARS

The companion technique to the hauling system described above is the method of cleaning a pitch using jumars and self-belay, rather than being belayed by the leader and climbing in the normal way. There are many schemes of sling arrangements for jumarring. Some people prefer to attach one jumar to the seat harness and the other to a foot sling. Others use two Perlon slings ending in web foot slings. (The Perlon slings pass easily through the seat harness.) The most common and simplest technique for big climbs when aid slings are being used anyhow is to clip the aid slings to the jumars.

The jumars should first be prepared by tying a short sling of 1-inch webbing to the bottom of each. The sling should pass completely around both the front and the base of the jumar, forming a figure-eight around the corner to distribute stress, as shown in the illustration on page 226. Other slings of hardware can be clipped into these. (As with any sling material, check frequently for wear or loosening of knots.) When aid slings are clipped to the jumars, correct heights are usually achieved by using a higher step in the sling attached to the lower jumar. The climber should also have a sling running to his waistband from each jumar. The sling to the lower jumar is a safety sling;

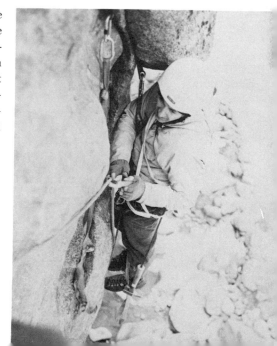

Following a pitch on jumars. Here, the climber is using his jumars for a belay while his *étriers* are attached directly to the placements. This method is often easiest when following a traversing pitch. On a pitch that goes straight up, it is simplest to jumar directly up the rope. Proper safety precautions, discussed in the text, are essential when seconding with jumars.

the one to the upper jumar occasionally serves as a safety sling also, but it is often used for tension and should be adjusted accordingly. Those using aid slings with Robbins's sub-aiders attached, as discussed on page 307, will find that the sub-aiders work well for safeties to the harness. Some climbers use rubber bands to keep the aid slings on their feet or use special jumar-ring slings. A little pressure with the feet works quite well, however, or one can use a girth hitch in the *étrier.*

The procedure used in seconding the pitch goes this way. The climber waits until the leader has signaled him that the climbing rope is anchored at the other end and ties into it if necessary. (He will normally be tied in already.) He releases the haul bag when signaled, and he can then begin to clean. The jumars are clipped onto the rope, making sure that the safeties are on, particularly if the rope does not go straight up, and the aid slings are clipped onto the jumars. The climber can then step into his slings, clip or tie on his safeties, and untie from the anchor. On reaching a placement, the climber will often find that he cannot unclip the rope until he has moved his weight above the anchor. This is done by standing in the lower sling, removing the upper jumar from the rope, clipping it in again above the anchor (making sure the safety catch is in the proper position), and putting all the body weight on the upper ascender. The rope can then be unclipped and the placement cleaned.

A couple of safety procedures should be mentioned here. *Always tie into the end of the climbing rope.* Always tie into the jumars, particularly the lower one, which is removed from the rope less often. The second attachment can also be managed by tying the two jumars together. There are many schemes—the important thing is to follow one as a matter of course. Periodically, accidents involving jumars happen, and because of the places where they are normally used, many of these mishaps are fatal. Several additional precautions can be used. A prusik knot can be tied between the ascenders as a back-up, one that has the advantage of being non-directional. Some climbers use a single Gibbs ascender as a back-up; it will trail the climber without having to be moved by hand. I prefer to tie a figure-eight loop in the rope every 30 feet or so and clip it into the harness, besides being tied into the end of the rope. The security is sure, and the procedure not excessively time-consuming or inconvenient.

There are several ways to follow a pendulum with ascenders. One should be particularly careful in pendulum maneuvers with jumars, since it is not too difficult to get mixed up and clip them in the wrong way on some pendulums. If the pendulum is long, one can jumar up to the pendulum anchor, set a prusik safety on the other side, rig a carabiner brake or belay plate rappel below the jumars, untie from any loops in the rope, transfer the jumars—one at a time—to the other side of the pendulum anchor (they may be pointing toward the ground, if the rope goes down to the next anchor), and, hanging from the jumars, rappel down until one is at or below the next anchor. Once he is safe from taking a nasty swing, the climber can clip into a loop in the rope, untie from the end, and retrieve the rope from the pendulum. On short, easy pendulums, it may not be necessary to rappel; one jumar can be moved past the pendulum point and the other left behind it. The rope is fed out gradually through the second jumar until the climber reaches the bottom of the pendulum.

17

SMALL EXPEDITIONS

Sooner or later a lot of climbers get the urge to climb in mountains that are bigger or wilder or colder or snowier than the ones that can be found closer to home. Or they want to climb peaks or faces that no one has ever done before. So they go on an expedition. There are numerous kinds of expeditions. Big expeditions are the kind that climb Everest and the other giants (so far at least), cost a lot of money, are very efficient, and to many climbers represent the antithesis of what climbing is all about. Big expeditions are worse than useless unless they are very well organized. With this characteristic assumed, a large expedition is far more likely to be successful and safe on a really big mountain than any small group of anarchists can ever be. This book is not about big expeditions.

PLANNING

A small expedition is something that you put together, preferably with some friends, to satisfy that itch for the far-away ranges, whether they are in British Columbia or Patagonia. This will not really allow you to shortcut the planning, however—simply to put it on a more personal scale. All that is intended in this chapter is to suggest some of the problems you should keep in mind. You should start thinking about the trip as far in advance as possible and use every source of information available.

The first point to consider—and be very careful about—is the people going on the expedition. The most important

The lure of far ranges is compelling to many climbers. Some are huge and some small, but remoteness and lack of knowledge lend a special quality to their call.

thing you have going for you is that all the members know each other, like one another, and have climbed together to test their relationships and to learn their mutual strengths and weaknesses. If you give up this advantage by running a "mail-order expedition" or by going with people you don't like, you are risking a lot of extra problems. If you can't get along with somebody in a two-day climb of a local peak, how will it be sitting out a week-long storm with him in a small tent? Things are far simpler if the members of the expedition know and like one another, have planned the expedition together, and are fairly well agreed on the goals. Expeditions are not likely to be enjoyable if half the party is mainly interested in trekking around the country while the other half is bound for glory on a major technical climb. In this situation, everyone is likely to be frustrated in their goals and to have a miserable time to boot.

As a matter of course one should read all the literature available concerning the area first, obtain whatever maps can be had, and talk with any friends that may have been in the general region. The standard mountaineering journals are usually the best starting point. Correspondence with members of earlier expeditions may be helpful, as may letters to local residents and officials.

A few of the matters that may have to be considered follow:

Permission. Some sort of authorization may have to be obtained in many regions, and inquiries should be made well in advance. In some countries, limitations are made on the number of parties allowed in an area to prevent adverse impact on local economies. Some have fees. Even in the United States, application well in advance may be required. McKinley is an example of a peak where advance permission is necessary.

Equipment. A careful listing of equipment that will be needed should be prepared early in the game, so that decisions can be made about what members of the expedition already own, what will need to be purchased or made, how much it will cost, and so forth. A discount may be available if everything is bought at once. Don't forget spares, replacement parts, and repair kits.

Fuel and Stoves. Different fuels are more readily available in different parts of the world, and transportation costs and regulations may require your taking stoves that can use a locally obtainable fuel.

Food. You will have to decide how much, if any, will be purchased locally, after considering costs, weight, availability, customs regulations, and so on. Be sure to consider the preferences of all the party members and to read the literature. If you are going to higher altitudes than some members have been before, expect that tastes will change. Many cannot tolerate greasy foods at altitude, for example. Food is very important, affecting both morale and performance, and it is worth spending a good deal of time and effort getting everything just right. The fact that you have climbed lots of local peaks on chocolate and salami does not mean you will be happy and aggressive after living on them for a month. Packaging is important, both for preservation and to save time on the mountains. Many expeditions have found it convenient to prepackage everything into small cooking units and then into two-man-day bags, at least for food that is to be used in the mountains. If food is purchased locally, you may have to budget time to get it packaged. Finally, be sure to take enough, both in quantity and variety. Variety is not only the spice of the menu; it also ensures that if something becomes utterly unpalatable after a certain number of days or a certain altitude, it will not abort the trip.

Customs. Make sure that you have anticipated problems and expenses with customs and immigration officials as far as possible. Talk or correspond with people who have been to your destination as recently as possible. If any problems seem possible, be sure that the member of your expedition with the greatest resources of humor, tact, devious nature, and tolerance is available to get your stuff through. Particularly if you are going to Asia, try to get help from someone who lives in the area and has experience. Allow for extra time and expense.

For U.S. citizens driving into Canada, there are limits on the amount of food that can be brought in duty-free, although Canadian customs officials are unusually courteous and understanding. Supplies being taken through to Alaska can be sealed at the border to be carried on without charge.

Medical Supplies and Skills. If you have a doctor as a member of the expedition, consult with him, and don't forget to suggest the possibility that he has as much chance of getting sick or injured as anyone else. If you have no doctor, you will have to consider carefully the skills and medical supplies that will be necessary to provide a reasonable margin of safety, perhaps consulting with a physician as part of the process. Use *Medicine for Mountaineering* as a starting point.

Also in this category are inoculations and various prophylactic measures. *Investigate the shots that may be needed and make sure everyone gets them.* Remember that in many countries of the world, one is risking serious illness by eating raw fruits or vegetables or drinking local water. Oddly enough, there are mountaineers who don't really believe in germs, at least not when applied to them. On a return journey, it is every man for himself; but since an illness contracted on an approach can affect everyone by the time it shows up high on the peak, these matters should be discussed beforehand, and there should be a meeting of minds. See the appendix for literature.

Party Size. This is a question which depends pretty much on who is interested in a trip and can come, on the feelings of the climbers, on the difficulty and size of the mountains, and on the isolation of the range. You should consider logistics, particularly if someone becomes ill or is unable to acclimatize. Accident and rescue problems should be squarely faced. You may want to run a two-man expedition to a major Alaskan peak, but you should carefully consider the risks involved—they are far greater than those faced by a four-man party. Don't forget possible problems if someone has to pull out at the last minute, particularly if you are climbing a peak like McKinley, where minimum party regulations are imposed by the authorities.

Transportation. With an idea of the weights involved, you can start to think about getting to the base of the climb, whether you are going by car, plane, boat, or whatever combination you can think of. Check into the prevailing situation if you are planning to use porters. Many expeditions use small planes to get them or their supplies to base. You should find out as much as you can about local pilots and try to get someone who has the recommendation of previous expeditions. If you plan to use the pilot to pick you up also, or to check you in case of emergencies, make sure that everything is very clear on both sides. When is he to fly in? How many times, if the weather is bad? If you want the man to check on you, make sure he understands what you want and have authorized and that you are promising to pay for it. Ask his advice. If he has had a lot of experience flying in climbing parties, he may be able to give helpful information.

Communication. You may be required to have communication with someone off the mountain. Even if there is no official requirement, you may still wish to have some sort of radio communication within the party or with someone outside as a matter of safety. This should be investigated well in advance. It would normally be cheaper to rent or borrow radios, and arrangements will be easier to make if you start soon enough. As a supplementary or alternative communication method with the outside world, an air flyby may be arranged for radio or visual communication. Contingency plans, in case of bad weather, lack of radio communication, and so on, should be well understood by everyone involved.

Litter. Plan your gear, supplies, and transportation to leave everything as you found it. Just because you're on an expedition, you don't have to leave your garbage.

TACTICS

The style of climbing you decide to use will depend on many factors. You may simply be setting up a base camp and climbing in pretty much the same style as you do closer to home, and when climbing objectives are relatively small, this is the standard method. On big peaks, there are two possible approaches. The traditional expeditionary style is to build up a chain of camps and supply dumps on the mountain gradually, with fixed ropes on sections between them that are difficult or exposed enough to require belaying. There are major advantages to this type of approach. Both retreat and advance in case of bad weather are vastly simplified, leaving a generous safety factor. If climbers become fatigued, they can move down the mountain fairly readily, rest, and move up again. The disadvantage of this method is that it tends to require all the resources, size, logistics, and regimentation of a big expedition. It also can get to be very dull. Ninety-five per cent of the climbing is reduced to ferrying loads up the mountain. The style also has an air of overkill to many climbers on many mountains.

The second possible choice is to climb alpine-style. That is, the climbers carry their equipment with them, moving their camp up the mountain, and going as quickly as possible. Safety is sometimes enhanced when the technique works, because objective dangers are reduced by speed—one is in the line of fire for a shorter time. In general, however, the risks are greater with this style of climbing on big, remote mountains. If something happens, retreat may become difficult or impossible. Reserves will be less, since the climbers cannot carry so much food or equipment. Parties are smaller, and rescues become even less feasible than they might be with more manpower, fixed ropes, and a line of camps.

Actually, small expeditions will usually fall somewhere in between the two extremes. There is a great attraction now in trying to do bigger peaks in a style closer to that used at home. Some routes on some mountains are quite impossible to conceive of in this way. The current activity on technical routes on the world's great peaks—the South Face of Annapurna, for example—could not be even attempted by a small alpine-style party, but there is more and more activity by small groups doing technical routes on other large or extremely difficult mountains, in the Andes, Alaska, and Patagonia, for example. There are also many climbers interested in small, alpine-style assaults on the non-technical routes on the giants. The balance chosen by any particular group will depend on their own aspirations and aesthetics. On those choices will depend the direction of modern mountaineering.

It is important for anyone considering expedition climbing to do as much reading and talking to experienced people as possible in order to avoid major mistakes and to fill in gaps in his own experience. Such careful planning enforces consideration of the real problems and thus tends to act as a sobering influence.

It is also important not to become careless when traveling

on snow-covered glaciers. Precautions have been mentioned before, but on expeditions where very heavy packs are normally carried, perhaps containing vital equipment, the consequences of a fall into a crevasse must be taken very seriously. Self-rescue devices should be attached to the rope; climbers should be belayed when necessary; and ropes of more than two are often desirable. Chest harnesses in addition to pelvic ones prevent a heavy pack from upending the climber in a crevasse fall.

If fixed ropes are to be placed, both ropes and anchors for them must be brought and carried up the mountain. Many schemes have been tried with varying success, and it is impossible to set hard-and-fast rules. Diameters of about ¼ of an inch are fairly light and give a reasonable margin of strength for most fixed-line uses. Larger diameters are required for high-angle climbs. Low-stretch rope has significant advantages, particularly on traverses, and some parties prefer polypropylene for fixed line because of low stretch and better resistance to cutting. Great care must be taken to protect fixed lines from abrasion. Several deaths have resulted from ignoring the ease with which nylon can be cut under stress. It must also be remembered that a low-stretch rope cannot withstand high-impact loads or heavy tensioning on traverse lines.

A technique to prevent jumars from twisting off small fixed ropes on traverses. The carabiner attached from the sling to the fixed line keeps the body of the ascender more or less parallel to the fixed line.

Fixed lines are customarily ascended using mechanical ascenders, either for actual climbing or self-belay. If jumar ascenders are used, the usual care has to be exercised in making sure the safety is closed; but with small-diameter lines some extra precautions are in order to make absolutely sure that the ascender cannot twist off the line, particularly when the rope runs horizontally or diagonally up. The method shown on the preceding page is one way to prevent this possibility. A prusik or Bachman safety is also prudent.

Fixed lines have to be anchored frequently enough so that rope stretch does not become too much of a problem, particularly on traverses. When available cracks can be used, nuts or rock pitons are the anchors of choice. Deadmen make good snow anchors, although a few pickets should be carried to provide less directional anchors for traverses.

Finally, the problems of altitude should be considered, if the climb is planned in one of the mountain regions with peaks much higher than those with which the group is experienced. Acclimatization is perhaps the most important factor, and it is one which is too often neglected in modern climbing, with planes available to fly the expedition in and with short vacations into which everything has to be squeezed. The climbers should remember that acclimatization is important both to prevent acute altitude sickness, which is often fatal, and to improve performance. Whether one has climbed high before or not, the body's adjustment to altitude is lost rapidly, so anyone who has been at lower altitudes for a few days or more will have to readjust to altitude. Packing in separate loads serves this purpose well.

A good strategy on expeditions is to carry high and sleep low; that is, a load is packed up and a high camp set, and the climbers then drop back down to their previous camp to sleep. This procedure pushes the body to acclimatize to the high altitude, but allows somewhat more comfortable sleep and reduces the possibility of severe altitude sickness, especially pulmonary edema. All expedition members should be acutely aware of the symptoms of high-altitude pulmonary edema, so that if any member begins to suffer, he can be got to a lower altitude while he is still able to function. Otherwise he will almost certainly die. This problem is discussed briefly in Chapter 18, but members of small expeditions to high-altitude peaks should read all the available literature and discuss treatment with a physician.

18

EMERGENCIES

This whole book is, in essence, a catalogue of ways to stay out of trouble while climbing in the mountains. Preparation is the most important feature of any plan to avoid or handle emergencies in the mountains—preparation in terms of physical conditioning, mental attitude, and equipment carried. Just as there is no shortcut to becoming a mountaineer or rock climber, there are no shortcuts to preparation for the unusual circumstances that may cause trouble.

Most mountaineering accidents are caused by inexperience and carelessness, and the same elements are usually the factors that make minor incidents into serious ones. Reading accident reports or accounts of rescue missions tends to become tiresomely repetitive: attempting routes beyond the ability or equipment of the party, inadequate clothing for the mountains, ignoring fatigue or deteriorating weather, splitting a party in conditions of stress, and similar obvious errors keep cropping up again and again. There are exceptions, but the great majority of accidents occur when the basic principles of safe wilderness travel and mountaineering are violated.

Mountaineering is not an inherently safe sport. It always entails some unavoidable risks, and some forms of climbing carry more risks than others. Perhaps the most basic rule for reasonable safety is to avoid going beyond one's ability so that risks are not being taken that are not fully understood. A climber can only evaluate or prepare for possible emergencies if he avoids getting in way over his head.

FIRST AID AND EMERGENCY MEDICINE

Granted that most mountaineering casualties can be prevented altogether, accidents do occur, there is a good chance of their being serious, and the circumstances of climbing are such that a convenient ambulance and hospital emergency room are not likely to be handy. It behooves every climber to become as skilled as possible in the techniques of first aid and emergency treatment of the injured, and to see that his climbing companions are similarly trained.

Competence in handling medical emergencies requires study, training, and practice. Common sense is a great help, but it is not sufficient. For this reason, no general treatment of first aid is included here. It is best learned by taking courses designed to train people to deal with such emergencies, and by reading as widely as possible in the excellent literature devoted to the subject.

The first aid courses offered free by the American Red Cross are suggested as the logical starting point for climbers. The texts for these courses have recently been revised, and the courses themselves greatly expanded in scope, with the new Standard First Aid Course covering essentially the same ground as the old standard and advanced combined. After going through the Red Cross courses, the mountaineer can study with profit the other literature listed in the bibliography, and perhaps organize a course locally using the outstanding text, *Medicine for Mountaineering*, as a basis.

Besides the material generally covered in good first aid courses and books, several environmental illnesses are particularly common in mountaineering, and they should be understood as thoroughly as possible.

HYPOTHERMIA

Because of the severe weather that is common in the mountains, and the fact that shelter and fire are not always available, mountaineers are particularly vulnerable to cold injury. Frostbite is the best known, but usually occurs in victims already suffering from hypothermia—chilling of the body core.

When heat loss to the environment exceeds the heat production of the body, a number of changes begin to occur. Blood circulation to the surface of the skin and all the extremities except the head is progressively reduced to prevent chilling of the vital organs in the head and body core. Eventually, to preserve life, the body will even allow the extremities to freeze, sacrificing them to retain heat in the trunk. At the same time, as actual cooling of the trunk and the brain take place, rational thought and vital processes begin to deteriorate.

All the measures which have been discussed before and which should be well understood by mountaineers must obviously be taken to prevent the loss of body heat in cold weather. Measures against allowing insulation to become wet, and the preventive one of carrying clothing that retains some insulating value when wet, are especially important. Because the head continues to get a good blood supply, it loses tremendous amounts of heat, and head insulation is thus very important.

Rather than repeating all the strictures on how to keep warm that have already been discussed, however, what needs to be emphasized is that a person beginning to suffer from hypothermia is *often completely unaware of the fact.* The chilling dulls his thoughts to such a degree that he may act quite irrationally, particularly in failing to take measures to halt the progressive loss of heat that will kill him if it is not stopped. He may shiver, or he may not. His skin is likely to be pale, and bluish at the lips, nails, and mucous membranes. He may be acting strangely, stumbling, or speaking in a dull fashion. It is vitally important to recognize these symptoms in a companion and to take steps to get him warm. The longer one waits, the more active warming must be. Besides getting the affected person out of wind and wet clothes and providing insulation, it may be necessary to provide external heat with hot drinks and warm bodies.

Mountaineers should also note that in case of other kinds of injuries, shock and hypothermia tend to go hand in hand, feeding on one another, so that cold weather can turn a minor injury into a major medical emergency.

HIGH-ALTITUDE PULMONARY EDEMA

This problem is less common than hypothermia, but it is nearly always fatal unless caught in time, and it strikes quite unexpectedly. It is one form of altitude sickness, but unlike many others is very serious. It is marked by a cough and shortness of breath, both of which soon become constant. The victim will feel weak, his chest will be tight, and he may be dizzy and nauseous. Gurgling can be heard if the victim exhales as much as possible. Physical effort causes considerable distress. Pulse is rapid, and bluish lips and nails will appear. As the ailment progresses, the cough brings up frothy liquid, and the victim becomes weaker. Without oxygen, the only treatment is to get him to a lower altitude, which usually produces rapid recovery. It is important not to delay evacuation if pulmonary edema is suspected, because the victim soon becomes unable to help himself.

Pulmonary edema can occur at any altitude above 9000 feet, although it is more common at high altitudes. People previously acclimatized who descend to lower altitudes and then return seem particularly prone, as do fairly strong climbers pushing hard. Perhaps this is because these groups are more likely to push their bodies hard without considering altitude problems.

HIGH-ALTITUDE CEREBRAL EDEMA

Another form of acute altitude sickness is cerebral edema, swelling of the brain due to accumulation of fluid there. As with pulmonary edema, with which it may be associated, it is important to recognize the symptoms as quickly as possible and to begin evacuation of the victim *immediately*, as soon as cerebral edema is suspected. Getting the victim to lower altitude is the most important treatment, since brain-shrinking drugs, if you have them, act very slowly.

Headache is the primary symptom of cerebral edema, and anyone with an acute headache at high altitude should be watched. Deterioration in the victim's capacity for abstract thinking also indicates cerebral edema. Unconsciousness follows. Note that giving the victim of cerebral edema any strong sedative or pain killer will probably result in death.

RESCUES

It would be difficult to attempt here to cover the techniques of rescue, which have become a specialized branch of mountaineering. Literature is mentioned in the section on additional reading. At an elementary level, with which parties can deal themselves, rescue techniques are not much different from mountaineering methods. Any injured climber who can still walk must be assisted and belayed on any terrain where he might be injured if he fell, even on ground that would normally be trivial. A combination of first aid judgment and mountaineering judgment have to dictate whether it is wise for a party to try to get an injured person out.

With a severely injured person, the best that one may be able to do is to get the victim to a place where first aid can be given and a rescue awaited. Carrying a hurt person out requires a lot of manpower, and technical evacuations involve large quantities of hardware as well. Obviously, when the party consists of more than two people, one stays with the victim. If the victim must be left alone, great care must be taken to try to ensure his comfort and safety. Head injuries in particular may lead to irrationality, so that leaving the victim in an exposed place may be very dangerous.

PREVENTING AND HANDLING EMERGENCIES

There has been an attempt throughout this book to emphasize safety for many reasons, even though the essence of climbing is adventure. Climbing is not an inherently dangerous sport, even though some kinds of climbing are quite hazardous. Even the safest and least serious climbing takes place in situations of great potential danger, and the climber must rely completely on his own skills, on those of his companions, and on his equipment to maintain his margin of safety.

The basic ways to avoid emergency situations are to allow wide margins for error, to not attempt climbs beyond one's ability, and to reinforce both equipment and judgment with safety back-ups whenever possible.The margin one allows for safety should become a habit one applies to all potentially dangerous climbing situations. The more experienced climber is more knowledgeable and can often work closer to his limits, but good climbers rarely fall into desperate situations by accident. Overconfidence, competitiveness, egoism, and the like are the most common causes of accidents among moderately experienced climbers. These are the reasons why the new Yosemite *Guidebook* does not brag, as the old one did, that "very few climbers have been hurt while climbing in the Valley, and a fatal accident is seldom heard of." The old guide went on to describe the relatively few objective dangers in the Valley. These persist; it is unsafe climbing which has caused the accident statistics to pile up.

Handling emergencies, like their prevention, is largely a matter of preparation. Spending the time needed to learn to belay properly, to tie off a fallen climber and haul him to a safe place, to perform self-rescues in case of crevasse falls, jammed ropes, and a host of other possible difficulties is the only way to be prepared for real problems when they occur. There is no substitute for learning first aid and emergency care, practicing it frequently, and carrying medical supplies. Anticipation of possible emergency situations, preparation for them, and practice of the techniques necessary for getting out of trouble make for safe and enjoyable climbing.

A FINAL WORD

While climbing is never likely to become the national pastime, it has become an established and lucrative sport. The problems of crowding, overuse, and commercialization have suddenly emerged—problems which once seemed remote in American climbing. Competition, which has always been present in various forms, suddenly seems to be a danger as climbing becomes a more popular activity.

There are many problems which the American climbing community must come to grips with and solve in some fashion, ranging from those associated with crowding and the quality of the climbing experience to those of safety and the training of fledgling mountaineers. As a group, mountaineers and rock climbers are in some ways ill-equipped to deal with these difficulties. There isn't a single organization in the United States that unites or represents the climbing community. In the past there hasn't been an expressed need for such a group. The American Alpine Club seems to be trying to fulfill this role, which in current circumstances is probably a desirable one, but only a tiny fraction of the body of American climbers belongs to the A.A.C.

Despite the many problems currently facing the climbing community, most climbers continue to view the sport in a wholly romantic way, and I include myself in this group. We feel that climbing and mountaineering offer a beauty and depth of experience that are achievable in few areas of modern life. But these rewards are not automatic. They cannot be purchased in climbing shops or gleaned from guidebooks. The aesthetic experience, deep insights, and adventures in high places are pretty much a return for a love of the mountains and a dedication to climbing.

GLOSSARY

No attempt is made here to present a comprehensive list of climbing terms. Most of the words included are used in this book in one place or another, and they are given brief definitions here so that the reader will have them in one readily accessible place. A few other commonly used words that do not appear in the book are included also.

ABSEIL—**Rappel.**

AID CLIMBING—Climbing using slings, rope, nuts, and other paraphernalia for physical assistance in climbing, not just for protection or belay anchors. On ice, aid generally refers to the use for direct support of screws or other hardware which is left in place, rather than being attached to the feet or held in the hands. Aid is distinguished from **free climbing.**

ALPINE—The term can refer to the highest biological life zone or to the European Alps, but in American climbing usage it normally describes climbing similar to that found in the Alps. Thus, an **alpine route** would normally be a fairly long climb with a mixture of technical rock, snow, and ice.

ANCHOR—An attachment to rock, snow, or ice, using a sling, nut, or some other device or collection of them; particularly the attachment used to secure the belayer.

ARÊTE—A sharp ridge, which may either angle up to a peak for some distance or merely separate two gullies on a face.

ARREST—To stop a slip or fall on snow, ice, or steep grass using the ice ax as a brake.

ASCENDER—A mechanical device used to climb a rope. Ascender knots serve the same purpose.

BASHIE—A piece of malleable metal threaded with a light sling of wire or nylon. It is smashed with a hammer to make it conform to a cranny in the rock. Used for hard direct aid.

BAT HOOK—A device invented by Warren Harding to speed long bolting pitches of direct aid. A skyhook or cliff hanger is ground down so that it will fit into a shallow drilled hole. The use of bat hooks is quite controversial, because the holes rapidly erode to a rounded state.

BELAY—To secure a climber by passing the climbing rope around something firmly tied to the mountain, normally the belayer's body, in such a way as to produce enough friction so that an accidental fall by the climber could be safely held. Used as a noun, the belay can refer to the belayer's wrap around his body and his grip on the rope, to the spot where a suitable arrangement for belaying can be set up, or to the objects to which the belayer can tie himself. On difficult climbs where no ledges are available, the belayer may have to hang from the anchors. This is called a **belay in slings** or **hanging belay.**

BERGSCHRUND—The gap which often forms between a glacier or snowfield and the rock above it, or between a glacier (which moves) and the stationary snowfield above. Crossing a *bergschrund* can present a major problem when it is large, particularly late in summer.

BIVOUAC—A bivouac is a stay on a mountain through one or more nights with minimal equipment. On long climbs, bivouacs are often planned. Also used as a verb.

BIVOUAC SACK—A lightweight, waterproof bag with one or more face openings to conserve warmth and provide protection against the elements. They are made for one, two, or three occupants.

BOLLARD—A short column or mushroom of snow or ice formed by chopping or stamping out the surrounding material. It is used for a rappel or belay anchor and must be large enough to support the forces involved.

BOLT—An anchor which is placed in a hole drilled in the rock for the purpose. There are many types of bolts. Essentially, all of them work by exerting outward pressure inside the drilled hole. The **bolt hanger** is the metal piece which is attached to the bolt and has provision for attaching one or more carabiners; depending on the type of bolt, it may or may not be removable.

BONG or BONG-BONG—A very wide angle piton, 2"–6" thick, named for its tone when hit.

BOULDER—This name for a large piece of rock has been appropriated as a verb to describe the types of climbing problems a boulder can present: difficult or extremely hard moves close to the ground. Bouldering is an excellent training exercise for big climbs and has become a sport in itself.

BUCKET—A relatively large hold with a raised edge, ideal for a secure and easy grip.

BRAKE BAR—A device designed to slip over a carabiner so that the rope can be doubled over to create friction for rappels. It serves the purpose of the **carabiner brake** system illustrated in the text.

BUTTRESS—A buttress is one of the main supporting masses of a peak or wall; normally it is a very steep, rather broad ridge.

CAGOULE—A long, very roomy, waterproof parka which can serve as protection against wind and rain, and which is large enough so that the arms and legs can be drawn inside in a bivouac.

CAM—Camming refers to the action of several kinds of anchor placements which tend to expand and jam more securely under an outward pull. Some chocks and nuts can be cammed if they are placed so that an outward pull rotates the nut toward a wider cross section. **Cable cams** have the pull come on a cable exerting force against a wedge, jamming the wedge more securely as the cable is pulled. The **Lowe cam-nut** uses a spring-loaded cam attached to a bar on which the force is exerted. Camming placements require a good deal of experience to use safely and effectively, but they have the advantage over the more common jamming placements that they can often be used in openings and cracks with parallel sides.

CARABINER—An eccentric metal ring with a spring-loaded gate in one side which can be used to clip the running rope to various anchors or to fasten pieces of rope, sling, or hardware together quickly and securely. It is one of the most versatile and important pieces of modern equipment, and every serious climber will have to own a number of them. An **oval carabiner** is, logically enough, shaped like an oval, with the gate on one side. In a **D-shaped carabiner,** the side opposite the gate is straightened. This provides a good deal of additional strength by shifting the load away from the gate and hinge, which are the weak points on an oval, but many climbers object to some handling characteristics of D's. In a **modified D,** one end is larger than the other, allowing more room to clip in slings and rope but retaining the strength of the D. The strength of carabiners deserves considerable attention from the climber.

CARABINER BRAKE—A method of clipping carabiners together so that the rope can be run through a number of friction-producing bends, enabling the user to handle considerable loads safely. One type of carabiner brake is shown in the section on rappelling. Using the same principle, more friction can easily be added in situations where it is needed, such as rescues.

CHALK—Athletic chalk can be bought in bar form and carried in a bag for dusting the hands in difficult climbing. The marks made on the rock are unsightly, however.

CHICKENHEAD—A conveniently shaped rock projection with enough of a knob on the top for a sling to be securely cinched around it.

CHIMNEY—A long cleft in rock or ice, wide enough so that the body can fit between the two sides, yet narrow enough for the climber to be able to exert pressure on both walls at the same time. The technique of climbing chimneys is often to wedge the body by pushing on both sides at once, gradually working one's way up; thus **chimneying** refers to this method of climbing. The narrowest chimneys, into which one can just struggle, are called **squeeze chimneys,** and as the gap becomes wider, different parts of the body are used to bridge it: in the narrowest, heel-and-toe and hand-and-elbow; foot-and-knee or knee-and-back as the gap becomes slightly wider; feet-and-back and left-against-right hands at the most comfortable size; and finally, at the widest, a scissors spread of the legs from one side to the other. A **flaring chimney** is wider in the front than the back, and will require a narrow chimney or jamming technique at the back and a wider bridge on the outside of the body.

CHOCK—A term derived from **chockstone,** a rock which is wedged into a constricted section of a crack or chimney. A chock is constructed, usually of metal, specifically for jamming in cracks and other crannies in the rock. It is often called a **nut,** because the original type of chock was a machine nut picked up along the railroad tracks on the way to some British cliff climbs. Chocks are normally threaded with steel cable or with nylon rope or webbing to allow carabiners to be clipped to them.

CHOP—In climbing, chopping usually refers to the removal of the end of a bolt with a hammer or something else, rendering it unusable (but leaving part of the bolt and a scar). Most commonly, bolts are chopped when they are placed by later and less competent parties after the route was originally climbed without them. Unfortunately, bolting and chopping contests have often resulted in unsightly rows of scars and chopped bolts. When bolts must be removed for aesthetic or safety reasons, it is usually better to pull the bolt and fill in the hole with an epoxy-sand mixture.

CHUTE—A relatively steep and narrow cleft extending down a face, into which avalanches and rockfall are quite likely to be channeled. Water, snow, and debris, as they fall down a mountain under the influence of gravity, will tend to erode channels or enlarge other cleavages to form a drainage system from the mountain. On steep terrain, a system of grooves and crevices will be formed in the rock, snow, and ice. The terms for these features are somewhat interchangeable, but each has certain connotations. **Gully** is the most general term. A **couloir** is usually fairly steep, forming a direct line up the formation in which it is set, and often providing the main drainage for a whole face. A **chute** is likely to be narrower and steeper than a couloir, and a number of chutes may feed into a couloir. A chute may narrow into a chimney, particularly at the top.

CLAW—Clawing is the technique of climbing steep ice or hard snow using both hands and feet to drive sharp climbing tools into the ice, using them as holds. Normally, **crampons** with protruding front points are worn on the feet, and an ice ax or ice hammer is held in each hand. Clawing (**front-pointing**) is distinguished from climbing in balance with the weight directly over the crampons and from cutting steps and using them for making progress.

CLEAN—Cleaning a pitch means removing all the hardware placed by the leader.

CLEAN CLIMBING—This is a relatively new concept, and its meaning may be slightly different in different areas or groups. Essentially it refers to climbing which leaves the rock unscarred and undamaged after the climbing team has passed. Natural anchors and nuts are preferred to pitons that scar the rocks. The use of chalk may well come to be considered undesirable for the same reasons.

CLIFF HANGER—A type of **skyhook** made by Chouinard.

CLIP IN—To attach oneself to the mountain by means of a carabiner snapped onto an anchor.

COL—A pass; a low point in a ridge, usually a rather rounded or gentle one.

CORNER—In describing the features of a rock wall or face, corner refers to an angular feature, usually at something like 90°. An **outside corner** is a protruding vertical rib of rock. An **inside corner** is the included angle between two faces of rock that come together to form a roughly vertical intersection with an angle between them of between perhaps 60° and 120°. An inside corner may also be called an **open book** or a **dihedral.** A **left-facing** or **right-facing open book** refers to the direction toward which the inside corner opens.

CORNICE—An overhanging lip of snow which forms on the leeward side of a ridge when snow is blown across it. Cornices present several dangers to climbers. They are often difficult to see from the opposite side of the ridge, so that one can walk out onto the overhanging cornice without realizing it. When approaching from below, the climber may find it very difficult and strenuous to bypass or cut through the cornice. Falling sections of cornices can be dangerous in themselves and frequently trigger avalanches on the slopes below.

COULOIR—See **chute.**

CRACK TACK—A very short piton used for difficult direct aid in marginal cracks. Similar to a **rurp,** but used in slightly different types of situations.

CRAMPONS—Metal frames with spikes protruding from the bottoms, designed to be strapped onto the climber's boots and to bite into ice or snow, so enabling him to ascend steep slopes without cutting steps or improving his security in steps. Different types of crampons are discussed in the main text.

CREVASSE—A deep crack in the ice of a glacier, resulting from the stress of the glacier's movement over uneven ground. Crevasses range from narrow fissures to huge chasms in size. Because they normally form as a glacier flows over an irregularity, they tend to run parallel to one another, at least in one area. Less reliably, they commonly extend perpendicular to the direction of glacial flow. When a glacier is bare, with no recent snows or winter deposits covering it, crevasses often represent grave obstacles; but they tend to be less dangerous because they can be seen.

A layer of snow will form bridges over the crevasses, but it will also conceal them, baiting a trap for the unwary. Travel is normally perpendicular to the direction of crevasses, or in a staggered line, to prevent more than one climber from falling into the same crevasse. Conventional wisdom puts the minimum number for safe glacier travel at three, because of the difficulty of crevasse rescue.

DEADBOY—A small plate-type **deadman** for use in hard snow.

DEADMAN—An object buried in snow or earth with an anchor line tied to it, so that the anchor line is held by all the material in front of the deadman. Rocks, logs, packs, icicles, and many other objects can be used for deadmen. A more sophisticated device for snow is a cabled metal plate, angled from the line of pull, so that it absorbs energy as it dives into the snow, giving more holding power than the snow in front of the plate alone could provide. These are discussed in the main text, as are **flukes** —plates designed to be self-orienting as they are pulled through the snow.

DIHEDRAL—See **corner.**

DIKE—A vein of stronger rock which protrudes from the weaker rock surrounding it. It is formed by molten material working into a fissure in the surrounding rock. A dike is always fairly long, but it may be only a few inches wide and protrude only a little, or it may be many feet thick and stick out quite a way.

DIRECT AID—**Aid climbing.**

DOWEL—A direct aid tool for difficult routes which is somewhat controversial. A dowel is a short cylindrical piece of aluminum which is driven into an undersized, shallow, drilled hole and tied off with a piece of webbing. It requires less drilling than a bolt.

DROOP—The amount of downward curve in the pick of an ice ax or ice hammer. It is important for severe ice climbing and is discussed in more detail in the text.

ÉTRIERS—Short ladders used in direct aid climbing. In the U.S. they are generally made by tying loops in 1″ nylon webbing. Europeans often use rope to which aluminum rungs are fixed.

FACE—A steep, broad side of a mountain or pinnacle. A mountain may have several faces with ridges or buttresses in between. A **face** generally refers to a mountainside at least steep enough to present serious climbing problems.

FACE CLIMBING—Although a particular face of a mountain may have routes involving wide varieties of climbing techniques, **face climbing** refers to climbing on steep terrain using small protruding holds, rather than chimneys or cracks, for example.

FIFI—A hook, widely used in Europe to hook *étriers* into placements. A fifi has a small eye in the top so that it can be retrieved from above with light cord attached to the climber. Fifis are most useful on climbs that alternate between free climbing and direct aid, since it is often difficult to move up from direct aid to a free section and reach back to unclip the *étrier.* Fifis are not widely used here, however. Some climbers like to use a fifi to attach a waist line to direct aid placements on overhanging rock.

FLUKE—See **deadman.**

FREE CLIMBING—Climbing in which slings, nuts, pitons, and other anchors are used only to protect the climber in case of a fall, not for climbing progress. Distinguished from **direct aid.**

FREE SOLO—A climb on a difficult route, alone and without a rope.

FRENCH TECHNIQUE—Climbing on hard snow or ice with the crampons planted flat on the slope and the body in balance, with no step-cutting and with the hands and ice ax used mainly for balance. Distinguished from step-cutting, **clawing,** or **front-pointing.**

FRICTION CLIMBING—Climbing with the sole of the shoe or boot placed flat against the rock for friction, rather than hooking the edge of the sole onto small holds or jamming the boot into cracks. Friction climbing describes the type of climbing where this technique predominates. Few routes are pure friction routes, so many prefer the term **slab climbing. Friction shoes** are rock-climbing shoes which are very tight-fitting and flexible, so that they are best suited for friction technique. **Smearing** is a friction technique used on steep, scooped holds, where the sole is squashed into the hold to gain maximum adherence.

FRONT-POINT—See **claw.**

FROST WEDGING—The action of water in loosening rocks on a mountain, seeping into cracks in liquid form and then freezing and expanding, exerting tremendous forces and prying the crack wider. Frost wedging often causes heavy rockfall when the sun begins to shine on the face of a mountain. The freezing water loosens blocks overnight which remain held in place by the ice until it is remelted in the day. The same phenomenon occurs during spring thaw.

GENDARME—A tower or pinnacle along a ridge. Gendarmes often present significant climbing difficulties for parties on ridge routes.

GLACIER—A permanent field of snow and ice that is slowly moving down a mountainside or valley. Snow deposited on top and at the upper end of the glacier is gradually transformed into ice by snow metamorphosis, by pressure, and by alternate thawing and freezing. A **permanent snowfield** or **icefield** differs from a glacier in that it is not moving downhill. Major glaciation is responsible for many of the most spectacular features of mountain terrain. At the moment most glaciers in the world are receding, particularly in North America; that is, they are melting away at the bottom faster than snow is building on top. The characteristic features of glaciers —crevasses and icefalls—result from the flow of the river of ice over uneven terrain. The **crevasses** are small or massive cracks that form as the ice deforms; icefalls are great jumbles of crevasses and blocks of ice that form as the glacier slowly cascades down cliffs along its path. In most U.S. ranges, such as the Rockies and the Sierra Nevada, the remaining glaciers are rather small and have few crevasses or icefalls. In the Northwest, in Canada, and in Alaska, however, great and very active glaciers remain to challenge the mountaineer.

GLISSADE—Used as a noun or a verb, this is the technique of descending snowfields by sliding. It is one of the fastest and most pleasant ways to descend a peak, but it is full of dangerous pitfalls for the unwary. A **sitting glissade** is performed on the seat of the pants, while in a **standing glissade** the soles of the boots are used like skis. In both cases the ice ax is used to provide control, with self-arrest or a belay available in case the glissade goes awry.

GULLY—See **chute.**

HANGER—Generally refers to a **bolt hanger,** a small metal device that attaches securely to the bolt and has a hole large enough to admit one or more carabiners. Hangers may be made of aluminum or steel, with steel providing a better safety margin. Depending on the type of bolt and the design of the hanger, the hanger may remain permanently with the bolt or be removable. On older routes and infrequently ascended ones, spare hangers and the machine nuts that hold them on have to be carried. Both the nut and the hole in the hanger must be of the correct size, ¼" and ⅜" bolts being the most common. **Keyhole hangers** have become popular in a few climbing areas. The large carabiner hole is slipped over the end of the bolt (which can have either a nut or a wide head), and the hanger then slides down with a slot gripping the bolt head. A carabiner through the hole locks the hanger on. The keyhole hanger is removable, and this type of hanger must be carried on routes where the original ascent party used keyholes on rivet-head bolts.

HERO LOOP—A small loop made from 18–30" of ½" or ⁹⁄₁₆" webbing, which can be used for a number of purposes, particularly in difficult direct aid. A loop can be used to tie off a piton that cannot be driven in all the way; to provide a higher tie-in to a nut with a long runner; to prevent rope drag or leverage on an anchor; and so on. Originally, the term *hero loop* referred to the use of a short loop to provide a very high step, above the top one in an *étrier*, for a very long reach on a direct aid move.

HORN—A projecting piece of rock, over which a sling can be hung for an anchor.

ICEFALL—As described under **glacier,** an icefall is a chaotic mass of jumbled ice resulting from a steep section in the glacial bed. Because of their ruggedness and instability, they can be extremely dangerous. Icefall is also commonly used now to describe a frozen waterfall, which can provide interesting problems in technical ice climbing.

JAM CRACK—A more or less vertical crack which is climbed by wedging or jamming different parts of the body and then pulling up on them. Finger jams may be less than an inch wide, toe jams an inch or a few inches, and a heel-and-toe jam nearly a foot wide. **Jam** is also used to describe both the technique of climbing such cracks and an individual hold of the type. Thus, a **fist jam** is a hold created in a cranny by inserting the hand and expanding it by making it into a fist. Jamming is generally a rather strenuous type of climbing.

JUMAR—The trade name for a Swiss mechanical rope-gripping device. This type of ascender is so widely used for self-belay on expeditions and for seconding and hauling on big walls that the name has been anglicized and is used as a verb as well as a noun.

KERNMANTEL—Describes the construction of ropes which have a core protected by an outer braided sheath (mantel). In modern kernmantel ropes the core (kern) is generally made of one or more braided units.

KLETTERSCHUE—The German term for tight-fitting, flexible rock-climbing shoes.

KNIFE EDGE—Used to describe a very sharp ridge crest, with precipitous exposure on both sides.

KNIFEBLADE—A horizontal piton with a very thin blade, made from chromolly steel. The thicker knifeblades, when well placed, may offer adequate protection. Thinner ones are useful mainly for direct aid.

LEAD—To lead is to climb a pitch first, without an upper belay, thus incurring the risk of longer falls than would normally be experienced by the climbers following, if they were to slip. The **leader** also has the responsibility of placing whatever anchors are required for the protection of the party. A **lead** is the distance between one belay spot and the next, or the climb up that distance (also called a **pitch**). A **long lead** is one in which the whole length of the rope is pulled out, so it would be nearly 120', 150', or 165', depending on the customary rope length of the climbing area.

LIEBACK—This is a strenuous climbing technique in which adherence to two vertical holds is gained by pulling back against one with the hands and pushing the feet against the other. The principle is the same as chimneying, except that the full force of opposition must be sustained by the hands, arms, and shoulders. Liebacks are perhaps most often used for a move or two, but in difficult climbing they can be used to ascend long vertical flakes, open books, and offset cracks.

MANTLE (or MANTLESHELF)—A ledge at chest height or above which must be climbed by pulling up with the arms, flipping the elbows up, and pushing the body up until the feet can reach the ledge. **Mantle** is also used as a verb to describe the action of making such a move. Difficult mantles can be made onto fairly small holds.

MIXED CLIMBING—In classical mountaineering, the term refers to climbing involving rock, snow, and ice techniques. The versatility demanded by such "alpine-type" climbing puts extra demands on the climber's skill and may tax the rock climber new to the high mountains. **Mixed climbing** may also refer to alternating free and direct aid, and this usage is common in pure rock-climbing areas.

MORAINE—A heap of rock which has been or is being transported by a glacier. Moraines of various sizes will be found both on and around active glaciers and in previously glaciated areas. The size of the moraine and the boulders that form it are influenced by many factors, but several common features and forms can be mentioned. Moraines bear a superficial resemblance to talus piles resulting from rockfall, but a moraine is often more unstable, because a boulder deposited by melting ice is less likely to drop into a stable position than one that has crashed down from far above. A **terminal moraine** is deposited at the snout (lower end) of a glacier as the ice melts, and a glacier may have several terminal moraines below it, reflecting different periods in its history. A **lateral moraine** is formed by rocks collecting along the sides of a glacier, primarily as a result of glacial cutting of its walls. Melting may leave the lateral moraine deposited in the valley. When two glacial valleys meet, the confluence of the glaciers will bring the two inside lateral moraines together in the middle on the larger glacier that flows down the valley below the confluence; this central line of debris is a **medial moraine.** Very large glaciers that result from the joining of many smaller ones may have a number of medial moraines.

NAIL—Nailing is the ascent of cracks using pitons for direct aid.

NÉVÉ—Old and well-consolidated snow that has been reduced to a dense layer of granular crystals by alternate melting and freezing. When frozen it presents climbing problems similar to glacier ice.

NUT—See **chock.**

OPEN BOOK—See **corner.**

PEG—A British term for **piton.**

PENDULUM—A direct aid technique used to get across a section of blank rock or a rotten area from one crack system to another without having to use bolts all the way across. The climbers move high in one crack system, place an anchor, move back down, and swing across to the second system. A pendulum may be relatively easy, but is often quite difficult and usually involves complicated logistical problems.

PERLON—The trade name for a European type of nylon. The molecular structure is actually slightly different from that of the nylon commonly made in the U.S., but the properties are virtually identical. Because ropes imported from Europe are made of Perlon and are of **kernmantel** construction, Perlon is often used as a synonym for kernmantel in America.

PIN—A **piton.**

PITCH—The route or distance between one belay stance and the next. It may be a full rope length or considerably less. Thus, one speaks of "leading a pitch," or says, "The third pitch is the hardest on the climb."

PITON—A metal device with a tapered blade that will wedge into a crack in the rock when driven with a hammer and an eye or ring through which a sling or carabiner can be attached. Many types of pitons are illustrated and discussed in the text.

PROTECTION—A general descriptive term for the means a leader uses to ensure that a slip would not result in serious injury or death. **Protection points** refer to places where some kind of running belay can be attached to the rock or mountain—runners, chocks, pitons, bolts, or whatever. Hence, if someone says, "That climb can be adequately protected with nuts," he means that a properly experienced party can make the climb safely without resorting to pitons or bolts. To say that the protection on a pitch leaves something to be desired means that suitable spots for anchors are sparse or insecure.

PRUSIK—A knot (named after its inventor) which can be tied around a rope, and which will jam under tension but can be moved when the load is removed. The standard ascender knot. It can be used to ascend a fixed line, to tie off a fallen climber or a load, to extricate oneself from jammed rappels, and so on. Used as a verb, it means to climb a rope by means of prusiks or other ascender knots or mechanical devices.

RAPPEL—To descend by sliding down a rope, using some sort of wrap around the body or around a mechanical system to produce enough friction to control descent. The rope is normally doubled so that it can be pulled down afterward. The **rappel point** or **anchor** is what the rope or the sling holding it is fastened to at the top. Some of the many systems of rappelling are discussed in the text.

ROOF—A severely overhanging section of rock. A small roof may project only a few feet, while some formidable roofs on great walls may extend out dozens of feet.

ROPE—Mountaineering ropes, which are now always made of nylon (except for some special-purpose lines), are discussed extensively in the text. A **laid** rope is one made by successive twistings of individual nylon fibers and then of the yarns and strands made from them; while a **kernmantel** rope has a braided sheath over a core of one or more braided strands. A **rope** or **rope team** may also refer to a group of climbers roped together. To **rope up** is to tie together with the rope. Thus, a rope-up point is the place where the climbing becomes sufficiently serious to require roping. **Roping down** is another term for rappelling.

RUNNER—A loop tied or sewn from webbing or rope which is used for anchors and running belays. A runner may be looped over a flake, horn, or block, threaded through a hole in the rock, or attached to a nut, piton, or bolt. Standard-size runners are made from 1″ webbing or 9-mm (⅜″) rope, but smaller sizes are often used for some purposes. The use of runners is discussed extensively in the text.

RURP—A very thin, short piton used for marginal direct aid in very narrow cracks, fissures, and seams in the rock. The name is an acronym for *realized ultimate reality piton*. Rurps were invented by Yvon Chouinard and they are made by his company. They are similar to CMI's crack tacks, but each has certain advantages.

SCREE—Large quantities of small stones, usually in a **scree slope**. Scree is formed from the debris that falls from mountains and cliffs as they erode. **Talus** is the term used for larger blocks, and the piles of debris from decomposing mountains often consist of talus fans below with scree slopes above. Unless they are stabilized by dirt, scree slopes tend to be quite unstable; and although they are not dangerous, climbing them can be exhausting and boring, since the climber tends to slide back most of the way for each step he takes.

SECOND—The second man on a rope, usually a rope of two, whose tasks include belaying the leader and removing the protection placed by him. **Seconding** is performing these tasks.

SELF-ARREST—The technique of stopping a slip on snow or slippery vegetation, mainly by using one's ice ax for braking. A basic and essential mountaineering technique.

SÉRAC—A large block or tower of ice. Séracs form in areas of glaciers where tumbling or squeezing causes the ice to break up, primarily in icefalls; they are often extremely dangerous, since they eventually topple over, and anyone who happens to be in the way will be killed. The likelihood of a sérac's falling at any particular time will depend on the actual icefall, on temperatures, and on a host of imponderable factors.

SKYHOOK—A steel hook used in difficult and often tenuous direct aid routes to hang *étriers* from small flakes, ledges, and crystals, permitting upward progress without the climbers' having to resort to bolts.

SLAB—A flat piece of rock resting at an angle; it may be small or may form a whole face of a formation. A slab tends to be smooth and the holds small, although there is no precise meaning, and the actual surface may be polished smooth or filled with solution pockets. The connotation of **slab climbing** is that friction techniques predominate.

SLING—A loop of webbing or rope, either carried for use as a **runner** or tied through a nut or other protection or aid device. Uses for slings of many sizes are innumerable in climbing, and many are discussed in the text. A **sling belay** or **belay in slings** is a belay on a vertical wall where no suitable places to sit or stand are available, so that the belayer has to hang in slings suspended from anchors.

SMASHIE—A **bashie.**

SMEAR—See **friction climbing.**

SNAP-LINK—A carabiner.

SOLO—Climb alone. It is used both as a noun and as a verb. Soloing is sometimes done without any belay, although various self-belaying methods have been devised. Solo climbing at any level is considerably more demanding and hazardous than climbing with companions.

STIRRUPS—Direct aid slings made like little rope ladders with aluminum steps. They are no longer used much in this country.

SUNCUPS—Concave depressions formed on the surface of a permanent snowfield or a glacier by uneven melting and then by concentration of the sun's rays in the concavity. Large suncups can be several feet deep, so that crossing deeply cupped snow can be a considerable chore.

TECHNICAL CLIMBING—This is a rather loose term, because of variability of style and capability among climbers, but it makes a very useful distinction. Technical routes are those requiring the hardware of modern climbing and the ability to use it. Technical climbing is distinguished from classical techniques relying mainly on ice axes, threading the rope behind gendarmes, and the motto that in really exposed places, "The leader must not fall." In general, technical routes are those classified as fifth and sixth class.

TENSION TRAVERSE—A direct aid technique for passing a holdless section. The leader places an anchor, clips the rope through it, and pushes or pulls his way across while leaning out on the rope. Similar to a **pendulum,** except that the latter is usually longer and requires hanging from the rope and anchor, rather than simply pulling against them. As with a pendulum, the logistics for getting the second across and retrieving the rope may be complex. Retreat may also be impossible unless a fixed rope is left.

TIE-OFF LOOP—A short loop, generally of ½" or ⁹⁄₁₆" webbing, used to tie around a piton that can be driven only part way into a crack, to reduce leverage on the piton.

TRASHIE—A **bashie** that has been left on a route and that is strung with a nylon sling. The sling soon rots, and the metal blob is useless as well as unsightly.

TRAVERSE—A section of a route that goes horizontally across a cliff or face. Traverses may be easy walks along ledges or difficult passages. The problems of protecting traverses are often complicated, because a fall will cause the climber to swing down in a pendulum-like movement, and he will end off the route even if he is unhurt. A traverse is likely to be as hazardous for the second as for the leader, since he does not have an upper belay. The leader has to be careful to place protection for the second as well as himself. Protection for the leader will be placed just before a hard move, while protection for the second goes in just after.

UNDERCLING—A move or series of moves made by reaching down with the hands and pulling up on a down-facing hold to push the feet against the rock. Somewhat strenuous.

VERGLAS—A thin coating of ice deposited on rock. It makes for very difficult climbing, because it is generally too thin to allow effective use of crampons, although the rock is as slippery as a pure ice slope. It is produced by freezing rain or by a cold snap that freezes meltwater.

WALL—A steep cliff or face, vertical or nearly so. The term is used to refer to small features on a mountain and also to name great faces of extreme difficulty. A **big wall** in the U.S. is likely to refer to a major vertical rock climb of 1000 feet or more, perhaps requiring bivouacs in hammocks suspended from the rock. More generally, a wall will be a great mountain face. In an unfortunate use of the term, individual routes have sometimes been called walls, particularly in Yosemite, as with the Muir Wall, a route on the Southwest Face of El Capitan.

ZIPPER—A series of very poor direct aid placements, all of which can be expected to pop out one after the other if the leader makes a false move.

BIBLIOGRAPHY

No attempt is made here to list all the books about climbing that have appeared since it began to be viewed as a worthwhile activity. So many literate and thoughtful people have climbed and written about their experiences that the list would be very long indeed. The selection here is merely a sampling to get the interested climber started.

JOURNALS AND MAGAZINES

Accidents in North American Mountaineering. Published annually by the American Alpine Club, 113 E. 90th St., New York, N.Y. 10028.
American Alpine Journal. Published annually by the American Alpine Club, address above.
Ascent. Published annually by the Sierra Club, Mills Tower, San Francisco, Calif. 94104.
Canadian Alpine Journal. Published annually by the Alpine Club of Canada, Banff, Alberta.
Climbing. Published bimonthly, Box 962, Aspen, Colo. 81611.
Mountain. Published ten times a year, 56 Sylvester Rd., London N.2, Great Britain.
Off Belay. Published bimonthly, 12416 169th Ave. S.E., Renton, Wash. 98055.
Summit. Published ten times a year, P.O. Box 1889, Big Bear Lake, Calif. 92315.

BOOKS ON TECHNIQUE

Backpacking and Camping
Bridge, Raymond. *America's Backpacking Book.* New York: Charles Scribner's Sons, 1973. Paper edition.
Fletcher, Colin. *The New Complete Walker.* New York: Random House, 1975.
Manning, Harvey. *Backpacking: One Step at a Time.* Seattle: Recreational Equipment, Inc., 1972. Paper edition.
Map and Compass Work
Kjellstrom, Bjorn. *Be Expert with Map and Compass.* New edition. New York: Charles Scribner's Sons, 1976.
Rutstrum, Calvin. *The Wilderness Route Finder.* New York: Macmillan, 1967. Paper edition.

Winter Travel

Bridge, Raymond. *The Complete Snow Camper's Guide.* New York: Charles Scribner's Sons, 1973. Paper edition.

Brower, David. *Manual of Ski Mountaineering.* San Francisco: Sierra Club, 1962.

LaChapelle, E. R. *The ABC of Avalanche Safety.* Denver: Colorado Outdoor Sports, 1961.

Snow Avalanches. U.S. Department of Agriculture booklet 194, 1961.

Tejada-Flores, Lito, and Steck, Allen. *Wilderness Skiing.* San Francisco: Sierra Club, 1972.

Climbing Technique

Chouinard Equipment Catalogue. Published by the Great Pacific Iron Works, P.O. Box 150, Ventura, Calif. 93001.

Ferber, Peggy, ed. *Mountaineering: The Freedom of the Hills.* 3rd ed. Seattle: The Mountaineers, 1974.

Forrest Mountaineering Catalogue. Available from 5050-M-Fox St., Denver, Colo. 80216.

Henderson, Kenneth A. *Handbook of American Mountaineering.* Boston: Houghton Mifflin, 1942.

May, W. G. *Mountain Search and Rescue Techniques.* Boulder, Colo.: Rocky Mountain Rescue Group, 1973.

Rébuffat, Gaston. *On Ice and Snow and Rock.* New York: Oxford University Press, 1974.

Robbins, Royal. *Advanced Rockcraft.* Glendale, Calif.: La Siesta Press, 1973.

Robbins, Royal. *Basic Rockcraft.* Glendale, Calif.: La Siesta Press, 1971.

Smith, Phil D. *Knots for Mountaineering.* Redlands, Calif., 1971.

Wheelock, Walt. *Ropes, Knots and Slings for Climbers.* Glendale, Calif.: La Siesta Press, 1960.

A Sampling of the Inspirational, Devotional, and Terrifying

Abbey, Edward. *Desert Solitaire.* New York: McGraw-Hill, 1968. Paper edition.

Beckey, Fred. *Challenge of the North Cascades.* Seattle: The Mountaineers, 1970.

Bonatti, Walter. *The Great Days.* London: Gollancz, 1974.

Bonnington, Chris. *Annapurna South Face.* New York: McGraw-Hill, 1971.

Buhl, Hermann. *Lonely Challenge.* New York: E. P. Dutton & Co., 1956.

Harrer, Heinrich. *The White Spider.* New York: E. P. Dutton & Co., 1960.

Harvard, Andrew, and Thompson, Todd. *Mountain of Storms.* New York: New York University Press, 1974.

Herzog, Maurice. *Annapurna.* New York: E. P. Dutton & Co., 1952. Paper edition.

Hornbein, Thomas. *Everest: The West Ridge.* San Francisco: Sierra Club, 1965. Paper edition.

Houston, Charles S. *K2: The Savage Mountain.* New York: McGraw-Hill, 1954.

Hunt, Sir John. *The Conquest of Everest.* New York: E. P. Dutton & Co., 1954.

Irving, R. L. G. *The Romance of Mountaineering.* London: Dent & Sons, 1935.

Muir, John. *The Mountains of California.* New York: Doubleday, 1970. Paper edition.

Mummery, Albert F. *My Climbs in the Alps and the Caucasus.* Reprint of the 1896 edition. Somerville, Mass.: Quarterman, 1974.

Rébuffat, Gaston. *Starlight and Storm.* New York: E. P. Dutton & Co., 1957.

Roberts, David. *Mountain of My Fear.* New York: Vanguard, 1968.

Sayre, Woodrow W. *Four Against Everest.* New York: Tower, 1971.

Scott, Doug. *Big Wall Climbing.* New York: Oxford University Press, 1974.
Terray, Lionel. *Borders of the Impossible.* (Also published under the title *Conquistadors of the Useless.*) London: Gollancz, 1963.
Whymper, Edward. *Scrambles Amongst the Alps.* New York: Transatlantic, 1970.
Young, Geoffrey. *Mountain Craft.* New York: Charles Scribner's Sons, 1920.

GUIDEBOOKS TO CLIMBING AREAS

Guidebooks are constantly being revised, going out of print, or being replaced. They are also quite variable in accuracy and usefulness, depending on both the author and the nature of the area being described. One expects far more accurate and useful descriptions in a guidebook describing rock climbs in a popular and well-developed area like the Shawangunks or Yosemite, where weather and varying ice conditions play a relatively minor role and where most routes have been repeated many times by many climbers, than in a remote mountainous region, where many climbs have been done only once and descriptions must be gleaned from sketchy accounts or faded memory. Stopping at a local climbing store is one of the best ways to get route advice, information on regional climbing ethics, and up-to-date guidebooks. In some climbing areas, guides that do exist are not publicized to avoid attracting large numbers of people.

This section is bound to be incomplete, but it should provide a starting point. Addresses are included for some of the privately published books. Most guides are not distributed through standard publishing channels. They are best obtained through stores that specialize in climbing.

EASTERN U.S.

The Appalachian Mountain Club, with headquarters in Boston, publishes many hiking guides, but climbing guides to many eastern areas either do not exist or are hard to find. There are spots with good technical climbing on Mt. Katahdin in Maine and in New Hampshire's Presidential Range, for example, for which information is scarce.

Climber's Guide to the Mount Washington Valley, by Joseph Cote, includes such fine outcrops as Cathedral and White Horse Ledges. Write 659 Hall St., Manchester, N.H. 03104.

Cannon: A Climber's Guide, by Howard Peterson, covers the best-known New England cliff. Write Three Owls Productions, Box 575, South Lancaster, Mass. 01561.

Shawangunk Rock Climbs, by Richard Williams, covers the most popular Eastern rock climbing areas. New York: American Alpine Club, 1972.

Climber's Guide to the Adirondacks, by Healy, covers some other New York climbing. Available from Eastern Mountain Sports, 1047 Commonwealth Ave., Boston, Mass. 02215.

Climber's Guide to the Quincy Quarries, by Crother and Thompson, covers a local
area in greater Boston and should be obtainable from Eastern Mountain Sports if
it is reprinted.
Climbing in Eastern Massachusetts, by Steve Hendrick and Sam Streibert, discusses
the rocks around the Boston area. Available from Milgamex Co., Box 133, Wayland,
Mass.
Climbing Guide to Ragged Mountain, by the Yale Outing Club, is a pamphlet guide
to a nearby cliff.
A Climber's Guide to Seneca Rocks, by F. R. Robinson, covers the favorite rock-
climbing area in the middle Atlantic states, in West Virginia. Available from the
Potomac Appalachian Trail Club, 1718 N St. N.W., Washington, D.C. 20036.
Pittsburgh Area Climber's Guide, by Ivan L. Jirak, discusses cliffs within a few hours'
drive of the city, including Seneca Rocks. Available from the author, 205 Sheldon
Ave., Pittsburgh, Pa. 15220.

MIDWEST

Climber's Guide to the Mississippi Palisades, by Kolocotronis, is about an area along
the Mississippi River in Illinois. Available from Eastern Mountain Sports, address
above.
Climber's and Hiker's Guide to Devil's Lake, by David Smith and Roger Zimmerman,
gives routes for this area in eastern North Dakota. Published in Madison, Wisconsin.

ROCKY MOUNTAIN REGION

Climber's Guide to the Rocky Mountains of Canada—South, by William Putnam and
Glen Boles.
Climber's Guide to the Rocky Mountains of Canada—North, by William Putnam,
Robert Kruszyna, and Chris Jones. Together these guidebooks cover the finest
mountains in North America which do not require expeditions to reach. Both are
published in New York by the American Alpine Club and the Alpine Club of
Canada, the first in 1973, the second in 1974.
Climber's Guide to Glacier National Park, by J. Gordon Edwards, discusses routes in
Montana just south of the border. San Francisco: Sierra Club, 1966.
Technical routes in most of the U.S. Rockies, from Montana to New Mexico, have been
mercifully unrecorded in guidebooks. By and large, climbers interested in the
Rockies will have to research routes in old climbing journals or find their own.
Montana has a number of fine climbing areas, but, except for Glacier National Park,
there are no guidebooks. The same is true of Idaho, except that a guide to the
magnificent climbing in the Sawtooths was published in *Off Belay,* February 1975.
Guide to the Wyoming Mountains, by Orrin and Lorraine Bonney, is a monumental
work that covers the climbing in this large area as well as one book can. Chicago:
Swallow, 1976. Portions of Bonney's Guide, covering the Tetons, the Wind Rivers,
the Absorokas, and the Big Horns, have been reprinted in four separate *Field Books,*
which are a bit more manageable in size and format, but only the first two were
available when this was written.

Specific route descriptions for many of the routes on Devil's Tower, in northeast
Wyoming, can be obtained from the Superintendent, Devil's Tower National Monument, Devil's Tower, Wyoming 82714.

A Climber's Guide to the Needles of the Black Hills of South Dakota, by Bob Kamps,
gives route descriptions for the group of pinnacles just over the border from Devil's
Tower. New York: American Alpine Club, 1972.

A Climber's Guide to the Teton Range, by Leigh Ortenburger, is the standard guide
to one of America's favorite climbing areas. The full 1965 edition is currently out
of print. Until a new complete edition is published an abridged version is available
from San Francisco: Sierra Club, 1974.

Guidebooks to the rock-climbing areas in southern Wyoming, such as Veedauwoo,
have been published, but they are often not promoted to avoid attracting a large
number of people.

Guide to the Colorado Mountains, by Robert Ormes, is confined to nontechnical
routes. Chicago: Swallow, 1970.

A Climber's Guide to the Rocky Mountain National Park Area, by Walter Fricke,
covers one section of the Colorado mountains. Available from the author, #45, 1720
South Marshall Rd., Boulder, Colo. 80303.

Long's Peak: Its Story and a Climbing Guide, by Paul Nesbit, gives additional cover-
age to the highest peak in the Park. Available from Norman Nesbit, 1075 10th St.,
Boulder, Colo. 80302.

Roof of the Rockies, by William Bueler, is a history of Colorado climbing rather than
a guide, but it includes a lot of route information unavailable elsewhere. Boulder,
Colo.: Pruett, 1974.

High Over Boulder, by Pat Ament and Cleveland McCarty, is the standard guidebook
to the rock climbs around Boulder, Colo., but it is currently out of print.

Eldorado, by Pat Ament, is a guide to one of the canyons near Boulder. Available from
Paddock Publishing, 1115 Pearl St., Boulder, Colo. 80302.

Guide to the New Mexico Mountains, by Herbert Ungnade, includes technical climbing information. Chicago: Swallow, 1974.

The area between the Rockies and the Sierra and Cascade ranges has several good
climbs, but little guidebook information. A partial guide to the desert climbs in the
region by Steve Roper was published in *Ascent,* 1970.

Granite Mountain Guidebook, by David Lovejoy, covers the Arizona outcrop. Available from Outdoor Action, Prescott College, Prescott, Ariz. 86301.

THE COASTAL RANGES

The Coastal Ranges of British Columbia, which offer some of the finest climbing in the
world, are not covered by a guidebook. Research in climbing journals is the best
alternative available to those interested.

Guide to the Interior Ranges of British Columbia—North, by William Putnam, covers
half of the central mountains of the province. Until the companion volume is published, a copy of the 1969 edition, which covered north and south, might be found.
The new one is published in New York by the American Alpine Club, 1975.

The northern Cascades are also not covered by guidebooks at this time.

Routes and Rocks in the Mt. Challenger Quadrangle, by D. F. Crowder and R. W.

Tabor, describes some routes in one section of the northern Cascades. Available from Recreational Equipment, P.O. Box 24827, Seattle, Wash. 98130.

Cascade Alpine Guide, by Fred Beckey, covers the southern half of the Washington Cascades. Seattle: The Mountaineers, 1973.

Squamish Chief Guide, by Gordon Smaill, covers one of the main rock-climbing areas in the Northwest. Available from Hard, Box 35236, Stn. E, Vancouver V6M4G4, Canada.

Guide to the Leavenworth Rock Climbing Areas, by Fred Beckey and Eric Bjorstad, covers another popular rock-climbing area. Seattle: The Mountaineers.

Climber's Guide to the Olympic Mountains, by Olympic Mountain Rescue, discusses these fine Washington peninsular mountains. Seattle: The Mountaineers, 1974.

A Climbing Guide to Oregon, by Nicholas Dodge, discusses routes farther south. Touchstone Press, P.O. Box 81, Beaverton, Oreg.

Mountaineer's Guide to the High Sierra, by Hervey Voge and Andrew Smatko, unfortunately excludes routes that are above fourth class in difficulty, though a companion volume is promised eventually. San Francisco: Sierra Club, 1972. The older *Climber's Guide to the High Sierra,* 1965, now out of print, has all the significant routes of the later book, in addition to the technical routes to that date.

Climber's Guide to Lake Tahoe and Donner Summit, by Eric Beck, covers the rock climbs in this section of the northern Sierra. Tahoe City Parks Department, Tahoe City, Calif., 1974.

Climber's Guide to Yosemite Valley, by Steve Roper, describes the routes in America's greatest rock-climbing area. San Francisco: Sierra Club, 1971.

Pinnacles Climber's Guide, by Chuck Richards, lists the routes in this group of spires south of San Francisco. Recreation and Travel Enterprises, 1974.

Day Climber's Guide to the Santa Clara Valley discusses another local climbing area south of San Francisco. Available from Stark-Craig Publishers, P.O. Box 986, Morgan Hills, Calif. 95037.

Climber's Guide to Tahquitz and Suicide Rocks, by Chuck Wilts, lists the routes of Southern California's favorite rocks. New York: American Alpine Club, 1974.

INDEX

397